Praise for Sex, Teens, and Everything in Between

"Finally! A book on adolescent sexuality by an expert who talks to teens about sex and relationships every day! *Sex, Teens, and Everything in Between* provides a window into the real issues that today's adolescents face and an essential road map to help parents and youth navigate this thorny new world."

—**Julianna Deardorff**, coauthor of *The New Puberty: How to Navigate Early Development in Today's Girls* and Associate Professor, School of Public Health, UC Berkeley

"*Sex, Teens, and Everything in Between* is the ultimate relationship guide for teens of all orientations and identities. Teens will find the information, tools, and wisdom to support their development of personal and sexual agency. These pages are loaded with familiar scenarios, each followed by helpful perspective and a breakdown of potential choices and outcomes relating to each situation. Shafia provides readers the fuel to make the consent conversation clear, relevant, and applicable for everyone, acknowledging the interconnected factors of social media, normalized hookup culture, internet porn, and gender norms."

—**Cindy Pierce**, author of *Sexploitation: Helping Kids Develop Healthy Sexuality in a Porn-Driven World*

"Adolescent sexuality has become more complex and the issues surrounding it more difficult than ever before. Shafia is a rational voice for parents, caregivers, and kids on this difficult and sometimes awkward topic. *Sex, Teens, and Everything in Between* is a must-read for the parent, caregiver, and educator who would like to understand the teen universe of all things sex and proactively and thoughtfully engage with their teens around these challenging topics."

—**Debra Wilson**, President of the Southern
Association of Independent Schools

"Shafia is not only an elite educator but also a passionate and dedicated advocate for teens. *Sex, Teens, and Everything in Between* perfectly encapsulates her mission at the cutting edge of sex education: teaching adolescents how to become people of integrity with regard to sex and relationships. We are respectfully horny for this book."

—**Nick Kroll** and **Andrew Goldberg**, creators of *Big Mouth*

"As a sex educator, I know that these are the real issues that teens have questions and concerns about. I really appreciate Shafia's candid discussion about teen sexuality, including many topics that they would likely be afraid to bring up with their own parents. Her book is very inclusive and discusses perspectives and motivations that would be eye opening to parents. What a great resource to help teens navigate the sexual decisions of our modern culture and make smart choices. I wish everyone could have a Shafia as their personal counselor!"

—**Ivy Chen**, professor at San Francisco State,
Department of Sociology and Sexuality Studies

"This extraordinary and comprehensive work by Shafia Zaloom appears just in time; she has fashioned her life's work as a health educator into a bold and powerful framework that answers pressing questions about budding sexuality and consent. However, the book does far more; it holds each of us accountable for doing our part to help adolescents develop intimate relationships rooted in communication and care. The author has rendered a great service to parents and educators. You must read her unflinching treatise on developing socially and emotionally sound adults."

—**Dr. Louis N. Wool**, Superintendent of Schools, Harrison Central School District, New York State School Superintendent of the Year 2010

"Shafia Zaloom has created a road map for every teen, every parent, and every family navigating the sometimes frightening intersection of loving, healthy relationships, sex, and digital technology. Zaloom is a gifted educator who approaches her work with compassion, a deep knowledge of the lives of today's teens, as well as candor—and well-placed humor. She shows us that underlying teens' complex relationships with technology and sex are the age-old human needs for caring, connection, and respect."

—**Esta Soler**, President, Futures Without Violence

"These are the conversations every parent wants to be having with their teenagers. The pages are filled with sensitive, honest, and utterly urgent case studies that give us insight into the importance and delicacy of sexual consent. Shafia provides an unflinching examination of consent education—we can't afford to look away."

—**Bonni Cohen**, documentary film director of *Audrie & Daisy* (as seen on Netflix)

"Sex educator Shafia Zaloom has written an utterly remarkable book. Open to any page—or even a random paragraph—and you will discover the bottomless depth of her wisdom, experience, and expertise. Far from the minimalistic 'stay out of trouble' approach to sexual health education so common in the U.S., Ms. Zaloom shows parents how to speak to their teens about sexual decision-making through a sex-positive lens grounded in the values of empathy, kindness, respect, responsibility, mutuality, and joyful intimacy. Within that humanistic framework, the issue of 'sexual consent' becomes, ultimately, a virtual no-brainer."

—**Deborah M. Roffman**, human sexuality educator and author of *Talk to Me First: Everything You Need to Know to Become Your Kids' Go-To Person about Sex*

"Zaloom's timely book is a deeply insightful exploration of the complexities surrounding consent, sexual abuse, and healthy relationships for teenagers. An urgently needed and indispensable guide for educators and parents."

—**Kirby Dick**, documentary film director, *The Hunting Ground*

"Talking to our children about sex, consent, and healthy relationships has never been easy, but for this generation of parents, it can understandably be overwhelming and even scary. *Sex, Teens, and Everything in Between* gives you the information you need and really must have to navigate this tricky terrain—for you and your child. As the mother of two teen boys, I read this book with urgency and was so glad to see Shafia's balanced and thoughtful advice. So don't wait until you think your children are sexually active or you think they're mature enough. In today's world, it is imperative to start talking to our children as soon as they and their friends are interacting with social media. *Sex, Teens, and Everything in Between* shows you how, with both wisdom and tools to help you have the conversations that will keep your child safe and healthy."

—**Rosalind Wiseman**, *New York Times* bestselling author, *Queen Bees and Wannabees*

"This is a terrifically valuable guide to perhaps the most fraught, complicated, and profound dimension of teens' lives—healthy sex and love. I don't know another book on this topic that anchors itself so deeply in the nuances of teens' actual experiences—what they fret about, desire, fear, and hope for. Nor do I know a book on this topic that so successfully avoids platitudes and that provides so many specific, insightful, and practical recommendations for parents, educators, and teens themselves. Zaloom also has a fine moral compass, a capacity to listen deeply, and the wisdom that only comes from many years of experience working with teens. Every teen and every parent and educator—and every other adult who interacts with teens—should read this book."

—**Richard Weissbourd**, Senior Lecturer on Education, Faculty Director, Human Development and Psychology; Codirector of Making Caring Common Project, Harvard Graduate School of Education; author of *The Parents We Mean to Be*

Sex, Teens, & Everything in Between

The New and Necessary Conversations Today's Teenagers Need to Have about Consent, Sexual Harassment, Healthy Relationships, Love, and More

Shafia Zaloom

Published by Sourcebooks
P.O. Box 4410, Naperville, Illinois 60567-4410
(630) 961-3900
sourcebooks.com

Library of Congress Cataloging-in-Publication data is on file with the publisher.

Printed and bound in the United States of America.
SB 10 9 8 7 6 5 4 3 2

To my students and children,
for being my greatest teachers and inspiration.

Table of Contents

Foreword

By Mike Riera, PhD

Author of *Staying Connected to Your Teenager*

Head of School at the Brentwood School

Most parents of teenagers live in dreaded anticipation of having "The Talk." Indeed, some pass altogether on this essential dialogue and count on schools to cover this spectacularly uncomfortable conversation. Others have this lecture one time and in a one-way dialogue, like Sergeant Joe Friday: "Just the facts, ma'am." Trust me, nothing memorable comes from this approach other than mutual discomfort and tacit agreement to end the talk as soon as possible. Still others assume a level of pre-understanding in their teenagers and typically offer a few throwaway lines akin to *Just let me know if you have any questions.* This places all of the anxiety with the teenager, which is exactly where it does not belong. Without solid information, teenagers are prone to act on both the need to socially fit in with their peers and the influence of their hormones. That's a volatile mix at best.

In an ideal world, our children have these conversations with trusted adults in a variety of contexts: home, school, physicians' offices. More than anything, they need to be ongoing dialogues, not just one-time talks. In schools the conversations are with trained adults and at regular intervals—in human development classes and various health presentations. The same is true in physicians' offices, as the annual checkup provides an ideal time. But this is not the case at home, with parents. To begin with, parents need to make the time and broach the subject, which, no matter how you cut it, is awkward. Personally, I have always counted on the car for these conversations, because when sitting side-by-side there is minimal eye contact. Best of all, we are in a sealed environment with no way out—for either of us! On top of this inherent discomfort is the reality that compared to the professionals, we are significantly underprepared in terms of our contemporary base of knowledge. Despite this stacked deck, having these conversations at home with the people who are raising them and love them the most is much more important and impactful than with the other professionals in their lives. Welcome to parenting teenagers!

While the list of all the wrong ways to approach this topic could go on and on, the reality is that there is only one right way to address this topic at home, and that is through the parent-child relationship in dialogue with one another. This means that once the conversations get going there are no scripts to follow. There is no playbook. Whenever these interactions are productive it is because of mutual respect and vulnerability.

Fortunately, Shafia's book comes to the rescue. While her words will not necessarily relieve your anxiety about these conversations, they will prepare you for the questions that your teenager comes back to you with, as well as follow-up questions on your end.

I have known Shafia professionally and personally for over twenty years, and her understanding and care for teenagers is palpable. I have marveled watching her engage a room full of young people discussing the intricacies of relationships, biology, and desire. She is courageous, knowledgeable, and, as this book will reveal, humble. As a result, teenagers open up to Shafia in ways unimaginable to most adults. For the reader, this is a gift, as this book takes the express route into the minds of todays' teens on the topic most near and dear to them, sexual relationships. Trust me, whether you realize it or not, you have a lot to learn, and this book covers it all.

Finally, understand that while having these conversations with your teenager is important to their well-being, they are also essential to your ongoing relationship with them. When you venture into this arena, they will recognize how uncomfortable you are, which will prove yet again how much you love them. Plus, years later, sitting around the family dinner table, it will make for some great storytelling!

Introduction

My daughter's phone is on the table next to me when I hear it ping—a text message from a friend. I glance over at it.

"Damn girl," Jason writes. "Nice legs. When do they open?"

I freeze. Mei Lan is only twelve years old, and she and Jason have been buddies since kindergarten.

"Why did Jason text that to you?" I ask her as she takes the phone. "That is so disrespectful—not OK!"

She drops the cellphone in her backpack and strides off to her room, swinging her blond pigtails. "Chill out, Mom." She turns and smiles at me. "It's a joke, no big deal. He's just being a guy."

I am stunned by Jason's text. I love him. He's a great kid, and his parents are close to us. Besides, both he and Mei Lan are so young!

Five years later, thinking back on that shocking moment, I know he was just parroting some lines he heard in a movie or video game—and that Mei Lan was doing what the culture teaches girls to do: don't push back, don't be assertive, don't make a fuss.

They were only playacting at twelve, but these days, at seventeen, Mei Lan, Jason, and many American teens are steeped in a culture that glamorizes sexual aggression and hooking up without emotional connection. It's tough to make good choices in an atmosphere that normalizes porn, conducts personal relations on impersonal screens, and hypersexualizes every aspect of popular culture. Our kids are bombarded with messages about sex and relationships online and from Snapchat and Instagram, as well as from their friends, movies, songs, ads, video games, and TV. When I saw my nine-year-old, Maddie, twerking and singing "my milkshake brings all the boys to the yard" as she pulled on her pajamas, or heard my fifteen-year-old, Kyle, yell "take that, bitch!" while playing a video game, I knew that I have to keep talking to them regularly about sex, relationships, and values.

As parents, we have to be part of that conversation. And teens have to be able to ask hard questions about how to take care of themselves, make decisions that reflect their values, and stay safe. Those conversations are often difficult, even for me—and I've been talking to teens about sex for twenty-five years. It's my job. As a health educator, I've worked with thousands of adolescents and parents at independent, parochial, and public schools, published curricula on teen development and health education, consulted with schools on youth development programs, and trained their teachers. I specialize in creating safe educational environments in which teens can speak openly about touchy, messy issues involving friends, relationships, drugs, alcohol, and sex. They ask honest, real-life questions, like:

- "How do I get my ex to delete the naked pictures he has of me on his phone?"
- "I'm not ready to have sex yet, but should I give this guy a blow job so I won't be prude-shamed?"

- "If I'm drunk and she's drunk, and she says yes and we hook up but then she changes her mind, can I get in trouble?"

- "How do I tell my friends that I'm afraid of having sex with my girlfriend?"

These are awkward questions. But life and sex can be awkward too. And if teens don't have a chance to talk frankly about these issues, they can end up at physical, emotional, and even legal risk. We have to talk to our kids—not just about the mechanics of sex, but also about boundaries, reciprocity, love, the law, and how to treat people and have happy, healthy, rich relationships throughout their lives. Today more than ever, teens need to know how to stay safe, take care of themselves, and keep other people safe too.

THE HAZARDS OF HOOKUP CULTURE

Let's get one thing out of the way. Sex is a healthy, normal part of life, and so is age-appropriate sexual discovery in the teen years. Intimate, enriching sexual relations are among the great joys and privileges of being human. Healthy physical exploration and connection is like a great conversation. It fully engages two people who are paying close attention and actively listening to each other. It's fun, rewarding, and leaves each partner wanting more.

Sexual harassment and assault, on the other hand, is a form of bullying. It's a way for one person to exert power and control over another. It can be coercive, aggressive, and violent. For the person on the receiving end, it can be frightening and its consequences damaging.

Sexual well-being—like overall well-being—is about feeling respected and safe so you can be vulnerable and intimate with another person. But the hookup culture that is common in many high schools and colleges promotes a very different set of norms. The focus is on peer pressure, impulse, intoxication, and impersonal sex acts that involve genitalia but not the complex, emotional human beings they're attached to. Teens afraid of "catching feelings," as they put it, are taught to be cool and detached and that sex is about performance and competition.

Many teens believe that everyone is hooking up sexually, but that's a myth. According to a 2015 study by the Centers for Disease Control and Prevention (CDC), nearly 60 percent of U.S. high school students are virgins—up from 46 percent in 1991. And the vast majority of young people—85 percent, according to a 2017 study conducted by Making Caring Common at the Harvard Graduate School of Education—want to have sex within a serious romantic relationship. Still, the hookup myth persists, crowding out healthier attitudes about human connection.

The Making Caring Common study also found that many young people are not learning how to form caring, lasting love relationships—in part, because parents aren't talking to them about these deeper forms of human relations. Teens aren't learning about authenticity, trust, loyalty, respect, and commitment. They're not learning how to listen to themselves—how to say yes or no because they really mean it—and how to recognize and respect other people's verbal, physical, and emotional cues.

If teens do not hear these messages early, it can lead to trouble. I often hear from former students about disrespectful and nonconsensual sexual experiences they've had in college—like Jasmine and her friend Aaliyah. When the girls were freshmen, two upperclassmen, Zach and Brody, invited them to their residence to hang out and party. Jasmine didn't drink much alcohol in high school, but everyone was playing a drinking game that night, and she got into it. When the game ended, Brody took Aaliyah into his bedroom, and Zach led Jasmine into his room and closed the door. Jasmine, feeling a bit woozy, fell onto the bed, and suddenly Zach was on top of her, kissing her and unzipping her jeans. Jasmine struggled beneath his weight and said, "Stop, don't, I hardly know you," but he told her to relax. She doesn't remember much after that, but she woke up naked in Zach's bed. Her head pounded, she felt sick to her stomach, and her clothing was strewn all over the floor. While Zach slept, she got dressed and left his room, and it began to dawn on her that she had been sexually assaulted.

Jasmine said that when she got back to her dorm, she scrubbed herself in the shower, trying to clean off the filth and disgust she felt inside and out. Then she sat on her bed, shocked and numb, tears streaming down her face. What if she was pregnant or had a sexually transmitted disease? When her roommate, Nelly, walked in and saw her crying, Jasmine confided everything she could remember. Nelly immediately found the campus sexual assault reporting number and called it. In less than half an hour, a student representative arrived and told Jasmine about all her options. Jasmine decided to have a rape kit done and file a formal report of nonconsensual sex.

When Zach learned about the report, he was studying for a test. He was instructed to come in for an immediate interview, even though he would have to miss an important study group. Angry and distracted, Zach headed to the meeting. He wondered if he should call his parents, but his dad would flip—that would be a nightmare. Would he need to get a lawyer? This could get really bad—and the timing sucked. He had a big exam to take, he had just applied for a teaching assistant job, and he was planning to go to business school in the fall. Was this going to ruin everything? The previous year, a girl had accused his friend Tray of sexually assaulting her. Tray got suspended for a whole term and was trying to appeal his case. He wasn't sure if he'd be allowed back on campus for graduation.

Experiences like these are devastating for everyone involved, and they are way too common. The Association of American Colleges & Universities reports one in every five women is sexually assaulted in college, and the CDC reports one in four is assaulted in high school. More than a third of the victims are between twelve and seventeen years old. Many are sexually abused when they're drunk, drugged, or incapacitated. Most of the time, they're acquainted with their attackers.

National media has focused on explosive sexual abuse stories in colleges across the country, from Harvard to Stanford and countless colleges in between. But the problem starts earlier: sexual assaults are common in high schools. In Northern California, for example, a seventeen-year-old athlete was recently tried in juvenile court and convicted of a felony—oral copulation by force, violence, duress, menace, or fear—for sexually assaulting a fifteen-year-old girl. Two months earlier, that same boy had been accused of forcing a fourteen-year-old girl to give him oral sex in a school bathroom. Before the assault, he had harassed her and sent her naked photos of himself on Snapchat. After she filed a report, the school changed his schedule so she wouldn't have classes with him, but she saw him on campus and began skipping lunch to avoid him. Feeling bullied by other students, she often stayed home from school. Her grades started to drop, and she became suicidal.

As one of the victims wrote in a statement to the court, "Common sense is taking no for an answer when someone says they don't want to engage in sexual activity with you. Common sense is not forcing someone's head down when they're choking and pulling away." Common sense, certainly, is teaching our teens about the importance of sexual consent—what it is, how to ask for it and give it, and the potentially crushing consequences of ignorance.

Most teens actually do crave guidance on this issue, according to new research, but they're not getting it from adults. Parents who haven't had much sex education themselves, and sex educators who are restricted by limitations placed upon them by other adults—such as administrators, parents, lawmakers, etc.—are often misinformed and fear inciting sexual promiscuity (for which there is no empirical evidence). So there are few educated adults available to teach kids that you shouldn't pressure someone to hook up with you or have sex with someone who's intoxicated or impaired. As a result, many teens are dangerously unprepared to navigate the risky sexual landscape they're growing up in. When they're little, we teach them how to look both ways before they cross the street, and when they're older, how to drive legally and safely. But we're not teaching them the crucial physical, emotional, and legal rules of the road they need to know about sexual consent.

THE KEYS TO CONSENT

The basics are easy to talk about at any age. I often start by asking students how they feel when people grab french fries off their plates at lunch without asking. In all my classes, almost everyone says that behavior bothers them.

"This is a consent issue," I tell them. "People assume that they can take your fries without even asking you. Consent is all about asking permission and respecting your right to give an answer."

Sexual consent, to be sure, is more complicated than french fries, but the rules are clear: it has to be affirmative, conscious, voluntary, and ongoing. You can revoke it at any time. Silence or lack of protest is not consent. People can't give their consent if they're sleeping, unconscious, impaired, or under the influence of drugs or alcohol. And people can't legally give consent if they're under eighteen and their partner is over eighteen years old.

We absolutely have to teach teens these ground rules, because—for both victim and perpetrator—their lives, their educations, and their futures depend on it. For survivors of assault, the impact can last a lifetime. They may initially experience everything from disbelief, victim-blaming, and harassment, to retaliation from peers, administrators, and parents. Over the long term, they may struggle with anxiety, depression, post-traumatic stress disorder, eating disorders, and thoughts of suicide. All schools and colleges that receive federal funding are legally required to respond to, promptly investigate, and remedy campus sexual harassment and assault. Perpetrators also experience both short- and long-term consequences. They can be suspended, and their academic and athletic careers may come to a complete halt. If their case goes to criminal court, they can face jail time, and they may have to register publicly as a sex offender for the rest of their lives.

As parents, we want to keep our children safe and raise them to have successful, fulfilling lives. Today, that includes teaching them about consent—in high school or even earlier—to help prevent situations that can derail or possibly destroy their futures.

START THE CONVERSATION

In the wake of national sexual abuse scandals, many colleges and universities have developed sexual consent training programs. But by the time young people are in college, they've already established patterns of sexual behavior. Many expect undergraduate life to be an intensive four-year seminar in drinking and sexual encounters. As a result, most of these college programs are too late to have a significant impact. To prevent sexual assault, we have to get in front of the issue by talking to teens about consent while they're still in high school.

In my classes, which have been covered by the *New York Times* and NPR, I teach teens how to identify potential risks and benefits, access the information they need, develop strong self-awareness, practice empathy, understand their limits, and know the difference between healthy and unhealthy vulnerability. They need to know how to make good decisions, engage in introspection, understand sexual consent, and learn from their mistakes. It's a lifelong process.

As of 2017, however, California was the only state that required public high schools to teach students about sexual consent. As a result, there is a huge information gap nationwide, as well as serious risks for teens who don't know the rules. To fill this vacuum, parents have a vital role to play, but so many don't know where to start. Most of us never had these kinds of conversations with our own parents. Meanwhile, the digital world has changed how young people communicate, relate to one another, define personal identity, and form their expectations about sexual behavior. How do we talk to our teens about sexting, porn, sexuality, consent, relationships, and love? About listening for emotional cues, living with integrity, and expressing their capacity to care for other people and feel affection?

Adolescence is a time of discovery, yet not all teens are, or should be, experimenting with sexual relationships. Every person has an inner sense of readiness and knows when it's the right time for them. But every high school student—whether they're engaging in sexual activity or not—is exposed to all of these issues through their friends, the media, and the online world every day. As parents, we have to break the silence and talk with our teens about healthy relationships and sexual consent, without shame, guilt, or judgment. It's a matter of protecting our kids from and preventing harm.

Talking about these topics can be difficult for both parents and teens. It helps to be open and direct, deal with conflicts as they arise, and create a safe space for talking and learning about sensitive topics. Choose a time when you're together and doing something ordinary—like riding in the car, cleaning up the kitchen, or sharing a late-night snack. You might start by talking about a movie that features many examples of healthy and unhealthy relationships—*Superbad* comes to mind. Ask what your teen thinks about some of those friendships. Keep the discussion brief, and let your teen determine how deep you go. Then wait a few days before continuing the conversation. Again, find a relaxed time. Mention a sexual assault or harassment scene in the movie and ask what your teen thinks about it. It's not about lecturing or covering all your points in one conversation. It's about finding opportunities to exchange thoughts and feelings with your child—layering information, a little at a time, throughout adolescence.

In my classes, I ask students what they think about challenging issues, and then we brainstorm ways to deal with them. Asking a person for consent, for instance, can feel intimidating or like a buzzkill in the middle of a passionate moment. So I ask my students to suggest how they might do it. One class came up with the phrase "you good?" as a way to check in verbally with a partner without sounding awkward or uncomfortable. Similarly, parents can start conversations by asking their teens what they know about certain issues, how they feel about them, and the best ways to deal with them if they come up. It's a dialogue, a give-and-take, and an exploration for parents and teens together.

I am hoping that my book will help. *Sex, Teens, and Everything in Between* is the first complete sexual consent guide for parents and teens in the United States. This book is filled with practical tips and crucial information teens and parents need to know about giving and asking for consent, high school and college policies, legal issues, love and relationships, how teen brains respond to sex and trauma, the effects of pornography and cultural expectations, ethical issues, support, and prevention. Every chapter features an up-to-date, easy-to-read discussion of key issues, plus conversation starters for parents and unflinching answers to the unfiltered questions that teens ask. Filled with vivid examples and survivor stories, it also includes essential, step-by-step guidance for your teens on issues like what to do if you're sexually assaulted and what to do if you're accused of sexual assault.

This book is based on my decades of experience as a leading educator in the field of adolescent sexual decision-making and a consultant for award-winning documentaries, including *The Hunting Ground* and *Audrie & Daisy.* It is the first book that meets the urgent need for explicit, accurate information about adolescents and sexual consent. Parents want to know how to keep their children safe. Teens crave credible information, support, and guidance. *Sex, Teens, and Everything in Between* will give them the tools they need to cultivate healthy relationships, honor their sense of values, and prepare for and deal with challenging issues in today's world.

CHAPTER ONE

Yes Means Yes

What We Mean When We Talk about Consent

Blake and Ava are both seniors. They've been flirting with each other and strategically walking by each other's classrooms so that they "happen" to see each other. One day, they are together in a small classroom, where they are printing out an assignment. They are standing close to each other, and there is some casual touching and joking that makes them laugh. Blake looks at Ava and pauses to take in her expression. He sees eager anticipation. She moves closer, puts her hand on his waist, and steps forward. Their faces move toward each other and he whispers, "This OK?" She nods as their lips come together in a kiss.

Blake and Ava are equally engaged in what's happening. They are attentive to each other's facial expressions and body language. Blake's subtle yet clear question affirms that they both desire what is about to happen, and Ava gives consent not only by nodding yes but by moving toward Blake as she pulls him close to her.

Sexual consent is an agreement, one in which both people accept and want what's happening between them.

Sexual consent is an agreement, one in which both people accept and want what's happening between them. It's what makes sexual activity between people legal. It protects the fundamentals of human dignity: mutual respect and physical and emotional safety. Respect is treating others the way *they* want to be treated. We are all individuals who have different standards and unique desires, preferences, and limitations. Enthusiastic sexual consent emphasizes care; it is an affirmation that both people care about their partner's experience and want it to be good, even if it's only for physical gratification.

How do we even know if we're ready to explore sexuality with someone else? Each person has an individual sense of readiness, and only that individual can know when the time is right for them. The ability to make that decision requires self-reflection and preparation. First and foremost, a person needs to have the capacity to consider someone else—to think of a person other than themselves. Then there is the question of safety and sexual communication. Does someone know what their own boundaries are? What they need and want to feel secure? How to let people know what they want and listen for what their partner needs? Sexual consent is fundamental to engaging in this process of discovery.

There is a growing body of research and reporting, much of which is cited in this book, that reveals the challenges young people face when navigating sexual relationships. Statistical evidence and narrative expressions of nonconsensual, unethical, and unsatisfying sex has heightened awareness and raised flags for more comprehensive and sex-positive sex education, so that we may all engage in healthier, happier, more satisfying relationships.

> Jackson and Zara have been in a romantic relationship for close to a year. They are in Zara's bedroom and have been making out and exploring each other's bodies—over and under clothes. Jackson reaches into Zara's underwear. In an intimate pause, they pull back slightly within the closeness, their foreheads touching, and Jackson whispers, "This feel good?" Zara nods and says, "Yeah." She puts her hand on his and guides him a bit, then asks, "What about you?"

Sexual communication is normal and healthy between people who are sexually active with each other. Jackson asks for consent during a natural pause that is intimate and contributes to a deeper understanding of what feels good for both him and Zara. He could have also asked "you good?" or "this OK?" They also could have talked about what they are interested in exploring even before the sexual activity began ("How far do you want to go?"). Zara affirms her desire for what is happening and embraces the opportunity to guide Jackson in a consensual way. In turn, she asks what he wants. Their dynamic is balanced.

Many of my students are concerned that talking during sexual activity will be awkward or ruin the moment. These also are some of the same students, regardless of gender, whose sexual experiences have been, in their words, "eh, OK, I guess" or "uncomfortable but I didn't want to say anything." I ask them if that's the moment they were worried about ruining with communication, then suggest that some dialogue could have made the moment better.

Consent is about educating others on how to treat you and listening for how others want to be treated. It is important because how we treat each other matters.

As consent has become a topic of national conversation, in particular because brave people have come forward to tell their stories of unwanted sexual attention and assault, responsible adults understand that it is essential to teach young people about the issue. Consent is about educating others on how to treat you and listening for how others want to be treated. It is important because how we treat each other matters. Since teenagers are concrete thinkers, and many don't have experiential context, it is helpful to use real examples.

For young people to understand sexual consent, it is important to make a concrete connection between consent in daily life and consent in the context of sexuality.

Consent is at work in many of our daily interactions. For instance, if I hit you and I have your consent, that could be boxing. If I don't, it could be assault. If I take your bike and ride it to the store to get a sandwich, if I have your consent, I could be borrowing it. If I don't ask you, I might be stealing it.

And then there is the french fry metaphor that I referenced in the introduction of this book. I use this comparison all the time in my classes to take the issue of consent from the abstract to the real world. It usually goes like this:

I'll ask a classroom full of teens, "How many of you like french fries?" Hands shoot up and there is a buzz. "Don't you love that moment?" I continue. "You're in the cafeteria, you buy a plate of fries. They smell so good; your ketchup is on the side, and then you sit down at a table of your friends…and suddenly hands dart in and start grabbing fries. How many of you are actually OK with that? Raise your hands."

Maybe one or two raise their hands, sometimes in a class of a hundred students.

"How many of you are not OK with that?" Everyone else's hand goes up.

"This is an issue of consent, even if it's a lot different than a sexual encounter. Those are your fries, and people are just grabbing without asking. It may not even cross some people's minds that they should ask. People get impulsive with french fries—they're really good. What's going on with that dynamic?"

One student will typically say something like, "For the most part, I'd be OK with sharing my fries, but there's something uncool about not asking. It's a bummer, like geez, they're my fries, at least you could ask first instead of just helping yourself."

From there, I encourage students to think about what they're saying and the broader implications, and I ask, "What's so important about asking?"

"Because I paid for them and they're mine!"

"So they belong to you?"

"Yeah!"

"Manners show you care about people."

"Because it really means they respect your decisions. Like if you said no, they wouldn't do it, but if they don't ask, then they don't even care about what you want."

"Yeah, friends should care and respect you."

I encourage them to think about their role: "How many of you actually say something when it happens?" A smattering of hands. "What do you say?"

"Dude, uncool."

"Hey, what's up with that?"

"If it bothers the rest of you, what gets in the way of speaking up?"

"It pisses me off, but I let it go because it's french fries."

"Yeah, I don't want to be jumped all over like it's no big deal."

"Or judged because I should be cool with sharing them."

"How is this about consent?"

"Consent means you need permission. Giving someone the chance to say how they feel and what they want. Ask if you want a french fry!"

"Yes! That's called agency. Your right, ability, and power to choose for yourself. OK, now how does this apply to sexual consent?"

"Respecting people's right to give an answer. To be in charge of what's mine or yours if you're hooking up."

"Exactly. People get to choose how they touch and get touched because—what?—their bodies…"

"Belong to them!"

Jules and Remy have been friends for a long time. Recently, they've discovered each other sexually. Whenever they sleep at each other's houses, they sleep in the same bed. Their cuddling has become more intimate, and the sexual tension between them is building. One night, Remy is spooning Jules and quietly asks if she wants to hook up. Jules turns over and they make out and explore the sensuality of each other's bodies for what seems like forever. Jules pulls back slightly to catch her breath and looks into Remy's eyes. "How do you feel about oral?" Remy responds, "I don't know. I've never done it with another girl before. Let's just stay like this for a while. I'll tell you if I want to." Jules nods yes with a smile and they continue to kiss.

It's important that a consensual question allows for yes or no.

It's important that a consensual question allows for yes or no. Even better, it should offer an opportunity to communicate beyond that. The phrasing of Jules's question gives Remy the space to say yes or no. It isn't a manipulative or leading question. If it were leading, she might have asked, "Are we going to have oral soon?" The question assumes sexual activity and implies that oral is what Jules wants, which can add pressure or make Remy feel like she shouldn't disappoint her. Jules's question gives Remy the choice. Remy can then express her own desires and limits.

As individuals, we bring different values, beliefs, experience, confidence, and insecurities to a sexual encounter. Consent is meant to ensure that both people want what is happening between them. Sexual exploration is intimate—physically and emotionally. It has the potential to be enriching or destructive, depending on how we handle it, and in the context of our own values and sexuality. Sexual exploration and intimacy aren't bad; how we manage it is what matters.

Sarah and Hayden met each other through their youth group and have been dating for a couple of months. They have discussed the fact that they both have decided to abstain from sexual intercourse until marriage. Up until now they have been careful to keep their dates public and active while they get to know each other, so they won't be distracted by any sexual tension. One day, they are sitting on the couch watching TV at Sarah's house, and no one else is home. They've kissed once or twice before, and now they are making out. Their kissing gets intense, especially as Sarah begins to kiss Hayden's

neck. Hayden pauses for a second and asks, "Is this too much?" Sarah
thinks of their commitment to each other and says, "Yes. OK, maybe
we should go for a walk and get some ice cream or something."
Hayden agrees.

Sarah and Hayden are committed to abstinence and trying to figure
out the in-betweens of kissing and having sex. Practicing consent supports their commitment to their spiritual values and themselves, and it
also provides opportunities to pause and reflect on what actions they
believe align with their faith, what may be too tempting, and how to avoid
those temptations.

**Consent must be given in real time and ongoing,
which means you have to pay attention and
ask whenever another level of intimacy is
introduced throughout the sexual activity.**

Sexual consent is not manipulated, persuaded, or won over. It is not
silence, a lack of protest or resistance, and it cannot be assumed just
because there is a relationship or there has been sexual activity in the past.
It can't be given through text, email, social media, or electronic device,
and just because someone says yes to one thing does not mean they are
saying yes to other things. Consent must be given in real time and ongoing, which means you have to pay attention and ask whenever another
level of intimacy is introduced throughout the sexual activity. Consent
can also be revoked at any time.

Roz and Eddie are hanging out at a small party at a friend's house. Everyone has been drinking. Roz and Eddie are in chemistry class together, where they flirt sometimes. At the party, Roz is visibly intoxicated, but Eddie seems fine. Eddie suggests to his buddy that the others move to another part of the house so he and Roz can be alone. When they leave, Eddie moves in close to Roz. While they are talking, he puts his hand on her knee. Roz thinks Eddie is attractive and popular but knows he is notorious for hooking up with lots of girls and then bragging about it. She moves her knee out from under his hand, so he puts his arm around her shoulder and says, "You OK?" Before Roz can say anything, Eddie says, "It's OK" and starts to kiss her. Roz is in a haze, and concern for her reputation and how Eddie might be using her moves in and out of her mind. She pulls back a bit and manages to say, "Wait," but before she can catch her breath, Eddie whispers in between kisses, "You're so hot. I've wanted to get with you for so long." Roz wonders if Eddie thinks she's different from the other girls. They do talk and have fun as lab partners. Roz gives in to the kisses as Eddie slides his hand up her thigh.

There are several factors that make this a nonconsensual interaction. Roz and Eddie have used substances. Consent cannot be given if someone is incapacitated and their thinking and judgment is compromised by drugs, including alcohol. Eddie asks for consent but doesn't listen for an answer; he just assumes it. He registers the hesitation Roz has communicated with her body language because when she moves her knee out from under his hand, he asks if she's OK and says something that is meant to reassure her but—again—doesn't listen for her response. Roz also verbalizes that she wants to wait, which indicates she is not into what Eddie wants to do. Eddie ignores this and manipulates Roz's willingness with his comment about being hot and that he desires her. Eddie invokes gender roles to get what he wants. Girls are socialized to quantify their value based on how attractive, sexy, and desirable they are perceived to be—this is not equal. Eddie deliberately ignores the signal that Roz does not want to make out with him; he seductively takes charge and proceeds anyway. He doesn't allow Roz to express what she wants and needs. Eddie prioritizes what he wants to happen over Roz's perspective and experience.

Nick is a senior and Phil is a junior. They were friends who discovered their attraction for each other and started a romantic relationship. Their sexual exploration is intense and fun, but they haven't had intercourse. Even though consent was assumed for those experiences, there hasn't been an issue until Nick hinted that he wanted to have sex by saying, "Next time, I'm bringing a condom." He is making a declaration, not asking a question, and Phil doesn't get a chance to respond. The next time Nick and Phil are together and there is an opportunity to have sex, Nick initiates and Phil says, "Hey, whoa, what about the condom? And what about lube and prepping?" Nick says that he's clean and attempts to lighten the mood by pointing out that they don't have to worry about pregnancy. Phil suggests waiting because he wants to use a condom and do it right so it will be comfortable. Nick says, "Oh come on, you know you want to, just this once. Next time I'll bring one." Phil reluctantly agrees, but doesn't feel good about it, so while intercourse is happening, he says, "This doesn't feel right, let's stop." Nick answers, "In a minute. I'm almost finished."

An existing relationship does not equal consent. Not only is consent important when it comes to what two people are going to do, but also it is equally important to agree about how it's done. Phil wants to use a condom to protect against sexually transmitted diseases. Lubrication is also essential with anal intercourse because there are both involuntary and voluntary muscles involved. It's more difficult to consciously relax involuntary muscles, which can lead to unwanted pain. Phil communicates a personal boundary: he wants to wait. Nick tries to talk him into agreement with persuasive language and pressure. This is coercion and therefore not consensual. Also, consent can be revoked at any time. Phil retracts his consent because he does not like the experience and wants it to stop. Nick doesn't listen or respect his wishes, and he puts his experience and orgasm over Phil's welfare and consent.

Sometimes students will ask, "Wait, so if I am two strokes away from orgasm, do I still have to stop if the other person wants to?" The answer is yes. Consent and well-being must always be the priority. Not only is it a legal obligation, it is the foundation of healthy relationships.

On many occasions, while talking with my students, I hear "social media is life." Many come into my office to talk about their relationships and lead with "we were talking about [topic] and they said…and I said…" It is now my common practice to pause and ask, "Was this in person?" The immediate response is "Snap" or "text" or "DM," and they continue without missing a beat. Students will show me their texts and want me to deconstruct and interpret what's happened and what it means. I have to remind them that a face-to-face conversation during which they can see someone's body language, hear their tone, have the opportunity to ask questions, and know what they're feeling is the only way to accurately understand where someone is coming from. When it comes to consent as part of a sexual encounter, it has to be in person. Once two people come together physically, the context (what's going on with someone internally and what's going on in the external environment) that someone was working with through an electronic device may change. People have the right to change their mind, and sometimes sexual activity ends up feeling or being different than what someone expected. There are lots of variables that make up the context of a sexual situation, and they may shift and change while sexual activity is happening. There also are specific laws that protect young people from nonconsensual behavior in cyberspace.

> Charlie, a high school senior, and Jordan, a junior, have been flirting with each other all semester. They hook up at a party at a friend's house, kissing and touching each other intimately. Then Charlie unzips his pants and pushes Jordan's head down for oral sex. Jordan starts to perform it, but after a few moments, she pulls away, and says, "I'm not really into this." She doesn't realize that Charlie has recorded a video of her giving him oral sex and Snapchatted it to the entire soccer team.

Nudging or pushing someone's shoulder or head down to genitals is a demand, not an ask. It doesn't allow someone to freely express what they want. Everyone deserves sexual agency. The recording is nonconsensual because Jordan is seventeen, didn't know about it, nor was she asked if it was OK with her. If someone is under the age of eighteen, it is illegal to film, distribute, or receive anything sexually explicit through cyberspace. In addition, it is exploiting a moment that should be private. It objectifies and dehumanizes Jordan, her body, and her sexuality. It is also a form of harassment, because Charlie doesn't know if his teammates actually want to see what he recorded. The social status of his teammates and gender norms could get in the way of one of them saying no to this kind of Snap. It also assumes that they are informed about and OK with illegal behavior.

Social power dynamics are an important part of consent. When someone has more social power than another—like a boss over an employee, an older person over a minor, a team captain over a recruit, or an upperclassman over an underclassman—that person has an advantage, because the other may feel obligated to please them in their subordinate role, even if it isn't something they desire.

Exploring sexuality with others can be scary, confusing, and thrilling, and digital devices make every interaction more consequential. Consent must be given in person, during sexual activity, and whenever a new form of sexual activity is initiated. Many young people communicate and establish relationships through technology. This may provide a false sense of knowing someone, intimacy, or readiness to engage in a sexual relationship. With all of the abbreviations young people use (hu = hookup, wbu = what about you, dtr = define the relationship, etc.), they are in many ways abbreviating relationships. It is important to consider that the only way to truly know if you are comfortable and ready to be sexually active with someone is to actually spend time with them.

As adults, we can talk to teenagers about knowing whether they can trust someone and are ready to be more intimate. This means considering whether they are comfortable discussing issues such as consent, how far they want to go, what they are ready to do, etc. If their partner pressures, manipulates, or guilt-trips them into activities they don't feel ready for, they should consider whether this is a relationship they want to continue.

Sex educator, speaker, author, and my personal rock star, Emily

Nagoski, has a beautiful garden metaphor I use with my students to deepen their understanding of consent within the context of their sexuality. It goes like this: When you're born, you're given a little plot of rich, fertile soil, slightly different from everyone else's (a.k.a. your brain and your body). Your family and culture (the immediate and broader communities you're a part of) plant seeds and tend the garden. They also teach you how to tend it. Those seeds are the language, attitudes, knowledge, and habits about love and safety, bodies, and sex.[1]

Each garden is unique and has different needs depending on the vegetation those seeds yield. Some gardens may require extra sunlight and water, some may need extra fertilizer or shade, some may be drought-tolerant or need extra vigilance when it comes to weeding out toxic and invasive species. Over time, as you become an adolescent, you start to take on the responsibility of tending your own garden. While discovering what's in your garden, what it needs, and how to take care of it, you get to choose what gets pulled out and what gets to stay.

Consent is having the agency to decide who gets to enter your garden and what will happen while you're there together. It's the option to choose whether someone comes in and how they behave while they are there—do they play and frolic, or stomp and trample? Consent determines how long they get to stay, and whether they get to plant something or take anything with them when they leave. You should ask before entering someone else's garden. Honor it because it's theirs. And anyone you let into your garden should help it thrive.

PARENT–TEEN CONVERSATION STARTERS

My students give me the best advice for how to approach conversations with teenagers. Be concise and focused. Allow your teen to guide the conversation. Talk less and listen more. It's OK to say "I don't know." Stay open to different perspectives. Avoid letting the conversation become a family debate. Worry less about what your teen is doing and more about how they feel about it. Have many smaller conversations over time in different contexts. My students also emphasize the importance of selecting questions from the list below that will resonate with your own teenager. Every teen is unique and up to different things and dealing with different issues, so be selective with the questions you choose.

- In your own words, what is consent? What are some examples of consent that come up in everyday life?
- What's the value of consent? How does it relate to healthy relationships?
- What are some examples of asking for consent?
- What does it feel like when someone doesn't respect your right to choose for yourself? How do/can you respond?
- How can you connect your understanding of everyday consent to sexual consent?
- Why are some people trying to change the notion of consent from "no means no" to "yes means yes"? What is the difference, and do you agree or disagree?
- What are some examples of consensual questions for the following: asking someone out; deciding how you're going to spend time together; or being sexually intimate with someone?
- What are the circumstances in which consent cannot be given?
- What are some important characteristics of a sexual relationship beyond consent?

Resources

Everyday Feminism magazine has a helpful online comic strip titled *What If We Treated All Consent Like Society Treats Sexual Consent?*

STRAIGHT ANSWERS TO TEEN QUESTIONS

Why is "yes means yes" better than "no means no"?

"Yes means yes" comes from the media's coverage of recent affirmative consent laws ("affirmative" is the legal language used that requires someone to ask for agreement to initiate a level of intimacy). Until affirmative consent laws were created, the phrase "no means no" reflected widely held thinking around consent and sexual assault. It meant that if someone said no to a sexual act, the person initiating the activity should respect that boundary and stop what they are doing. This is still important. If someone doesn't want to engage in a sexual act, they can say no and the other person should stop or it might be considered sexual assault.

"Yes means yes" is an improvement on "no means no," because "no means no" *assumes* yes until that person expresses their discomfort by literally saying the word *no*. Ideally, all people would feel comfortable and confident enough during a sexual encounter to say no. Unfortunately, that isn't always the case, especially with young people. Asking for affirmative consent, if the question truly allows for either answer, expresses respect and care for a partner's sexual experience. It is also more positive because it affirms desire and hopefully leads to better sexual communication. It is the kind of communication that ideally should happen during sex and in healthy relationships. Beyond yes is *enthusiastic* consent, which means not only does the other person agree to what you're doing together, but also they genuinely desire it and they're excited about it.

What would be considered "another level of intimacy"?

An example of another level of intimacy might be going from making out with someone to taking their clothes off, or when two people are feeling each other up and one reaches into the other's pants. Another example is when someone goes from intimate touching to moving down the other person's body to give oral sex. Different people experience different levels of intimacy in different sexual situations. Some people may feel that kissing is more intimate than genital touching. Others may think that genital-to-genital intercourse is more intimate than oral intercourse. It depends on the person, so ask and pay attention to how your partner responds.

Do I have to ask for consent even if I'm really close to the person?

Yes, you must ask for consent even if you're really close to your sexual partner. A preexisting relationship does not equal consent. There are many benefits to knowing your partner. In a healthy relationship, trust and care are built over time. This allows for both partners to communicate without fear of being judged. Sometimes, consent is wordless between people who know each other really well. Communication happens with body language, facial expression, and pleasurable sounds. Still, paying attention to context is important for everyone. The context or circumstances that surround the sexual activity can change within moments and may influence how someone feels sexually, and it is important to understand that context may influence consent. And if the consent is wordless, the partners involved must be attentive to each other and make sure that whatever is happening between them is something they both want.

When do I have the right to say no?
When is it socially acceptable?

You have the right to say no at any time in a relationship or within a sexual experience. The answer to the second question will likely vary depending on who you talk to. We live in a sex-negative culture (one that focuses on objectification, sexualization, sex stigma, and body-shaming) that doesn't always promote healthy perspectives on sexuality, especially for young people. It may seem and feel like you have to say yes because that is what you see in the media or what you hear from your friends. A sex-positive and sexually healthy society would make it socially acceptable to say no to sexual activity whenever you feel you want or need to. Remember that you are under no obligation to engage in behavior you don't feel ready for, no matter the circumstances.

There are different ways to say no that you may want to consider. Within any type of relationship, be clear with your no. If you are in a healthy relationship, engage in a conversation with care and respect, so you can talk through what you're both thinking and feeling. What your partner wants matters. Being a considerate and generous lover is mature and responsible. Encouraging people to talk openly about consent, and the ability to say yes and no, benefits everyone. Everyone deserves that kind of respect from a partner, and it makes for a healthier relationship.

If you are saying no in a hookup situation, be clear and assertive. If you and your partner are engaged in a respectful sexual encounter and care about each other's experience, it should be OK to engage in open and honest dialogue. You could say, "I'm not comfortable with that but would be comfortable with [activity]." If your partner only seems to care about getting off physically and doesn't consider your experience, then be clear and direct with your no and end the hookup. Bottom line: you have the right to say no.

Can someone give consent if they are drunk?

No. The legal language of affirmative consent legislation for being drunk or intoxicated is "incapacitated." A person cannot give consent if they are incapacitated, which means they aren't able to think clearly because they are under the influence of a substance or drug (alcohol is considered a drug). The point at which someone becomes incapacitated is different depending on many variables, including genetics, size, tolerance, how much of a substance they consumed, what kind of substance they consumed, when and how they took the substance, if they had recently eaten, or if the substance had an additional substance in it. If someone reports a nonconsensual experience and the people involved were incapacitated, the police or authorities on a school's campus (if it took place at school) will investigate to determine whether the people involved were incapacitated and if this impacted the situation.

If I send a nude or "dick pic,"
does that count as consent?

No. You cannot give consent to sexual activity over a phone or other digital device, especially if you are under the age of eighteen. Nudes do not equal consent. In fact, unless someone asks for a nude photo, it can be considered sexual harassment. And if you're under eighteen, taking sexually explicit photos of yourself and "sexting"—sending nude photos—is considered trafficking in child pornography and is against federal law. Some states have teen sexting laws to deal with this common issue because the consequences for teens who violate federal law can be severe.

Remember, too, that what is on your device and what you send to others is essentially public. Just because the photos disappear from your phone doesn't mean that someone didn't screenshot and forward or save them. If you send a nude photo, you should expect that it will probably become public at some point and may be circulated. Would you want your family, employer, college admissions officer, or future romantic interest to see it? Probably not.

What if I'm comfortable doing something sexual with a guy but not a girl?

Your body belongs to you; you get to choose how to touch and be touched. The guidelines are the same for managing what's going on while you explore sexuality with someone, regardless of gender. No matter the person and how they identify, it's important to communicate your desires and limitations and to listen and ask for theirs. Mutual respect doesn't depend on how someone identifies. Communicate with a potential sexual partner in the moment. If they are safe and OK to be with you sexually, it's OK to do what you want and don't want. Period.

Isn't it OK to push just a little to try to persuade someone to go further? I'm not going to force someone, of course, but what if they just need a little convincing?

Nope. Not OK to push even just a little. The need for any sort of persuasion makes the situation nonconsensual. Coercion, or saying things like "C'mon, it'll feel good," "Just relax, don't worry about it," "If you like me you'll do this," or "Everyone does this, what's wrong with you?" is not consent. Adding social power or leverage to the dynamic is also not consent. Saying things like "C'mon, don't you want to be first pick of the team next year? You know I'm the captain," "If you don't do this, I'll have to post those pictures you sent me," or "You don't want everyone to know you're gay, do you?" is not consent. It is coercive and exploitive. It is manipulative, unhealthy, bullyish, and disrespectful to pressure someone into second-guessing themselves and compromising their emotional and physical safety; if taken too far it can even constitute assault.

Can consensual sex be regrettable?

Yes. If consent is asked for and given, without the influence of substances, the impairment of a mental or physical disability, coercion or age disparity (one partner is over eighteen, the other is under eighteen), then the sex is legal. Just because the sex is legal, however, doesn't mean it's right. If it isn't consented to for the right reasons—for instance, someone wasn't ready, the sex wasn't physically or emotionally safe, or someone else's well-being is impacted (like a friend is betrayed)—someone may regret having participated in it. Legal sex is not necessarily ethical or "good" sex. Ethical sex is legal and takes into account the well-being of the participants and others who may be impacted by their actions. Good sex is legal, ethical, and feels pleasurable and satisfying for both partners. To avoid regrettable albeit consensual sex, make sure you choose to engage in sexual activity for *your* right reasons.

CHAPTER TWO

It's the Law

Your and Your Child's Rights—and the Real-World Legal Consequences of Sexual Harassment and Assault

Before reading this chapter, know that it includes explicit accounts of sexual harassment, sexual assault, and rape. If you or someone you know has experienced sexual harassment, assault, or rape, remember that you are not alone. It's important to understand your options and how you can access support. There are resources and hotlines at the end of this chapter as well as an appendix in the back of the book for people who have experienced sexual violence. Please practice self-care, and consider whether you are able to read this chapter and how you can support yourself if the material triggers negative memories and reactions.

It's a Friday night and there's a bonfire at the beach. Forty high school kids are passing around a fishbowl full of assorted pills. Everyone is expected to grab some and wash them down with alcohol, including freshman Katya, and Tony, a sophomore. Within a couple of hours Katya can barely stand. Tony leads Katya over to a washed-up log a ways from the party to sit and chill. Tony and Katya start making out, then lay down in the sand. A couple of Tony's friends see what's going on and make their way over. They start heckling Tony. "Yeah, bro, get after it!" "Give it to her, dude. Yeah bruh, fuck her." Katya struggles to get out from under Tony but can't. She is whimpering "no." Despite Katya's refusal, Tony pulls his pants down and starts to have intercourse. After a minute, Katya is barely moving while Tony finishes. Several of Tony's friends record the event with their phones, send it out, and it goes viral in the school community and beyond.

What takes place between Katya and Tony is rape, a criminal act or felony. Katya is clearly incapacitated, so she cannot consent to any sexual activity. Tony initiates sexual activity and elevates it to the point of genital intercourse. In some states, from a legal standpoint, he is responsible for getting her consent, but doesn't have it because Katya can't legally give it while under the influence. In fact, she is audibly protesting. Tony's friends are complicit with their encouragement (and their failure to help Katya or prevent what Tony is doing), and the social media exploitation of recording and sending video is in violation of federal law (not to mention a really exploitive thing to do). On many counts, these acts of sexual violence are illegal, more importantly because they violate and abuse another human being. Consent laws are meant to keep people safe and protect those who are not able to make decisions for themselves at certain points in time. The law is meant to protect the fundamentals of human dignity. That other people find what takes place entertaining and respond by promoting it is outrageous and indicative of problematic cultural norms we all need to address.

Consent laws are meant to keep people safe and protect those who are not able to make decisions for themselves at certain points in time.

Nonconsensual sex is normalized in many aspects of American pop culture. Whether it be veiled by humor in comedies like *Superbad* and *Horrible Bosses*, or viewed in popular TV series like *Game of Thrones* and *Westworld*, or explicitly expressed in music like that of Tyga and Lil Wayne, teenagers are exposed to nonconsensual sexual dynamics every day. Human bodies are also regularly sexualized and objectified in magazines, newsfeeds, marketed products, advertisements on billboards and buses, television, mainstream movies, and porn. Teen brain development is a process that goes on into the early to mid-twenties for female-bodied people and the mid- to late twenties (even early thirties) for male-bodied people; experience shapes the neuroplastic teen brain and establishes patterns of behavior. Therefore, it is essential that we talk to teenagers about the images of sex they see every day and provide opportunities to identify and make sense of what behaviors are illegal and criminal as well as legal and ethical.

Teens also need to consider digital space as an extension of their personal space as they engage in relationships through their devices. They need to understand that taking, sending, and forwarding nudes is against federal law, and that imposing sexual dynamics into a text exchange needs to be consensual or it may be experienced as sexual harassment. If these same interactions carry over into real-time relationship dynamics, they may be experienced as sexual assault, which is a criminal offense.

Criminal charges refer to crimes committed that could lead to potential jail or prison time, monetary penalties, and other consequences. Civil charges refer to infractions where someone could be punished by fines for their behavior. Being charged criminally or civilly can affect a teen's ability to go to college or get a job; if they are found guilty of perpetrating sexual violence, they may have to register as a sex offender for the rest of their life, which can also make finding a place to live difficult. Bad choices can limit one's future options. The psychological and emotional impact of those consequences can also be life-altering. Both adolescents who experience sexual violence and those who perpetrate it require therapeutic treatment and rehabilitation. Since teenagers spend so much of their time at school, many of these dynamics (between survivor and perpetrator) may play out on campus grounds—during activities, free time, or even classes. The impact can affect a student's overall well-being, including academic performance, social standing, and self-esteem.

Katrina and Jake are both sophomores and in a mixed grade-level art class. Whenever Katrina looks up, Jake's eyes seem to be on her. Jake Snaps Katrina a picture with the caption "whats up." Katrina Snaps back with "not much." Jake Snaps Katrina a few times over the next few days. Katrina opens the Snaps but only responds with "hey." Jake then Snaps "down to hu," and Katrina responds with "im not into that." Jake sends a dick pic and continues to Snap one at random times to Katrina. Whenever Katrina enters the art room for class now, Jake's senior friends allude to Jake's attraction by whooping and hollering at him. As a result, Katrina dreads going to art class, where she feels bullied and unsafe. She becomes preoccupied with avoiding Jake on campus and starts to experience panic attacks. When that happens, she has to leave class and spends time alone in the bathroom trying to catch her breath and calm herself.

Depending on the state, sending naked sexual images while under the age of eighteen may violate teen sexting laws or federal laws that prohibit the trafficking of child pornography.

Katrina did not welcome or want Jake's sexual attention or photos; therefore, his persistent Snaps and sending of explicit images is sexual harassment. Depending on the state, sending naked sexual images while under the age of eighteen may violate teen sexting laws or federal laws that prohibit the trafficking of child pornography. Some states have teen sexting laws that are designed to target teens who send explicit images to other teens, making the crime less significant than a federal child pornography charge, which would apply if the people involved were adults. Depending on the circumstances, sexting may be a crime under federal law. In some states, especially those without specific teen sexting laws, anyone who creates, possesses, or distributes nude or explicit photos of a juvenile, even of themselves, may be charged with child pornography or related crimes, such as the sexual exploitation of a minor.

Since Jake is in Katrina's art class and is sexually harassing her, the educational environment has become "hostile"; that is, she is distressed by his presence because of the sexual harassment and is not able to learn and participate in class the way she would if the harassment were not happening. The unwanted attention from other, older students as a result of the harassment compounds the situation as well. This circumstance would violate many private school sexual harassment policies and invoke Title IX, a federal civil rights gender equity law in public schools.

Title IX of the Education Amendments Act of 1972 ensures equitable access to an education. While public secondary school leaders across the country have an obligation to ensure that students are safe at school, districts vary in their sexual harassment and assault prevention measures. It's important for parents to understand what school policies and procedures are, in addition to our children's and our own rights. Parents also need to be healthy sexuality educators for our children to prevent these incidents from occurring if possible and to prepare them to effectively handle situations. The consequences of sexual harassment and assault can be life-changing, not only from a legal perspective, but also from a psychological and emotional one. Today's social media exploitation, which compounds sexual violence and its consequences, can also have an everlasting public impact.

All of us deserve to be treated with dignity in cyberspace, just as we do in our relationships in our real-world environments. Social media and texting can be a lot of fun; they can also be a great tool for teens to stay in touch with friends and family, or network for school or employment opportunities. But when used inappropriately, they can carry legal consequences. It's important to remember that anything posted on social media remains there forever, and even if deleted, it is still discoverable by law enforcement.

At one point, when art class is over, Jake follows Katrina out of the classroom and toward the stairs. She doesn't know he is following her. Just before she steps down the first step, he pushes then quickly catches her from behind, his body pressed up against hers, arms around her, a hand on her breast, and whispers in her ear, "Don't fall." Before Katrina steadies herself, he has disappeared in the other direction.

The legal term for this type of unwanted sexual touching is sexual battery. Most states have a statute or penal code prohibiting the willful touching of another person in an offensive or harmful manner.

Hopefully, Katrina has the support of her parents. If your child tells you they have experienced harassment or assault, it's important to believe them and to be supportive. It's essential that your child knows that choices are available. Harassment and assault are disempowering experiences. It is important, then, that survivors feel they have the capacity to choose what happens to them after the incident. If Katrina chooses to, she can file a police report against Jake for the misdemeanor. She can also tell her school, which should trigger an investigation of the allegations to determine whether Jake's actions violate sexual harassment policies (in the case of a private school) or Title IX (in the case of a public school). Federally funded schools are obligated to protect their students from gender-based violence under Title IX. In either type of school, the consequences may range from suspension to expulsion, and could also include criminal proceedings if the school calls the police and the alleged victim presses charges. Both students should have their parents present during any conversation about the incident and should seek legal counsel. Katrina could also file a restraining order against Jake. Regarding the explicit photos, Jake may be treated as an adult and it could be on his record for the rest of his life.

Federally funded schools are obligated to protect their students from gender-based violence under Title IX.

Maria and Will go to the same high school and are talking over Snapchat. Maria, fifteen, likes Will, seventeen, and feels they are building trust, so she agrees to meet him at a party. Once there, the two have a couple of drinks of alcohol and spend some time together. After a while, Will leads Maria into a room upstairs. The lighting is dim, and Will closes the door. There are two other boys waiting in the room. Maria immediately expresses discomfort. Will says, "Don't worry, don't you trust me?" Maria responds with, "I do, but I don't think…" Will cuts her off, "Don't worry, it will be fun. If you like me, you'll do this." Maria is then pressured into giving oral sex to all three boys. Each act is recorded on one of the boy's phones.

For the next two months, Will tells Maria that if she doesn't perform sex acts for him and his friends, he will make her "Instagram famous." Many of the coerced sexual incidents happen in secluded areas on school grounds. Maria finally decides she can't continue and goes to the dean at their school. Within minutes, Will follows through on his threat and the videos are posted to a public Instagram page and are screenshot, downloaded, and circulated hundreds of times.

This predatory, methodical, and exploitive assault violates federal and state laws. The age of consent ranges from sixteen to eighteen, depending on the state. Maria is not of consenting age. Furthermore, she is intoxicated, so she is unable to consent and is coerced by manipulation and persuasive language into performing oral sex on the boys. The majority of states have statutes or penal codes identifying this as forced copulation. In addition, the photos and videos taken and circulated violate federal law, as Will is disseminating child pornography and using the photos to extort sexual favors. In addition, some of the sexual violence happened on school grounds and the continued harassment and stress of attending school with her perpetrators creates a hostile environment for Maria, which triggers Title IX. Let's take a look at what happens after Maria reports Will's assault and harassment.

Maria reports to her school's Title IX coordinator

Title IX prohibits discrimination on the basis of sex in schools that receive federal funding. It requires schools to address sexual violence promptly, thoroughly, and fairly, regardless of whether the incident is also reported to the police. All forms of sex-based harassment are prohibited, including sexual harassment, harassment based on a student's failure to conform to gender stereotypes, and sexual assault. It does not matter whether the harasser intends to harm; the harasser and the target do not need to be different sexes. And severe harassment, which would be determined in court, does not necessarily require repeated incidents.

Whenever possible, schools should obtain a student's consent before beginning an investigation; to protect the student's privacy and safety, school administrators should only disclose information to those involved in responding to the incident. When Maria goes to her school administrator or Title IX coordinator (every public school is required to designate at least one employee as the Title IX coordinator and make sure that everyone knows how to contact this person), they should do the following:

- Notify her parents.
- Present Maria and her family with options.
- Call Child Protective Services to make a confidential report (all teachers and administrators are mandated reporters).

Maria and her family decide
if they want to involve the police

Schools are usually not mandated to call the police, so that decision may be left to the child and parents. A great deal of effort has gone into training law enforcement to create and follow survivor-centered procedures. In fact, if the family or school call the police, a victim may request an officer who is trained to interact with survivors and is part of a Sexual Assault Response Team (SART), which provides a coordinated response of medical personnel, law enforcement, and sexual assault service providers in the victim's area.

If a family has difficulty accessing this kind of support, they can call the National Sexual Assault Hotline (1-800-656-HOPE). The staff will connect the survivor with a local sexual harassment service provider who can help them understand the process of getting help and reporting to trained law enforcement.

Maria's family asks for a forensic interview

Before anyone questions Maria, it is important for the family to request a forensic interview. Forensic interviews are trauma-informed interviews conducted by an individual who is trained in supporting survivors. The interview is intended to minimize the potential for retraumatizing the survivor with inappropriate questions, or by asking them to retell the events multiple times. The interview may then be used for various purposes. The infractions in this situation are many. If Maria's school doesn't address the situation effectively and efficiently, the family can file a complaint through the Office of Civil Rights at the U.S. Department of Education.

Maria decides if she wants to press charges

In addition to Maria's sexual assault, the social media exploitation may be reported and addressed as well. The Prosecutorial Remedies and Other Tools to end the Exploitation of Children Today (PROTECT) Act of 2003 makes it illegal to produce, distribute, receive, or possess with intent to distribute any obscene visual depiction of a minor engaged in sexually explicit conduct. Federal law also criminalizes causing a minor to take part in sexually explicit conduct in order to visually depict that conduct. Parents who allow this behavior can also be prosecuted (18 U.S.C. 2251). However, federal prosecution of juveniles for sexting is unlikely because The Federal Juvenile Delinquency Act (FJDA) provides that, where possible, juveniles should be prosecuted in state, not federal, courts. If found guilty, there is a wide range of penalties that may apply. In states that have specific teen sexting laws, the crime is typically a misdemeanor offense or a petty offense, which carries lesser consequences than if the state doesn't have teen sexting laws. If the sexting offense is considered child pornography, that is typically charged as a felony and has much harsher penalties.

If Maria's family presses charges, there will be juvenile proceedings. When a juvenile, such as Will, is suspected of violating a criminal statute, the procedure is different than that used in an adult criminal case. All states have special juvenile court systems for minors who get into trouble with the law. Will's family needs to retain legal representation through their local public defender's office or a private defense attorney, as well as counseling support so Will can be held accountable legally and therapeutically. During those juvenile proceedings, a prosecutor or probation officer takes over; they have discretion to dismiss the case, handle the matter informally, or file formal charges or "petition" the case. Most cases are resolved by mediation and/or a plea bargain. If the case is petitioned and a judge finds Will delinquent, there will be repercussions. Depending on the gravity of the case, consequences may range from continuum of probation and changing schools, to a residential sex offender program, to juvenile prison.

> Finn and Casey, who have been friends and in the same social group since freshman year, end up at the same party one night. It's a typical party scene with drinking games and shots happening in the kitchen. People are smoking marijuana and drinking in the main rooms of the house. Most people are staying over so that no one has to drink and drive. As the night winds down, people try to find space to settle down and sleep. Casey stumbles to the back of the house to find a room and passes out on a bed. Finn shows up and prods her to move over so he can lay down too. She mumbles something and goes back to sleep. A while later she wakes up because she feels weight on her body, pressure in her genitals, and heat on her neck. Casey's haze clears and she realizes that her pants and underwear are off, Finn's penis is inside her, and his face is in her neck; he is breathing hard as he orgasms. Casey pushes Finn off, gets dressed, and leaves as quickly as she can.
>
> After the incident, Finn acts like nothing happened. Casey avoids him whenever possible and changes her school schedule so they aren't in the same class. Over time, she falls into a depression and her grades begin to drop.

What happened between Casey and Finn violates state statutes and penal codes of forcible sexual penetration. Casey was asleep and intoxicated; there is no way she could consent to sexual activity. The incident occurred at someone's home, on private property. Since both Casey and

Finn are minors, it is illegal for them to drink alcohol and smoke marijuana, so the owners of the home may be legally liable for enabling underage drinking and any infractions that happen as a result, even if they didn't know there was a party going on.

In terms of Casey's options, she could report the rape to the police. As in Maria's case, Casey is entitled to a forensic interview and should be offered options so she can make informed choices about how to deal with the abuse. Casey's options are:

- To tell her parents or another trusted adult and ask for help.
- To report the incident by calling the direct line of the local police station or go visit it in person.
- To call the National Sexual Assault Hotline (800–656-HOPE) to acquire support and information about resources in her area.
- To seek medical help.

If she is examined or treated because of the assault, she can tell a medical professional that she would like to report a crime. While at the medical center, she could request a sexual assault forensic exam, commonly known as a rape kit. This won't require Casey to make a report but will provide crucial DNA evidence should she press charges later. The sexual assault nurse examiner (SANE) can inform her of the state's statute of limitations (the window of time to report a crime) in case she wants to wait and report in the future. If Finn is found guilty, the consequences could include missing significant amounts of school to participate in a sex offender rehabilitation program (either residential or outpatient), monetary fines, time in custody, probation, and registration as a sex offender for the rest of his life.

Even though the incident happened off campus, its effects are likely to play out at school as well. Casey doesn't feel safe and needs academic and therapeutic support. If Casey and Will attend a public school, Title IX should provide that assistance, assuming Casey knows how and chooses to access it. If they are students in a private or independent school, Casey can make a formal report and the school can investigate to see if they should adjudicate the situation with disciplinary proceedings under the sexual harassment policy. Either way, if Casey does not make a formal report, it is the school's obligation to ensure the safety and well-being of its students and should provide Casey with the psychological and academic support she needs.

If Casey were in college, she could also opt to use Callisto, a unique technology that supports survivors through the disclosure process. Callisto, a nonprofit organization that collaborates with some colleges, provides technology called Callisto Campus, which is designed to detect repeat perpetrators and empower survivors to make a reporting decision based on different options. The online system protects the survivor's anonymity and offers three options: to save time-stamped written records of sexual assault; report only if another victim reports the same perpetrator; and report directly to campus administrators without waiting for a match. Callisto Expansion enables victims to identify their perpetrator with the precondition that if there is a match, a Callisto counselor will reach out to the victims in person and advise them on their reporting options.

Sexual harassment and assaults take place within all social contexts. The majority of victims know their perpetrators.

The majority of victims know their perpetrators.

Jonathan is fifteen and plays club hockey for his local team. After practice, the coach has several players work with the team's athletic trainer, Mike, an all-star hockey player in his day; his team even won the collegiate championship. He's friendly and supportive and has kids of his own. The boys appreciate his enthusiasm and support. Sometimes after a tough workout or game, he recommends that Jonathan receive a neuromuscular massage in the trainer's room. Mike always stays in the room while Jonathan undresses and talks hockey while massaging him. When Mike gets to Jonathan's groin, his hand will sometimes move to Jonathan's crotch and fondle his genitals. This doesn't feel right to Jonathan, but when he tenses, Mike tells him to relax, and explains that he's just loosening up his hip flexors. Jonathan tries to breathe through it. During one session, Jonathan sees that Mike is visibly aroused, so he jumps off the table, grabs his clothes, and leaves. Jonathan feels guilty for what has happened and blames himself, so he doesn't tell his parents. Instead, the next time Mike puts Jonathan on the schedule for a massage, he tells his parents he wants to switch from his club team to his high school team, and they agree to the change.

Jonathan is a victim of sexual misconduct. Sexual misconduct laws include sexual harassment, sexual assault, exploitation of a minor, and any conduct of a sexual nature that is without consent. State laws vary in the way they define acts that constitute sexual misconduct and the age of consent. Currently, the range of consent for among the U.S. states is from sixteen to eighteen years old, so Jonathan cannot consent because Mike, the other participant, is an older adult and has social power over him. Jonathan's intuition about Mike's improper touching is correct. Mike is taking advantage of his position as an adult managing a kid's hockey team to exploit Jonathan's vulnerability and trust. This may also be considered statutory rape.

Statutory rape is a term that encompasses various laws regarding sexual misconduct.

Statutory rape is a term that encompasses various laws regarding sexual misconduct. The laws within the context of this term are intended to protect minors from being sexually taken advantage of by adults. As parents, we must educate our children on what is appropriate behavior from adults they interact with, as well as what is explicitly inappropriate. Let them know that you will protect them from such behavior. This behavior may happen in the context of any of the various activities our teenagers are involved in. It's a delicate balance: we don't want to make our children fearful or paranoid; we also want to encourage healthy relationships with adult guides and mentors. Exercise a balance of caution and calm. At the same time, kids should be informed of their rights and told how to deal with predatory adults. When a child discloses abuse, it is essential that we believe them and respond. This may include telling the appropriate authorities and pressing charges.

PARENT–TEEN CONVERSATION STARTERS

Teenagers need information about their legal responsibilities about consent from credible sources, as well as values education and guidance on how to apply that information to digital and real-life social interactions and relationships. It's important that we, as parents, educate ourselves so we can effectively inform our children. Here are some questions to get the dialogue going. If you don't know the answers yourself, suggest finding the information with your teen (see list of resources below).

- Do you know the legal definitions of sexual harassment? Assault? Rape?
- What values is the law trying to protect?
- What do you think motivates someone to violate the law?
- Do you know what the age of consent is in our state?
- Why do age of consent laws matter?
- How do these nonconsensual dynamics show up in high school?
- Have you ever experienced anything like what happened in any of the scenarios described in this chapter?
- Have you ever been witness to or heard about anyone experiencing anything like this?
- What is the sexual harassment policy at your school? Sexual assault policy?
- Does your school have a policy about cyberharassment? (for private school students; in public schools, this is included under Title IX)
- Are you aware of what Title IX is? (for public school students)
- Do you know who the Title IX coordinator is at your school and how to make a report?
- How could you help a friend access help if they are have been harassed or assaulted?

Resources

Equal Rights Advocates: https://www.equalrights.org/

RAINN: Reporting and the Criminal Justice System, Statutes of Limitations: https://www.rainn.org/articles/legal-role-consent

The National Women's Law Center: https://nwlc.org/

Know Your IX: https://www.knowyourix.org/

Futures Without Violence: https://www.futureswithoutviolence.org/

Stop Sexual Assault in Schools: http://stopsexualassaultinschools.org/

Articles

"David Schwimmer Made Six Short Films about Sexual Harassment: We Annotate
One of Them" by Claire Cain Miller, *New York Times*, January 26, 2018

"Stand Up to Sexual Harassment and Abuse: How Men Can Help Women" by
Zaron Burnett III, *Teen Vogue*, October 24, 2017

"A Gentleman's Guide to Street Harassment" by Zaron Burnett III, humanparts
.medium.com

STRAIGHT ANSWERS TO TEEN QUESTIONS

What is sexual violence?

Sexual violence refers to physical sexual acts performed by one person
without the consent of the other person or when the other person is
unable to give consent. It includes sexual harassment, sexual assault, rape,
domestic violence, dating violence, and stalking.

What is sexual harassment?

Sexual harassment is a term that was first coined in 1975 at Cornell
University by female activists in defense of Carnita Wood, an administrative assistant in the nuclear physics department. Wood was being sexually harassed by professors to whom she reported and was subsequently
fired, many believe because she protested the harassment. The term orig-
inated to describe a sexual power dynamic that originally happened in
the workplace.

The U.S. Equal Employment Opportunity Commission states that it is unlawful to harass a person because of that person's sex. Harassment can include unwelcome sexual advances, requests for sexual favors, and other verbal or physical harassment of a sexual nature. Harassment does not have to be of a sexual nature; it can include offensive remarks about a person's sex. For example, it is illegal to harass a woman by making offensive comments about women in general. Both victim and harasser can be either female or male and both can also be the same sex. Although the law doesn't prohibit simple teasing, offhand comments, or isolated incidents that are not serious, harassment is illegal when it is frequent or severe enough that it creates a hostile or offensive work environment, or when it results in an adverse employment decision (such as the victim being fired or demoted). The harasser can be the victim's supervisor in another area, a coworker, or someone who is not an employee of the employer, such as a client or customer.

What is sexual assault?

According to the U.S. Department of Justice (DOJ), "Sexual assault is any type of sexual contact or behavior that occurs without the explicit consent of the recipient. Included in the definition of sexual assault are sexual activities such as forced sexual intercourse, forcible sodomy, child molestation, incest, fondling, and attempted rape." Sexual assault occurs when a person engages in physical sexual activity without the consent of the other person, or when the other person is unable to consent to the activity. The activity or conduct may include physical force, violence, threat, intimidation, coercion, ignoring the objections of the other person, causing the other person's intoxication or incapacitation, or taking advantage of the other person's intoxication.

What is the difference between sexual harassment and sexual assault?

Generally speaking, sexual harassment is unwelcome sexual attention and can happen without people's bodies touching each other. Sexual assault is unwelcome sexual touching or activity, usually between two people's bodies. You can think of sexual harassment as *conduct* (how people behave toward others) and sexual assault as *contact* (how people touch each other). Both are considered sexual violence because sex is the mechanism by which someone imposes their power and control over another person. The impact of both sexual harassment and sexual assault can be traumatic and create a hostile environment where the victim experiences duress and hardship, which can lead to inequities in the workplace, school, or other venue.

Does sexual assault include rape?

Yes, the definition of sexual assault from the Department of Justice includes rape. The DOJ defines rape as "the penetration, no matter how slight, of the vagina or anus with any body part or object, or oral penetration by a sex organ of another person, without the consent of the victim." The legal definitions for terms like *rape, sexual assault,* and *consent* vary from state to state. Consent often plays an important role in determining whether an act is legally considered a crime. Three questions that states may use to determine consent as it relates to sexual acts are:

- Affirmative consent: Did the person express overt actions or words indicating agreement for sexual acts?
- Freely given consent: Was the consent offered of the person's own free will, without being induced by fraud, coercion, violence, or threat of violence?

- Capacity to consent: Did the individual have the capacity, or legal ability, to consent? (Source: https://www.rainn.org/articles/legal-role-consent)

For help with understanding any of this language, see the Consent Glossary in the back of the book.

What if assault happens between two people of the same sex?

There are many ways people can identify their gender and how it does or doesn't align with their sexual reproductive organs. The legal language of affirmative consent legislation and criminal law is inclusive of different sexualities and orientations; however, the media coverage and cultural interpretation of those laws may not be. You *should* get equitable legal protection under school policies and the law, no matter how you identify or who the perpetrator is. That is the point of Title IX, a civil rights gender equity law. Because there is still sex stigma in our culture surrounding different expressions of sexual identity, there may be added layers of complexity when reporting. There are many inclusive, positive resources now available for LGBTQQ+ (lesbian, gay, bisexual, transgender, queer and questioning, and additional identities) young people. Seek the support of your school's LGBTQQ+ advocacy group or contact the sexual assault survivor resources in the back of this book, specifically created to support LGBTQQ+ youth. These resources can provide guidance and moral support on how to report the assault and get the help you need. You are not alone!

If I had consensual sex at a party, could I be accused of rape?

If both partners agreed to have sex with each other, were not under the influence of any substances, and were of the same mind about what would happen, then the answer is no—*unless* you are over age eighteen and the other person is under eighteen, or the person has a physical, developmental, or cognitive disability that impairs their understanding of consent. In comparison, if you and/or your partner were incapacitated by any substances, the act is not considered consensual. Consent must be freely given and unambiguous. It is to your benefit to know your partner and what they want and don't want in your relationship, whether it lasts for fifteen minutes or three years. Consent requires both people to be self-aware, able to self-regulate, honest, and clear-minded. Drugs, including alcohol, often get in the way of that.

How do you prove in court that you had affirmative consent?

Within the criminal justice system, you are innocent until proven guilty, so affirmative consent isn't something you have to prove. Rather, the prosecution (who represents the alleged victim) has to prove that you didn't acquire it. You are not legally required to put on a defense, and you never have to testify. However, realistically, if the evidence is overwhelmingly against you, you may choose to testify if your lawyer recommends it. Remember that the criminal justice system is different from a disciplinary process in a school, which may take place under the guidelines of Title IX or private school policy.

When is it OK to drink and hook up?

Whenever anyone engages in a sexual relationship, there are some fundamentals that should be present: physical and emotional safety, mutual respect (which requires empathy), and sexual communication. Ask yourself at what point these values become compromised when drinking. Once these fundamentals are at risk, affirmative consent is compromised. Both partners should be in a state of mind that enables them to authentically express desires and limitations, and fully exercise autonomy and agency of their own sexuality. If one or both people are intoxicated, this may not be true. As a general rule, an individual under the influence cannot legally give consent. Drunk sex is an ethical and legal risk.

What should I do if the person says
I assaulted them but I didn't see it that way?

This can be tricky. There are legal and ethical responses to consider. First, find an adult you trust who can help you figure out what to do. Depending on the other person and what they are contesting, you may want to have a conversation with them. If they have reported or may report the incident, you might want to wait on further communication until you figure out what you want to do and what your rights are. It's important that you do not ignore what's happening and think that it's just going to go away. You should think carefully about the context and what happened during the interaction and determine to the best of your ability the truth from your perspective.

It's important that you be accountable for your actions. You may not have intended to hurt someone, but if they say that's the impact you've had, it's important to take responsibility. If you care about this person and feel you aren't at risk for legal consequences, have a meaningful and thoughtful conversation about what happened and how you can make it better. Express your genuine concern and see if they need resources for support. If you believe you are at risk of being formally or legally reported, consult your parents and an attorney. Therapeutic counseling can also be helpful if you are navigating a legal proceeding, and it is always confidential.

If I'm assaulted, who should I tell? The school or the police? My parents or my friends?

Sexual assault is a serious issue and can be disempowering and traumatic. It's important for you to think carefully about what you want to do. As difficult as the situation is, remember that you have options. You can tell a trusted adult. Possibilities include a teacher (who will be required by law to make a confidential report of the incident to Child Protective Services [CPS] and possibly to school administration); a school administrator (who is also required to make a report to CPS); your parents, who will hopefully provide moral support and help you decide how to move forward; a school counselor (who is also required to make a report to CPS; however, depending on the policies of their school, they may not have to share the information with your parents or other school adults); or a trusted friend. You may choose to go to the police, who will hopefully provide guidance and resources for support and investigate. You can also call a hotline (the National Sexual Assault Hotline: 1-800-656-HOPE) or check out the resources throughout this book. The most important thing to do is to get assistance from someone you trust and who is in a position to help you. There are potential psychological and physical risks if you remain isolated, so remember that you are not alone and that there are people who can and want to help you.

What if I tell on the person who assaulted me and they get mad and want to get back at me?

Retaliation is a common fear and the reason many people who are sexually assaulted don't report sexual assault. It's important that alleged perpetrators are held accountable for their actions so they don't continue to hurt people. It's up to you to decide, however, if that is more important than the possible consequences if you report the incident. An alleged perpetrator also can experience consequences for retaliation. A trusted school counselor or adult can help you figure out strategies for reporting an incident and dealing with any potential problems that may result. If confidentiality is important to you, make sure you have that right. Find out what your school's policies are and try to find out if they are typically followed. Some schools offer protection and support in different forms if someone retaliates. If you report the incident to the police, they can also take protective measures. If someone is bullying you online (as retaliation or otherwise), take screenshots, record or save what they are doing, and tell a trusted and responsible adult. This type of assault and bullying can be traumatic, confusing, and challenging. These destructive effects can often thrive in isolation. Make sure you get some sort of support from someone you trust. If you don't have that, there are hotlines and resources available to you in this book.

CHAPTER THREE

"You Good?"

How to Teach Consent—
and Keep It Sexy

> Nick had a crush on Eliza since the beginning of the school year, but
> he was always too shy and tongue-tied to talk to her. To his surprise,
> right before finals Eliza started flirting with him and invited him over
> to her house to study. Before he knew it, they were making out on
> her bed, and Eliza was into it, slipping her hands under his shirt and
> pulling him close. Nick started sliding his hand up her thigh, under
> her skirt—when the thought crossed his mind that maybe he should
> ask for her consent before taking things another next step. But he
> didn't know what to say, and he worried about sounding awkward
> and ruining the moment.

The thought of asking someone for sexual consent seems overwhelming
to many teens. If they're inexperienced and anxious, they don't want to
risk spoiling an encounter by saying something that might come across
as uncool. Many guys assume that they should "just know" if a girl wants
to become more intimate. And many girls, if they're taking the lead, think
they'll come off as "slutty" if they ask a guy for his consent. Too many
teens (and adults) don't know that healthy sexual encounters include

dialogue, feedback, and reciprocity. The media, after all, hardly ever shows scenes of couples having sex and communicating attentively with one another. But the truth is, asking for consent is not something that has to be hard or awkward. It's a natural human expression of caring and concern for another person.

Asking for consent is not something that has to be hard or awkward.

Devon and Katrina have been going out for eleven months, and one day after school, they started messing around at Devon's house. No one else is home, and they get to a point where intercourse might happen. Although they haven't talked about doing that, Katrina asks Devon if he has a condom. He said yes, and then asks her, "Are you up for sex?" Katrina smiles at him. "I think so," she says. "But go slow, OK?" Devon nods and puts on the condom, and Katrina guides him to intercourse. As they are having sex, Devon whispers to her, "You OK? Tell me what feels good." Katrina nodded and said, "OK. You too."

For Devon and Katrina, asking for and communicating consent is as natural as their physical connection. Their verbal check-ins express mutual caring, respect, and concern for each other's comfort and pleasure.

Sometimes, clear body language can convey consent—or the lack of it—as well as words.

Tina and Karen have been friends since they started high school. By the middle of sophomore year, Tina feels they have grown more emotionally connected. She mentions it to Karen, who tells her she is feeling the same way. That weekend, they watch a movie together at Tina's house. They started cuddling on the couch, and soon Karen looks at Tina questioningly. She nods, they start making out, and then Tina lifts the bottom of Karen's shirt, hinting that she wants to take it off. Karen helps her do it, and then Karen starts to unbutton Tina's blouse. She is fumbling with it, so Tina helps her. They make out a while longer, and then Karen asks, "You good?" "Yeah," Tina says. "Let's stay like this." So they keep making out and don't go any further.

Body language is a crucial part of their conversation. When Karen looks at Tina, and Tina nods and helps Karen unbutton her shirt, she is affirmatively giving consent. It is part of the natural physical flow of their encounter. But if there is any doubt at all about your partner's body language or facial expressions, you have to ask for consent verbally. It doesn't have to be awkward. As one of my students said, you can say anything in a sexy voice. It's a part of the caring give-and-take of healthy sexual encounters.

Sometimes, though, people can be ambiguous or change their minds about the level of intimacy they want.

Chris and Kennedy start making out after a party, and things get pretty heated and intense. Chris whispers, "Are you into oral?" Kennedy says, "Uh-huh," and starts to give Chris oral sex. But after a few moments, he pulls away from Chris and says, "I can't do this now." Chris asks, "Do you want to just stick with what we were doing before?" "Yeah," Kennedy says, and the two of them go back to making out again.

Checking in with each other is necessary whenever a partner initiates a new level of sexual intimacy.

Checking in with each other is necessary whenever a partner initiates a new level of sexual intimacy. There has to be a moment when the other person can say yes or no—verbally or through clear facial expressions or body language. Like stopping at traffic lights or stop signs when you're driving, pausing for consent is one of the rules of the road that every teen needs to know. It's about respect, caring, ethics, and the legal obligation to protect other people and keep them safe.

HOW NOT TO ASK FOR SEXUAL CONSENT

Let's be clear. Sexual consent is not silence or the lack of protest—and it's not about the absence of the word *no*. People can't give their consent if they're incapacitated by substances or have a cognitive disability. They can't give their consent if they're coerced. And, in some states, they can't give their consent if they're under age eighteen and their partner is at least two years older.

It's also important to know that consent is not the same thing as sexual arousal. If someone's partner has a genital response—like a spontaneous erection or a wet vulva—it doesn't mean that they've consented to sexual activity; genital response is involuntary. Consent has to be freely and clearly given. A partner's words are much more important than their genitals. And people can't give consent digitally, by texting or apps like Snapchat.

At the end of his senior year, Bret texts Marla, a sophomore, on a Saturday night, offering to pay for an Uber to take her to a party at a friend's house. Although they have hooked up a couple of times during the school year, Marla wants to take it slow. Bret has bragged to his friends that he was getting impatient and planned to "tap that shit" over the weekend. So he texts Marla and pressures her to get together with him. Marla texts back that she doesn't think she can make it to the party—plus, she adds, "You're a senior and I can tell you're drunk." But Bret keeps texting, asking her to come to his house and watch a movie with him or sleep over: "C'mon you know you want it ;)," he texts. "I chose you out of all the hot sophomores." Marla texts back, "Ok I will be there soon."

This is not consent, because Bret is using his social power to coerce Marla, and consent has to be given in person, in the moment, freely and clearly—even when the partners are in a caring relationship.

When Randy and his girlfriend, Leyla, are at his house one day after school, they are trying to get some homework done but start messing around. They have casually talked about oral sex before, and Randy wants to see if Leyla would be into it. So he gently nudges her down on him, whispering, "You're up for oral, right?" Leyla gives him oral sex. But afterward, when she moves back up to kiss him, Randy notices that her eyes are teary. He asks Leyla what is wrong, but she won't look him in the eye and doesn't answer. Finally, she tells him she is fine and leaves, saying that she has to get home.

Randy assumes that Leyla has consented to oral sex because when he suggests it, she doesn't answer. But he didn't really ask Leyla a question—he made a statement about what he wanted. Leyla's silence didn't mean that she consented. Sexual consent has to be asked for directly and given explicitly in the moment. Randy's body language—nudging Leyla down his body—was not a legitimate way to ask for consent either. It was just another way of telling her what he wanted. He didn't unambiguously ask Leyla if she wanted to engage in oral sex, and he didn't pause to allow her to say yes or no freely and clearly. Furthermore, consent can be revoked at any time.

> Emily and Matt have hooked up a couple of times at parties in their senior year and both feel fine about it. Emily has given Matt oral sex, and while texting one afternoon, they talk about going to the same party, hooking up, and having sex. They get together like they planned, find an empty bedroom, and begin to have intercourse with a condom. Soon, though, Emily whispers to Matt, "Wait—this doesn't feel right." But Matt continues having intercourse with her, telling her in a soothing voice, "Don't worry. You're doing great."

Matt is more concerned about his orgasm than about Emily's feelings. When Emily says that she doesn't feel right, he should have stopped. Instead, he is treating her like an object, prioritizing his own pleasure and sexual arousal over hers. Their relationship was friendly but superficial. Even though they have been physically intimate before, have friends in common, and feel familiar with each other through text messages, they haven't established a relationship of trust, caring, and authentic connection and communication. By ignoring Emily's wishes, Matt shows he is only in it for himself. By coercing her to let him "finish," he shows his lack of fundamental decency, respect, and care. He and Emily could have engaged in another form of sexual activity that they were both comfortable with, or if Emily wanted to stop altogether, he could have waited and relieved his sexual tension by masturbating later. The point is that Emily had the right to revoke her consent, and Matt had the obligation to stop. When he didn't, he was coercing and violating Emily and potentially placing himself in legal jeopardy.

People can't use their friends to facilitate consent either. Lauren, for example, has her eye on DJ and has her friend ask one of DJ's buddies if he is interested in her. Through the grapevine, DJ says he is. But neither of them is consenting to sexual activity. That has to be given in person, in the moment. Using friends as go-betweens may shield teens a bit from feelings of vulnerability and rejection, but it's more important to practice how to take healthy risks and communicate directly with people you may want to know better. Learning how to connect, convey your intentions clearly, and ask sexual partners for consent are essential interpersonal skills and the building blocks of healthy, respectful, caring relationships.

> **Learning how to connect, convey your intentions clearly, and ask sexual partners for consent are essential interpersonal skills and the building blocks of healthy, respectful, caring relationships.**

PARENT–TEEN CONVERSATION STARTERS

As I've pointed out before, teens are concrete thinkers, so the best way to approach the how-tos of sexual consent is to watch an interaction on a video, in a movie, or on TV, and talk about the episode together. It doesn't need to be a heavy conversation. Sometimes, as parents, we grab any opportunity to say everything we've always wanted to say about a subject. But it's better to take it easy, go slow, don't overwhelm your teen, and layer information a little at a time, over many separate conversations. You've probably already laid a solid foundation about the importance of personal boundaries, respect, and empathy, as well as your family values. Now that your child is a teenager, it is time to be explicit about how these values apply in the context of romance, love, and sexuality.

Be aware of where your child is developmentally, what media they are exposed to, and what sorts of messages they are hearing. If together you watch a scene of a sexual encounter, you can use the opportunity to ask your teen a few of these questions as part of the natural flow of conversation:

- How did the couple communicate what they wanted or didn't want?
- Was it clear and enthusiastic?
- Sexual exploration can be awkward sometimes. Did you notice any awkward moments? If so, how did the couple deal with it?
- How was consent given or not given? Was it with words only, or was there accompanying body language?
- How was consent explicitly asked for? Did the question allow for yes and no?
- When and how should it have been asked for?
- Did both people show care and respect for each other? In what ways?
- If they didn't, what could have been done differently?
- Did you see or hear any coercion?
- Do you think the scene was an accurate representation of what real-life sexual exploration is like?
- Did the physical intimacy express the couple's emotional intimacy?

- What values that we have raised you with were present or not present in what you saw?
- Was the sexual exploration safe and responsible? If not, what got in the way?
- Was there an unequal power dynamic?
- How did the couple feel about it afterward?
- Did both people walk away from the experience with their dignity?
- What was the impact of the sexual encounter on their relationship?

Resources

For younger teens, amaze.org has some effective films on consent for kids. Two videos in particular are "Consent" and "Saying Yes or No: What is Consent?"

For older teens, Planned Parenthood has a great collection of consent videos on YouTube. The messages and examples they provide are clear and effective for teenagers and young adults. They also are inclusive of different sexualities and political identities. It's best for you to watch them first and decide whether you feel they're appropriate for your teen:

"How Do You Know When Someone Wants to Have Sex With You?": https://www.youtube.com/watch?v=D-8isMT2u9A

"When Someone Isn't Quite Sure If They Want To Have Sex": https://www.youtube.com/watch?v=D-8isMT2u9A

"When Someone Doesn't Want To Have Sex": https://www.youtube.com/watch?v=QSDjSetlGiw

"When Someone Definitely Wants To Have Sex": https://www.youtube.com/watch?v=VmcGigHzpK0

After you share these videos with your teenager, you can ask a few of these questions:

- Based on our conversations and the videos, what is your definition of consent?
- How did the videos compare to other scenes of sexuality in the media that you've been exposed to?
- How did the video(s) change or deepen your understanding of consent?
- What might be an obstacle to practicing consent this way?
- What would make those interactions nonconsensual?
- How would you advise the characters to handle it?
- Were there any differences or mixed messages that came up when you watched the video, relative to our family's values?

For assertiveness training workshops, see André Salvage and Associates: https://www.andresalvage.com

As a parent, strive to model good communication and respect for personal boundaries; avoid using sexist language or reinforcing sexual stereotypes. You are by far the most powerful example for your teen, and your actions always mean much more than words.

STRAIGHT ANSWERS TO TEEN QUESTIONS

How do I even start the consent thing?

Ideally, consent starts before you actually engage in sexual activity. How you approach a relationship or express your interest in getting to know someone physically, emotionally, and intellectually is important. Whatever attention you give someone should be welcomed by them. If it's the very beginning of the relationship, the person you initiate a connection with should at least reciprocate curiosity and interest. If you are going to ask someone out, be considerate about how and when you ask. Make sure that your question treats someone with dignity, in a way that honors that person's value. Your actual question should also allow for a yes or no answer. You could ask, "Would you like to go for a walk in the park after school with me?" or "Do you want to go to the beach and chill to the sunset on Saturday?" or "Would you be interested in seeing a movie together on Sunday afternoon?" If you are in the same friend group, make sure you include "with me," "together," or "just the two of us," so you are clear that you are interested in them beyond friendship. Then respect their answer, whatever it may be.

Just like consent for sexual activity, if someone asks you out, your response is important. If you reciprocate the interest, you could just say, "Yeah, sure, what time?" or "Definitely, that would be fun." Then go do a happy dance. If you don't reciprocate the interest, you could say, "I appreciate you asking, but no thanks." If someone asks you out, they've given you a compliment, so it's important to treat them with dignity. A lot of my students get anxious about saying no to someone. Be honest and clear. Be aware of creating false hope ("not right now") to save yourself from the discomfort of saying no. Of course, if someone asks without respect or doesn't listen to your no and is harassing you, then be assertive with your no and find support from trusted adults and friends.

Do I have to ask for consent in a certain way?

Whenever you initiate a new level of sexual activity, you need to ask your partner for consent. Phrase your question so there is room for your partner to say either yes or no and communicate their genuine response.

Neutral questions like "You good?" or "Is this OK?" or "How do you feel about oral?" give your partner the opportunity to express their authentic desire and limits. On the other hand, questions like "Will you go down on me?" "Will you have sex with me?" or "I know you want it, right?" can make your partner feel obligated. Those aren't legitimate ways to ask for sexual consent.

Can consent be implied? Does it always have to be said, or can it be with body language?

Consent needs to be clear and unambiguous. Facial expressions and body language can count, but if there is any doubt, it's essential to ask verbally. Pay attention to your partner's face. If they smile at you, that can be a positive sign. If their body moves toward you in a relaxed way, even if sexual tension is building, that can be positive too. If your partner wraps their arms around you and applies pressure to your body in response to what you're doing, bringing you physically closer, this can also be positive. But if your partner stiffens, has their arms at the side, just lies there, is nonresponsive, or tries to position their body away from you or your touch, that's an indication that they are not into it, and you should stop and check in with them.

Do you have to ask for consent every ten minutes?

Consent is about mutual respect during all sexual activity. Exploring sex with people who want to explore sex with you is an affirmative thing. You should ask for consent whenever a new sexual activity or level of intimacy is initiated. It isn't about time on a watch, but the timing of the sexual exploration that is happening.

Some people may think you have to ask literally every ten minutes because there was misreporting on the *Today* show of a conversation in my class. The *New York Times* ran an article on how I teach about consent. One of my students asked a sarcastic question, "Yeah, what does that mean—you have to say yes every ten minutes?" I responded, "Pretty much. It's not a timing thing, but whoever initiates things to another level has to ask."

Within a couple of days, *Today* filmed another class and did interviews with me and my students. The piece that ran was two minutes and then Erica Hill and Matt Lauer had the following exchange:

Matt: "Did they come up with clear guidelines as to how often the question needs to be asked?"

Erica: "So there's been talk about every ten minutes. You sort of need to check in and make sure, OK, are we still, are we still good? And you and I were talking, Matt, too, some of the language that they come up with is awkward, especially in your teen years. What do you say?"

Erica's reference to consent every ten minutes came from my fifteen-year-old student's snarky question. The reality is that you have to ask whenever there is a shift in the type and intensity of sexual activity. Depending on the pace of what you're doing that could be thirty or sixty seconds later, or five minutes later, or fifteen minutes later, or yes, maybe ten minutes later.

How do I give and get consent without killing the mood?

Healthy sexual activity includes communication. Asking and consenting can be integrated into the rhythm of the moment. You can audibly whisper "You good?" or "This OK?" If your partner consents, they can simply say yes, which affirms desire. (However, it's important to be aware of different social pressures and messages that may get in the way of people expressing what they truly want. These issues are discussed in chapter 4.) If you start to unbutton your partner's shirt and then look into their eyes questioningly, your partner can show consent by helping you with the buttons or taking off their own shirt. This is reciprocal exchange. It doesn't have to be awkward, but the reality of sexual activity is that sometimes it is, and that's OK. Choose a partner you trust to get through awkward moments without judgment. Exploring sexuality with someone you can communicate with comfortably will ultimately make for a better experience.

How do I know if they really mean it when they say yes?

To know this, you need to be able to trust your partner. Trust is something that takes time to build. The more partners know and care about each other, the more probable it is that they will mean yes when they say yes. Alcohol and other drugs, however, can impair someone's ability to say yes and mean it. A yes from someone under the influence of substances is not reliable, while a yes from someone who is clear-headed and sober is more so. The better you know someone, understand each other's intentions, and care about each other's experience, the more you can trust your partner's words.

What if I really like someone, but what they want to do freaks me out?

Sometimes when we like someone, we're afraid to communicate that something feels unsafe, uncomfortable, or scary. We may not want to cause a conflict or come across as a *prude* (someone who is shamed for choosing not to be sexually active) or a buzzkill. But here's the thing—if that person is worth having a relationship with, they should care that you're genuinely into what you're doing together sexually. If they don't, it won't be a positive sexual experience or a healthy relationship.

What if I ask and they say no?

You have to ask for consent, out of respect, so your partner has the opportunity to say yes or no. And if they feel comfortable enough to say no, that's a positive thing. The next step is to ask whether they want to stop all sexual activity, want to continue what you were both doing before, or want to switch to some other sexual activity that feels better. If your partner wants to stop all sexual activity, it's essential to honor that. Find out if your partner needs space, if they want to talk, or if they want to spend time with you doing something nonsexual. Think about what you'd like to do as well and have a conversation about it. More often than not, the word *no* is not a rejection of your relationship. It may feel awkward, but getting through the situation together can deepen your personal connection.

What if I say yes to something, and then we're doing it, and it doesn't feel right, and I want it to stop? Can I do that?

Absolutely. Affirmative consent can be revoked at any time. Sometimes, we may think that we're up for something, but then once we start experiencing it, we realize it's not what we expected or wanted to be doing. So speak up. The words and tone you use will depend on how responsive your partner is to you and your experience. If you have a healthy and communicative relationship, you can say, "Wait, I'd like to stop. This isn't feeling right for me." If you feel you need to be more assertive, you can say, "This doesn't feel right—let's stop." But if your partner isn't listening to you, you can firmly say, "No!" "Get off!" or "If you continue, you will be assaulting/raping me." If someone totally ignores your request and is forcible or violent with you, use all your strength to get away, yell "No!" "Stop!" "Help!" and get to safety.

It's important to know, however, that it's common for people to freeze, physically and psychologically, when they're in an unwanted sexual encounter, making it hard or impossible for them to respond aggressively. That's one reason why it's so important for sexual partners to actively seek consent before any level of intimacy.

What if someone knows I've done one thing and assumes that, because I have that experience, I'll do it with them?

This is why "yes means yes" is so important. People shouldn't assume consent for any sexual activity even if it's a part of their partner's sexual history. Sexual exploration with each person, even with the same person in a different context, can be a different experience. Before engaging in sexual activity with someone, think about whether you feel comfortable setting limits, and if they will respect how you want to be treated and your right to decide what sexual activity you want to participate in together. If you are engaged in sexual activity and you feel respected, communicate what you want. It's your right to say "I'm good with this" or "Let's stay with this for now" or "I'm not ready to do that with you yet" or "No." If the person you're with doesn't listen and respond with respect, stop what you're doing because you are not being treated with respect.

If this occurs within the context of a relationship, it's important to talk to your partner, express your feelings, and resolve the situation. You should both be communicating with each other about what you want and need from each other. A healthy sexual relationship makes each other better and is mutually pleasurable. If your partner continues to ignore your boundaries, it's time to end the relationship.

If this happens in the context of a hookup, stop what you are doing and don't hook up with that partner in the future. If you decide to give them another chance, make sure you're really clear about your expectations. You deserve to be with someone who cares about your well-being and the sexual experiences you share.

If I say yes to one thing, do I need to say yes to another?

No. You have the right to say yes to the sexual acts you feel comfortable with, desire, and truly want to engage in. You also have the right to say no, continue doing what you're comfortable with, end the encounter, or decide to move forward. It's also important to communicate with your partner, learn what they want and need, and think about whether your desires are compatible. If you're worried about your sexual boundaries, it isn't a good relationship or hookup to be in.

What if I'm in it for the physical only, and I'm afraid that if I ask for consent, it will be misunderstood as emotional and as wanting more?

If you are engaged in sexual activity with someone for only physical pleasure, you should make sure that is what they want too. How your question for consent is received and interpreted will depend on the level of your sexual communication as well as your partner's intentions, understandings, opinions, values, and experiences. Asking for consent and getting an enthusiastic yes is legal, but that doesn't necessarily mean it's ethical. Ethical sexual exploration takes into account your partner's well-being. If you know they want more from you than just physical gratification, and you don't feel the same way, it is respectful to tell them. Then they can choose whether to say yes based on an honest understanding of the context of the sexual activity.

If I receive oral, do I have to give it back?

Positive sexual activity should be mutually desired. If you don't want to give oral, you don't have to, even if your partner gave it to you. Some people find giving and receiving oral pleasurable, and others don't. Some may like to give it, while others may like to receive. Different people experience pleasure in different ways. If you want to reciprocate with something pleasurable for your partner, ask them what would feel good, then consider whether you're comfortable with that. You should also explore and discover together what's pleasurable for you both. And if you're not ready for or don't like certain types of intimacy, it's important to be clear about that too.

Something I've noticed over the years is that I hear about boys receiving oral sex from girls but rarely hear about boys reciprocating and going down on girls. Like I said above, nobody should agree to sexual activity they don't want. And I suspect that the latter is in many ways because of double-standard gender norms that are addressed in chapter 4. If double standards are the source of your lack of reciprocity, it's time to take a hard look at what you're really in it for and if it's fair and healthy.

What if both people are drunk? Doesn't that make the power dynamic even?

No. If both people are drunk, neither can legally consent to sexual activity. There are levels of intoxication and variables for each individual that determine how drunk they are or are going to be throughout a sexual encounter. Because of that, their incapacitation cannot be the same or equal. If an investigation were to take place, the investigator would look into and try to determine how intoxicated both people were at the time of the incident if it is being contested. Remember, consent protects the fundamentals of human dignity: primarily respect, and physical and emotional safety. If both people are drunk, those values are compromised and put both people at risk.

CHAPTER FOUR

Sexpectations

Gender, Pressure, and Porn

When I check my work email on Sunday night, I see that Julia, a current student, has reached out. She wants to meet first thing in the morning. We schedule a time. A few minutes after I get to my office, Julia peeks through the crack of my open door. Her eyes are red-rimmed and swollen, and she looks washed out and serious. She manages a soft, "Can I come in?"

"Of course. Close the door. What's going on?"

Julia sits on the couch in my office and hugs herself tightly. Her hand is on her forehead and her eyes are downcast. She closes them and breathes deeply. Heavy silence fills the room, and she looks up at me with a furrowed brow and tight mouth.

"There was a party. And I was drinking. People were really drunk."

"Was it a big party? Were there a lot of people?"

"Yes. I hooked up with someone. He was drunk, too, but not so much that we didn't know what we were doing."

"Is there something you want to share about the hookup?"

"We did some stuff. Stuff I wanted to do. It was fine. I mean, I think I wanted to. We're friends, but…"

"But?"

"But when we left the room, he put his fists in the air like he had scored a goal and announced what we did. He literally told everyone. Everyone. I was fine with the hookup. It's the telling everyone that I'm not fine with. I mean, I wanted to hook up with him. But it was just so different than when I was with my boyfriend last year. It was just so…impersonal. And then he went and broadcast it to everyone. I mean, I guess I should have expected that, right?"

The tone of Julia's last question is rhetorical and questioning at the same time. "I don't know what to do."

Julia felt angry, sad, and ashamed. She was anxious that her reputation would be ruined and that she could get pregnant. The possibility of a sexually transmitted disease also weighed on her mind. She had two tests to take that day and had trouble staying focused. She felt like everyone was talking and looking at her with judgment. In several social circles, they were.

There are many things wrong with this situation: impersonal sex in the context of substance use (making it nonconsensual), the boastful exploitation of sexual intimacy, the bragging and gossiping and judgment. Julia did not want to provide the name of the boy involved for fear of social backlash, so his unethical, selfish, and egregious behavior went unaccounted for. But in my experience as a high school sex educator, Julia's experience is not uncommon.

What factors into this scenario, and how do we address it as adults and parents? How do we guide teenagers toward what has integrity? What do we want for them and what gets in the way?

There is substantial research that tells us the key to living a happy and healthy life is the quality of our relationships.

My friends with kids and the thousands of parents I've worked with want their children to be healthy, happy, good people. There is substantial research that tells us the key to living a happy and healthy life is the quality of our relationships. Good, close relationships ensure our health and well-being. People who are more connected are happier, physically healthier, and live longer than people who are less connected, and it's the quality of those close relationships that matters.[2] Robert Waldinger, director of the Harvard Study of Adult Development, one of the most comprehensive longitudinal studies in history, emphasizes the importance of "leaning into relationships." He also cites evidence that this is not a priority for many young people today. In a 2015 TED Talk, he references a survey of millennials who were asked about their major life goals. Eighty percent said that a major life goal was to get rich, and 50 percent said a major life goal was to become famous. Far fewer put a priority on developing and sustaining relationships.

Why do so many of our teens have trouble developing deep and sustaining relationships? We are steeped in a culture that constantly tells us to work harder and achieve and consume more. Teens are more exposed and connected to popular culture than ever before. Research by Common Sense Media found that teens who watch stereotypical gender representations in the media are more likely to value masculine than feminine traits, have more tolerant views of sexual harassment, support the belief that women are at least partially responsible for sexual assaults against them, and use media representations of romantic and sexual relationships as their own expectations for exploring sexuality with others.[3]

Given the inequitable and sexist messages our teenagers are bombarded with, how do we help them lean into caring, loving, and loyal relationships? Quality connection is built on authenticity and the capacity to tend to ourselves and others. This takes self-reflection, self-awareness—and lots of practice.

It also requires the capacity and willingness to be vulnerable. Despite some progress in terms of our social attitudes about gender norms and expectations, allowing oneself to be vulnerable is still challenging for many boys (and men). In one of my classes, for example, during a discussion about masculinity, many of the boys agreed that anger was the only emotion boys are encouraged to show. This can be challenging for boys. One young man shared that he had "trained" himself not to cry. Every other boy in the room snapped their fingers (an expression of resonance) in agreement.

In my classroom, we discuss gender through an activity during which we create three boxes, one with cultural norms of masculinity, one of femininity, and one for nonbinary genders. Without fail, every class comes up with the same list of traits for each of the binary genders. This has been the case for the twenty-five years I've been teaching. To cite a few examples, boys typically receive cultural messages that they should be emotionless, strong, in control, dominant, athletic, sexually experienced, rich, competitive, and that they should win at all costs. Girls receive cultural messages that they should be smart but not too academic or intelligent, sexually active enough to avoid being called a prude but not so much that they are judged a slut, submissive, emotional, sexy, thin with large breasts and curves, and easygoing about inappropriate behavior.

When we make observations about the qualities listed, what they most often notice is that a lot of the binary expectations are opposites of each other and keep each other in check (girls are expected to be passive, boys aggressive, for example), creating a gender paradigm. When we talk about the impact, the conclusion is that the lists don't allow either gender to realize their full humanity or true selves in how they connect with others, and that gender socialization has the potential to get in the way of authentic connection. As far as the nonbinary list, it is obvious that our culture is still overwhelmingly trans- and homophobic.

True courage in relationships requires us to open ourselves up to a connection with another person.

What resonates with all students is that vulnerability, for any gender, is seen as weakness.

Our culture is still sending this message, and we need to help our teenagers understand that in fact the reverse is true. True courage in relationships requires us to open ourselves up to a connection with another person, at the risk of rejection and emotional vulnerability, and that we learn how to ask for consent and guidance from our potential partners.[4]

Social scientist, researcher, and writer Brené Brown defines vulnerability as "our most accurate measure of courage." Citing Brown's book, *The Gift of Imperfection*, author and sex educator Cindy Pierce identifies guideposts to wholehearted living that are particularly important for developing adolescents. These guideposts include authenticity (letting go of what other people think); intuition and trusting faith (letting go of the need for certainty); creativity (letting go of comparison); play and rest (letting go of exhaustion as a symbol of status); meaningful work (letting go of self-doubt); and laughter, song, and dance (letting go of being cool and in control). [5]

I often speak with students who come to my office or approach me after a workshop to raise questions and issues about sexuality. The questions typically relate to relationships, how to talk about and acquire birth control or preventing STDs, coming out, concerns about a friend, how to know if they're ready to have sex, as well as issues of sexual harassment and assault.

In the past several years, some of my students are expressing new concerns; several boys have come to my office stressed because, as they put it, they think their "dick is broken." When they try to have sex with their girlfriend or a casual hookup, they experience premature ejaculation or they can't keep an erection. I'm getting concerning questions from female students, too, like "How do I suppress my gag reflex while giving a blow job?" or "How can I keep anal from hurting?" or "I have a sore vulva. What should I do?" I ask questions to better understand their concerns and encourage them to seek medical support if they need it. Through these discussions I've come to realize that the issues they're telling me about are a by-product of the toxic pressure they feel to participate in what I call *performance sex*, amped up and often aggressive sex acts that are a staple of media, pornographic films, and images on the internet.

When I talk to boys about where their ideas about sex and what it should look like come from, it usually comes down to media and their friends' boasts about their own sexual exploits, which are also typically influenced by media, mostly porn. Pornographic sex largely reflects traditional gender norms of dominance and control, of course, so boys' conversations about sex don't include their partners' experience but focus instead on cultural expectations of sexual conquest and endurance. The girls I talk to watch less porn but are still influenced, either directly or through their sexual partners, by its messages about what bodies and sexual performance should look, sound, and feel like. (There is a widespread assumption that girls don't watch porn as an outlet for pleasure, but I hear from many of the young people I talk to that some girls do.)

Porn is pervasive in our culture, so it should be no surprise that it is influencing our young people. Pornhub alone has 28.5 billion visitors a year. That's 81 million people per day, 50,000 searches per minute, and 800 searches per second. In 2017, 3,732 petabytes of data was transferred across the internet. That's enough data to fill the memory of every iPhone around the world.[6] You get the picture: pornography is available 24/7. It is accessible, affordable, and anonymous—and easily accessed without parental or legal oversight.[7]

In fact, porn has become America's default sex education.[8, 9] As I've discussed elsewhere in this book, many teens aren't getting adequate sex education in school, and their parents aren't talking to them about it, either. As a result, they are turning to porn to satisfy their very natural and healthy curiosity, but that's like watching *The Fast and the Furious* to learn how to drive.

As adults, whether we are pro-porn or anti-porn isn't relevant to our discussion about the implications of adolescent viewing. My students tell me there isn't a high school boy who hasn't looked at porn, which means that a middle school boy who watches it could see hundreds of explicit images of sex without even having had a first kiss. Many parents have no idea how much porn their teens are exposed to. We grew up in a very different world; back in the 1970s, '80s, and even '90s, porn was pretty hard to come by if you were a teenager. Maybe someone discovered a stash of *Playboy* magazines in a dad's closet, or an X-rated VHS or Betamax videotape. More often than not, porn was a still image, a photograph, or an illustration. Or it was erotica in a book with dog-eared pages that kids passed around. That type of pornography required the viewer to engage their imagination. The fantasy, whatever it was, came from the viewer's own mind. Today, most of the porn viewed (and masturbated to) is based on someone else's fantasy and is a multisensory experience. Teenagers, mostly boys, are conditioning their sexual response cycle with porn—a visual, aural, interactive activity in which there is a dopamine- and endorphin-reinforced response that an adult, porn producer, or director has conjured up to make money in a vast and highly competitive market.

High-speed internet has made very real and hard-core images widely available to anyone who wants to see it—and most teens, it turns out, want to see it. Parents who think their teens are not looking at porn should consider the research. A 2008 University of New Hampshire survey of over 560 college students, for example, found that 93 percent of boys and 62 percent of girls were exposed to online pornography during adolescence.[10] A 2009 survey of 29,000 students attending North American universities conducted by Michael Leahy, the author of *Porn University,* found that 51 percent of male students and 32 percent of female students first viewed pornography before their teen years (twelve and younger). Leahy also found that 64 percent of college men and 18 percent of college women spend time online for internet sex every week.[11] Another study concluded that, on average, boys are around thirteen and girls are around fourteen when they first see pornography.[12] It's important to note that feminist, "real life," and "healthy" porn exists. This isn't the porn I understand teenagers to be watching, however, since mainstream internet porn is free while niche pornography that some people believe is "healthier" is typically not.

Adolescents who visit sexually explicit websites are more likely to engage in high-risk sexual practices.

How does all this porn consumption affect teens? The *Journal of Adolescent Health* reported that adolescents who visit sexually explicit websites are more likely to engage in high-risk sexual practices, such as having multiple partners and using substances during sex, both of which have the potential to adversely affect reproductive health. They also are more likely to have permissive attitudes that vary by the amount of porn exposure,[13] which means adolescents may allow sexual behaviors that other people disapprove of.

To date, however, there have only been limited studies of exactly how porn influences behavior. The understanding of cause and effect is limited. We don't know, for example, whether individuals who engage in more risky sexual behavior are more drawn to pornography, or whether the pornography is causing the behavior. Likely, it's reciprocal.

Some experts believe that pornographic images that young people consume can condition their sexual response cycle, creating an appetite for increasingly extreme images. Our brains may be wired for desire during adolescence, but the cues and triggers are learned, not innate. We learn this from our external environment. Adolescents are developing their identities, including their sexual identities. When teenagers view porn habitually, their brains are modified to be aroused by and desire what they see, because when they view it (especially through digital delivery) there is a neurological biochemical reward that reinforces the cycle of stimulation, arousal, and orgasm.

Wendy Maltz, a well-known sex therapist, educator, author, and social worker, believes that porn can lead to a variety of maladaptive behaviors such as social isolation, mood disorders, sexually objectifying other people, and damage to self-esteem. She points out that porn exploits on the natural needs and qualities of adolescents, including sexual curiosity and the powerful desire to discover sexual pleasure. Porn also allows teens to avoid feelings of rejection and insecurity, because it gives the consumer the illusion of being wanted, accepted, and in control. Porn doesn't negotiate, talk back, or question what you're thinking, feeling, and doing. Of course, as I discuss in other places in this book, learning to experience rejection and to open yourself up to the wants and needs of another person are important skills to master on the road to maturity. Too much porn consumption, particularly if it is engaged in at the expense of real relationships, risks impeding that growth.

To date, there has not been definitive research on whether pornography is addictive.

To date, there has not been definitive research on whether pornography is addictive. Few parents will give consent for their children to participate in studies about compulsive porn viewing and its effects, for one thing, plus it's illegal to knowingly expose a minor to sexual media. Current research seems to indicate that while you can't actually be addicted to porn, it can be used compulsively for a variety of dysfunctional reasons. The concern with adolescents viewing porn is that it trains the brain so that they may develop a sexual response that can only be triggered by more pornography, which is often unrealistic and portrays misogynist images. Trained consistently in this one context, they'll have to retrain their body and brain to respond sexually in different contexts, including those with a real person.[14]

This is because porn creates unrealistic expectations about sex and how participants should look and act during sexual activity. Most of the pornography teens access can also be detrimental because it separates sex from emotions and is highly misogynistic in how it eroticizes the degradation of women. It also often creates a perception that sex is about conquest: women will naturally resist a man's advances, but in fact they wish to be forced. In other words, the concept of consent is not a common theme in pornography. That's not all: pornography also centers mainly on the male experience, with little attention given to the satisfaction of the female partner.

It's important to acknowledge that pornography didn't develop in a vacuum. It incorporates underlying gender assumptions and attitudes that pervade our broader culture and that our teens see widely reflected in the non-X-rated media they see every day. For boys, sexual dominance and conquest is glorified, while they get the message that expressing emotions and being vulnerable is not masculine. Meanwhile, girls tend to be trapped in a culture of politeness, effortless perfection, traditional gender norms of passive sexuality, and the very real fear of being considered a prude if they decline sex, or slut-shamed if they seek it out or actively engage in their sexual experiences. The easiest role for girls then is to be a passive participant, to go along with what their partner wants, and ensure that he enjoys the experience.

Given the environment in which our teens are growing up, how can the adults who care about them help counter the messages they receive not only from pornography, but also the other media in their lives?

As stated above, we don't know the precise cause-and-effect influence of pornography or other widespread cultural assumptions and gender expectations on our teenagers, but I see the evidence of both in the stories teens share when they come to me seeking guidance. With their permission and anonymity, I present the scenarios in class as a part of our lessons on ethical quandaries. We consider many.

Aisha is at a small party at a friend's house. Everyone is drinking. A few of the boys, including Jim (who Aisha has a crush on), have smoked weed. Last week, Aisha's friend Sophie told Jim that Aisha is interested in him, and the feeling seems to be mutual. Aisha and Jim talk, laugh, and hang out. Pretty soon the rest of their friends move on to the kitchen to find something to eat. Aisha and Jim are alone in the TV room, and he makes a move. They kiss and make out for a while. It feels great for both of them. Jim's hand goes up Aisha's shirt and then to the buttons on her jeans. Aisha starts to feel a little awkward, so she positions herself so he can't undo her jeans. Jim moves her hips back and persists. He whispers, "Don't worry, we'll take it easy."

In a classroom context, students immediately understand what's wrong with this situation: Jim is subtly pressuring Aisha to go further than she's comfortable with. They are also quick to identify what should happen next. I explain that, while there are worst- and best-case scenarios for how the rest of the night between Aisha and Jim unfolds, I'm really interested in what's realistic, given the culture and context they're navigating in that moment.

Aisha communicates a limit with how she moves her body. Jim recognizes her hesitation, and he responds by moving her to a position that gives him access to the button on her jeans while trying to reassure her. In my classes, the conversation tends to become binary and gendered. Girls will suggest that Aisha doesn't want to come off as prude by explicitly refusing Jim, because she really likes him and wants something to happen between them. The boys agree that Jim is being a jerk because he isn't taking Aisha's preferences into account. He clearly does not have her consent to go further sexually. At the same time, the boys in my classes usually venture that Jim may be a good guy and believes that Aisha wants to hook up. "He probably thinks that's what he *should* do," they will say.

In the rational, uncharged atmosphere of the classroom, the students will always accurately identify the problem from a legal and moral standpoint. The discussion will explore gendered socialization and how that gets in the way of communication. In this scenario, if Jim and Aisha communicated about how they are feeling, she could say that she would like to have some sort of relationship with him. Jim, for his part, may or may not want a relationship, but in the moment, he wants to take advantage of the hookup opportunity.

When we talk about what gets in the way of Jim and Aisha having a direct conversation about their intentions and desires, kids point to fear of rejection, inhibitions about talking directly about sex, fear the other person wants something different, and a resistance to making oneself vulnerable. Some of my students talk proudly about being able to have sex without emotional ties, and steer away from catching feelings, which makes emotional connection sound like a disease. Yet despite the bravado, in almost all of my students' journal entries, they express longing for connection and a caring relationship.

As adults in teens' lives, it's crucial for us to initiate conversations about how gender stereotypes—or "straitjackets"—can interfere with how we bring our true selves to a relationship. To encourage greater awareness in teens of what influences their relationships, it is useful to discuss cultural gender roles and the explicit and implicit messages students receive about their gender, and to reflect on how those messages may affect their relationships—not only with others, but also with themselves.

Jenna and David have been committed to each other in a romantic relationship for about a month. The pace of their sexual activity has been pretty slow but has recently become more intense. They really like each other. One day, David is exploring Jenna's body with kisses. Jenna is comfortable with everything they've done so far, but today there's a light on in the room, and Jenna is wondering what David thinks of her body now that he can see her naked. He moves like he's going to go down on her. Before he gets to her vulva, he looks up at her and asks, "This OK?" She responds, "Mmm-hmm." David pauses and then starts to give Jenna oral sex. Jenna stiffens and her mind starts to wander. She's never had someone go down on her, and she's heard that some guys joke about vaginal smells. What if she smells nasty? David can tell she is distracted and pauses what he is doing to ask, "Hey, is everything OK? Are you sure you're into this?" Jenna averts her eyes and doesn't know what to say.

Teens are exposed to fourteen thousand references to sexuality a year, according to the American Academy of Pediatrics. Rarely are those messages positive, nor do they contribute to a healthy understanding of sexuality. In any given class, if I ask, "Who has been sexually harassed?" every girl and nonbinary gender student raises their hand, as well as a smattering of boys. According to Harvard Graduate School of Education's Making Caring Common 2017 national survey and study of eighteen- to twenty-five-year-olds, titled "The Talk: How Adults Can Promote Young People's Healthy Relationships and Prevent Misogyny and Sexual Harassment," 87 percent of women reported having experienced at least one of the following during their lifetime: being catcalled, touched without permission by a stranger, insulted with sexualized words, having a stranger say something sexual to them, and having a stranger tell them they were "hot."[15]

When I ask about the nature of the verbal taunts, they're usually comments about how hot someone is, or something about their "nasty pussy," or whether they're "down to fuck." Young women pick up on the sexist language that is an integral part of sexual banter, especially among boys. It's common for aggressive language and action to be veiled in humor. The survey also found that many young people don't see certain types of gender-based degradation and subordination as problems in our society.

It isn't uncommon for girls to hear boys justify not reciprocating oral sex with excuses about vaginal odor or about pubic hair being "hella nasty." Teens are also inundated with messages through certain music and on social media. As I'm writing this, Kanye West and Lil Pump's song "I Love It" has been released and experienced great success. The lyrics include "I'ma fuck a bitch, tell her cousin... Then I fucked up on her cousin... Or her sister, I don't know nothin'... You're such a fuckin' ho and I love it." The song got over 50 million listens in its first week, and just yesterday it reached over 5 million in a single day. And then there are messages like the one on Instagram from Kim Kardashian advising that pineapple juice makes your vagina taste like a piña colada. When I asked one of my female students if this creates insecurity, she looked at me with wonder at my ignorance and said, "If women like that are talking about how vaginas taste and smell, girls will automatically start thinking, *Oh, should my vagina smell like a piña colada?*" Enough said.

Body image is directly related to one's capacity for pleasure. When Jenna and her boyfriend engage in oral sex, the internalized messages and insecurities that flooded her mind made it hard for her to relax and enjoy the experience. Jenna shared with me that she felt shame for being distracted by her negative thoughts and guilty for compromising hers and David's sexual experience. Girls who are valued for what their bodies can do rather than what they look like usually stand a better chance of surviving the onslaught of pressure to live up to an impossible ideal.[16]

David, for his part, is not only respecting the concept of consent, but also he values Jenna's experience enough to pick up that something is wrong and check in with her about it. He later shared that he had his own doubts about whether he was doing it right and needed Jenna's feedback to find out what felt good to her. Communication, as in all good relationships, was the key: eventually the two talked about it and gradually moved beyond their respective inhibitions to comfort and pleasure. It took time, patience, and care.

Just last week, Cole, a senior, approached me to talk about his relationship. He said his mother has always "pounded into [his] head" the concept of consent and the importance of paying attention to a partner's pleasure and of mutual respect when exploring sexuality. Up until now, Cole's relationships have been with girls who were comfortable talking about sex and telling him what they wanted and what they didn't.

In his current relationship, however, Wendy, the young woman he's seeing, is always drunk when they hook up. When they discuss the implications for consent, she tells him, "I prefer being drunk so I don't have to think about these things." She also expects the sexual activity to be initiated and led by Cole. If he asks her what feels good or how far she wants to go, she says, "I don't care. Just tell me what you want me to do." She also seems uncomfortable with Cole's efforts to give her pleasure.

Cole talked to his girlfriend, and it became clear that she'd never been in a relationship and had only experienced hookups. In the hookups, moreover, she was the one who did things for her partners sexually. Her partners did things *to* her but not *with* her. Her experiences exemplified how in popular media and porn in particular, women have things done to them, not with them. Cole wanted to know how to help Wendy and has a new resolve to encourage boys to avoid any objectifying and performance-based sexual behavior, based on the implicit and explicit messages they get from media and the broader culture.

I also hear teenagers talk about each other in objectifying ways a lot of the time, which makes authentic connection seem like a big deal, and of course, it can be.

> Luke and Kim have been public and exclusive with their relationship for about three months. They are into each other and invested in making it work. As seniors in their spring semester, they want to affirm their relationship by having intercourse. They prepare themselves with testing and birth control—the anticipation is high. Their sexual activity will get to a point when Kim will say, "I want you to fuck me." But when they try to engage in intercourse, it's awkward and uncomfortable. They try different positions but can't seem to find one that works for both of them. This frustrates them both and Luke loses his erection. The next couple of times they venture to have intercourse, they have the same experience. Luke is embarrassed and reassures Kim that it's not her. Kim is annoyed by this and snaps back, "I know it's not me." She grows distant, suggests they be free to hook up with whomever they want during their last two weeks of school, and finally ends the relationship.

Luke told me about this because he was desperate to save the relationship and was convinced that it ended because he "wasn't good enough in bed." We talked about the element of dirty talk that he felt he should embrace and be inspired by; however, he was able to realize it actually added a lot of pressure. Was he supposed to "fuck her" like they do in the movies or in pornography? He was thrown off by the awkwardness of exploring intercourse, which he didn't expect. The more awkward and frustrated they got, the more anxious Luke felt that he couldn't maintain an erection. Kim's lack of understanding and the lack of communication between them weighed hard on Luke and his self-esteem. Having received cultural messages that relationships are fundamentally about sex, and "good" media-like sex at that, he was convinced that he was at fault and doomed to be a bad lover for the rest of his life. Luke was so preoccupied with his performance that he completely forgot about his own pleasure as well as Kim's. He believed the experience was contingent on his performance alone.

Girls also frequently feel pressure to experience and express pleasure without communicating with their partner about their own sexual needs and desires. Female students share that girls look at sexual interactions in the media and think, *Oh, I guess I'm supposed to like that, and I should respond like that woman on the screen. Then I'll be considered good in bed and desirable.* Girls also learn from media images and gender socialization that they should prioritize male over female pleasure, and not risk damaging their partner's ego by advocating for themselves.

Sarah and Keith have been together for a couple of months. Their physical intimacy has progressed quickly, and they are both really into it. At first, they made out and felt each other up a lot before sex—there was tons of foreplay. Lately they just make out for a minute and then Keith grabs a condom. Sarah's usually on the bottom of missionary and it's uncomfortable when Keith starts without any foreplay. It feels better as they get into it, but it isn't always enjoyable to her. Keith often asks if it feels good and when they're done, "Did you come?" Sarah makes lots of pleasurable sounds and tries her best to fake an orgasm. She doesn't have the heart to tell Keith she didn't come and that the sex isn't that great. He's so kind and always checks in about how she feels and what she likes, so she doesn't want to make him feel bad.

Many girls I talk to are hesitant to explore their own bodies to find out what feels good to them. But understanding our own bodies and what gives us pleasure improves our ability to communicate to our partner. Many girls also believe that they don't have the capacity to orgasm, or that they've had an orgasm when they actually haven't. Faking orgasms is incredibly common among teenage girls who are sexually active, because they don't know how to reach orgasm themselves and can't communicate that to their partner, they are too shy or self-conscious to tell their partner what feels good, or they don't want their partner to feel sexually inadequate. In Peggy Orenstein's book *Girls and Sex*, she cites a study of college women by Sara McClelland, which found that "women tended to use their partner's physical pleasure as the yardstick for their satisfaction, saying things such as 'If he's satisfied, then I'm sexually satisfied.' For men it was the opposite: the measure was their own orgasm."[17]

Many of the same girls who aren't having orgasms say their sexuality is empowering, especially if they frequently hook up without an emotional connection. But exactly what do these girls mean by empowerment? The health, art, and technology departments at the school where I teach collaborated on a workshop on female empowerment in art. The workshop was conceived in response to the many nude images students were sending. Many girls argued that if they are proud of their bodies, why shouldn't they send images out to others? As part of the workshop, we asked the girls to bring in images they felt represented sexual empowerment. The one that stuck out the most to me was a picture of Nicki Minaj in black leather bondage lingerie, sitting in a provocative sexual position with a red patent leather stiletto over the neck of a man lying on the ground.

In response to the photos, a senior girl observed, "I think I've finally figured out why this isn't real empowerment. We want to be perceived as equal with the guys. We want to own our sexuality with confidence too. So we try to mirror what they do and how they do it. The problem is that we aren't boys, so it doesn't work. We kid ourselves into thinking what they want is what we want and don't take the time to figure out what that actually is for ourselves."

Empowerment is self-defined and earned through an internal process of self-awareness and actualization that includes all aspects of who we are.

Exactly. Empowerment is self-defined and earned through an internal process of self-awareness and actualization that includes all aspects of who we are; it certainly isn't built on the degradation of another human being (like a stiletto across a man's neck). Empowerment is a growth process through which we gain confidence by doing right by ourselves and others. If what we do to grow is ethical and has integrity, it isn't at the expense of someone else. Empowered sexuality comes from within, not from what we do to other people or what they do to us.

I contract with other schools on a regular basis to lead consent workshops. These workshops are open to all four high school grades. The room is full and there is rapt interest. After a short presentation and a substantive conversation with the group, it's time for the students to move on to their next elected workshop. A boy lingers after the rest of the students clear out of the room. He's a big kid, wearing a letterman jacket, and he fits the stereotype of the good-looking athlete.

His eyes scan the room and he softly says, "Hey."

"Hey, what's your name?"

"Kevin."

"Hi, Kevin. How was the workshop for you?"

"It was all right, but I still have a question."

"Sure, I'll do my best to answer."

"So you know how you said assault can happen to guys. Can that happen even if you're bigger than the girl?"

"It could. Is there a situation in particular you're thinking of?"

"I don't know. I mean, there's this senior girl and everyone thinks she's hot, and she's always coming up to me in the hallways and stuff. She says things like, 'Hey, Kev, you're a freshman, but you're hot. You should come hang out sometime and stuff.'"

"What's it like for you to hear that?"

Kevin looks at the floor—he's rocking back and forth.

"I don't know—it's all right, I guess. Once though, she grabbed me, you know. It was outside my pants, but she still grabbed me. She just keeps telling me I should hang out with her and her friends, I wish she'd just stop. Yeah, I wish she'd just stop, but like everyone likes her. She's a *senior*..." Looking down, Kevin pauses, and before I can respond, he glances at his watch and makes for the door.

"Oh man, I gotta get to my next thing. It's all good, really. Thank you for the workshop, Ms. Zaloom."

Kevin disappears down the hall. I find Jim, my counselor contact at the school, and let him know about the dynamic. He is grateful for the information and expresses his exasperation. Apparently, there are a couple of senior girls who have chosen a couple of freshman boys as their "projects."

Many teenagers, boys in particular, will laugh and cheer Kevin on when I bring up this scenario in my classes. This sort of gender double standard and the dismissal of Kevin's discomfort and confusion because he's being singled out by a popular girl, despite the age and social power differentials, comes at a cost to our boys. Contrary to masculine gender norms, many boys and men are sensitive and emotional. Many of my male students will confidentially articulate their insecurities and the pressure they feel to "man up" and conform to societal expectations.

Without guidance from the adults in their lives about how positive, pleasurable sexual experiences should look, sound, and feel, teenagers are working from the representations they see in media and pornography.

Without guidance from the adults in their lives about how positive, pleasurable sexual experiences should look, sound, and feel, teenagers are working from the representations they see in media and pornography: sex-negative images and messages that include hypersexualization, objectification, sex stigma, and body-shaming.

These create what I call "sexpectations," the normalized, cultural expectations about sex and sexuality that many teenagers are influenced by in their relationships. Sexpectations get in the way of teens practicing the communication that is essential for consensual, ethical, good sex and relationships; they also threaten their ability to have quality relationships that will determine their long-term happiness and health. Porn is a particular draw for teens who are sexually curious but also self-conscious or socially awkward, and those who fear vulnerability or being rejected. Humans also are wired to seek what is novel and respond to the sexual stimulation of porn through the reward pathway of the brain. This can lead to compulsive use.

One common sexpectation is sexual intimacy combined with drinking and drugs.

Lydia and James have been exclusively hooking up for several months. Whenever there's a party, they usually end up in a room together. Each time they get together, they take their physical intimacy to another level. Their hookup usually ends when James ejaculates. Lydia enjoys the physical closeness of skin-to-skin contact and the making out. The grinding can feel pretty good too—she can move her body in a way that puts pressure on her clitoris. The fingering is aggressive and uncomfortable for Lydia, but she doesn't say anything because she's afraid of hurting James's feelings. James usually gets a handy or blow job. The oral sex isn't reciprocated because James says Lydia doesn't groom enough of her pubic hair and it's just "too hard" to do.

After a party, Lydia sneaks James into her house and to her bedroom. They hook up in the usual ways and then get to a point when intercourse could happen. James asks, "Want to have sex?" Lydia responds, "Sure. I'll get a condom." James puts it on and Lydia guides him to intercourse. They are in the missionary position when James starts emphatically thrusting into Lydia for what feels like forever. The sex is starting to hurt. Lydia's vagina is dry, so she asks, "Did you come?" James replies, "Nah, damn it, whiskey dick," and they stop.

In Lydia and James's scenario, the priority is James's pleasure. Lydia doesn't want to offend James, and oral isn't reciprocated because James finds it "too hard," his excuse for not knowing what to do, buying in to the sexist myths about vaginas as dirty (they are one of the cleanest places on a person's body), or just not caring about or being invested enough in Lydia. James's comment about pubic hair reminds me of the many anonymous questions I get asking "to shave or not to shave?" It is also reminiscent of teen blog post exchanges I have seen, much of which is informed by porn. Some experts believe that hairless women in pornography is an effort to satiate the prepubescent pedophilic fantasy. I tell students it's their pubic hair, so they should do what they want with it, and it's important to have an honest understanding about their motivation. In my personal opinion, teenage girls are on their way to womanhood. They are not children anymore and should look it. Pubic hair also protects us from several bacterial and viral sexually transmitted infections. Boys also wonder about grooming because they hear it makes their penis look bigger. Ultimately, what one does with their pubic hair is an expression of sexuality. Agency and autonomy are essential components of that, so people should choose what they want to do for themselves.

Lydia and James's interactions center on James's orgasm. He isn't experienced or unselfish enough to notice that Lydia isn't aroused and the intercourse is uncomfortable, or that she isn't comfortable enough to say anything. There is also the issue of consent, which cannot be given while incapacitated by substances. The substance use is significant if James's ability to ejaculate has been compromised. In hindsight, neither Lydia nor James felt their sex was nonconsensual, but it certainly wasn't communicative or pleasurable. It begs the question of why teenagers feel like they have to be drunk to have a sexual experience. Is it because sex is not pleasurable? Because being drunk provides an excuse for behaviors that may lead to judgment from their peers? Is it because teens fear vulnerability, so it's easier to feel both uninhibited and courageous if they are inebriated? Is it because media, especially the porn industry, is "educating" teens on how to have sex and sets unrealistic expectations? From my conversations with teens, I believe all these factors play a part in this behavior.

Free internet porn is notorious for being heteronormative. Even gay porn is frequently from a hetero perspective, especially lesbian porn, which is more often than not created for male consumption.

Kai, Rex, and Luis are hanging out on a back porch at a party with Melissa, Patty, and Claire. Everyone has been drinking and some have smoked too. They're engaged in the usual banter with a lot of flirting and innuendo. Melissa and Claire have been friends for a long time and are very affectionate with each other. Rex dares them to make out with each other, saying, "C'mon, it's hot. We've all seen it!" Melissa and Claire are hesitant. Patty looks at them with "OMG" eyes, and Kai and Luis start to encourage them too. It's obvious that Melissa and Claire are uncomfortable, but they do it anyway, kissing for just a few seconds. When Melissa and Claire break apart, the boys are disappointed, saying, "Aw, that's it? C'mon." Melissa rolls her eyes and says, "Yeah, that's it. We're going back in." She, Claire, and Patty make their way back into the party.

Not only does this interaction minimize lesbian sex, but also the normalized "we've all seen it," the coercive "c'mon, it's hot," and "let's see it" behavior is insidious. The boys are enacting cultural objectification and view the situation as entertainment that they somehow deserve, whether the participants are willing or not. The girls obviously are annoyed, but the boys hardly notice; they are disappointed that something they feel entitled to has been withheld. Girls are socialized to not resist or express anger for fear of being perceived as uptight or bitchy. Instead of asserting themselves, they simply go inside. The boys' behavior goes unchecked.

Some of the gay male students I've spoken to have mixed feeling about the gay pornography they've seen. They acknowledge that it is misrepresentative of healthy sex but say that the very experience of seeing two men together within a sexual context is affirming. They see so few validating representations of gay sexuality that porn is at least helpful in supporting their same-gender attraction. Unfortunately, we still live in a transphobic and homophobic culture that isn't inclusive of all genders and sexualities.

Many of the gay boys I talk to express longing for companionship and true connection. The options are frequently limited, however, since many don't feel safe coming out. At the same time, seeking sexual experiences online can be risky.

Ben is a senior in high school who is gay and hasn't come out yet. He has been feeling restless and horny, so he turns on his computer in hopes of finding someone to chat with. He enters a gay chat room and starts messaging a guy who says he's thirty-three and lives a few states away. They chat for a while and Ben opens up about being gay in a school where not many people are out, and how sexually frustrating it can be. The guy asks if Ben wants to "cam," which Ben knows means to masturbate together with their webcams. Ben agrees, and once the video starts streaming, both guys begin to jerk off. The other guy asks Ben if he will show "face4face," which means that they would both show their faces through their cams. Ben has seen videos of people doing this (some post these as a form of porn) and has never wanted to do it himself. Still, this guy doesn't seem like a creep, so he makes an exception and angles the camera to his face. As soon as he does, the guy ends the call, logs off, and blocks Ben. Ben is left feeling rejected and mad at himself for breaking his rule; he's also scared that a video of him masturbating will end up online, making him "internet famous."

When Ben told me this story, I asked the reason for camming. He told me that camming provides an experience that is a degree closer to sex. He explained that while watching porn is passive, camming includes a real voice and a response. It has an interpersonal dynamic, almost like interactive porn. Frustrated that his desire to be with someone real made him break his rule, Ben is also scared. This experience is not one that will support his emerging sexuality and coming-out process in a positive way. Given pornography's pervasive influence, it's important that we talk to our teens about it. When we approach these conversations about porn, we shouldn't shame and punish teenagers for being drawn to it. It is normal to be curious about sex, and our teens are accustomed to searching the internet to learn about the world. And, as I discussed earlier, many teens aren't having discussions about these subjects with the adults in their lives. But as I've tried to emphasize throughout book, if we want the young people we care for to learn about healthy relationships, including sexual relationships, we have to step up and have these conversations, even if they are awkward.

It is normal to be curious about sex.

When I talk to the teens in my classes, I try to make some of the points below. Note: as a parent, it's a good idea to pick one or two points to start with and keep your initial discussions short. Your teen is more likely to listen (during your first and subsequent conversations) if you don't over-whelm them.

- Porn creates a fantasy world that represents a very limited picture of sexual experiences and virtually no relationship context. Bodies, male and female, are typically surgically enhanced and airbrushed. The violent and violating nature of the sex itself is veiled in exaggerated and contrived sexual responses (moans, cries for more, etc.) that appear pleasurable but likely wouldn't be in real life (particularly for the female participant). These images are not reflective of most people's sexual realities or healthy relationship practices.

- Porn is not created for educational purposes but for entertainment and financial gain. And it is a big business: according to some calculations, the worldwide porn industry's net worth is a staggering $97 billion. This means that the industry makes more money than the MLB, NBA, and NFL combined. Free internet porn is a highly competitive business, so videos must feature increasingly extreme content to attract eyeballs—and advertising dollars. And that is what most viewers are seeking: increasingly titillating fantasy and entertainment, not healthy or genuine personal or sexual interactions.

- There's nothing private about porn sex. It is accessible, free, and available for a global audience to see. Anyone with a digital device can watch it. Healthy sexuality includes a decided upon level of privacy between the people engaging in it. Intimacy requires trust and respect. Sexual activity, especially for teenagers who are just beginning to understand their sexuality, is very personal. Privacy is important so that people can focus on figuring out what they like and want without concern of being exploited in a public way. The more public our sex becomes, the less agency we have to control it.

- Porn performers are paid to mainstream their films, so marketing and branding are important and required. Porn stars have to enthusiastically participate in and promote their work. The documentary film *The Price of Pleasure* reveals that certain sex acts have a price tag. For instance, a blow job can be worth $300; anal $1,000; double penetration $1,200; gang bang $1,300 for three guys and $100 for each additional guy. The director of the porn instructs performers how to act and respond. Porn stars are acting according to their contracts: porn is contractual—and not always consensual.

- Porn is heterocentric and promotes bias and marginalization. There is also a lot of racism in porn, including exoticizing and fetishizing people based on their race or gender identity.

- Most performers are surgically altered and enhanced. In real life, for instance, breasts come in all shapes and sizes, and bigger doesn't necessarily mean better. In pornography, hair is removed and anuses are bleached.

- In porn the average penis size is 8 inches long. In reality, size doesn't matter when it comes to pleasure. Average penis size, when erect, is approximately 5 inches long, 1.5 inches in width, and 3.5 to 3.9 inches in circumference. Moreover, many people's sexual pleasure has nothing to do with a penis at all. There are lots of erogenous zones to explore on the human body. Within the context of vaginal intercourse, only 33 percent of women reliably orgasm with intercourse. That means about 70 percent rely on other forms of stimulation to have an orgasm.

- In most pornography, people are hairless from anus to navel. As human animals, it is normal and natural to have hair of varying amounts in these areas of our bodies. Pubic hair offers protection from most bacterial and viral infections. Since child pornography is illegal, some porn makers remove hair from women's genitals so they look more like young girls. In fact, the highly sexualized and prepubescent body that is so common in pornography may skew perspectives on what is an acceptable age to be sexually active.

- A ten-minute sex scene can take four hours to shoot. There's usually a lot of preparation, including sustained arousal fueled by Viagra and "fluffers," people on the sidelines who provide sexual stimulation. If the scene isn't exactly what a director wants, they can just retake the scene. It's manipulated and edited to elicit exactly what the director is going for. There can be awkward moments during real sex, and learning how to turn each other on, and the experience of pleasure together takes time, communication, and mutual respect and caring.

- Porn is largely geared for the male audience. In most porn films, women have something done *to* them versus *with* them. In real life, sex is, or at least should be, a reciprocal exchange, an intimate dialogue between two people even if just for physical gratification. Good sex is about equity and inclusive consensual experiences that are genuinely pleasurable. In real life, the woman in a couple may want to be dominant sometimes, or to act out fantasies of her own, but such scenarios are seldom represented in mainstream porn.

- Dirty talk, coming on your partner's face, exaggerated responses, violent or pounding intercourse, degradation, and objectification may be popular porn fare but they aren't necessary or required ingredients in real sexual relationships. Some people like dirty talk. Some don't. Some do it naturally, some can't bring themselves to, and some find it offensive and degrading. Some women like "facials" (I have yet to meet a teen girl who does) and some don't. This exposure to ejaculate also increases the risk of STDs.

- In porn there isn't usually any negotiation or protection. Healthy sex requires good communication, including asking for consent, and includes protection from unwanted pregnancy and sexually transmitted infections.

- In porn, bodies don't touch and hands don't explore like they would in real sex. For filming, it's all about the camera angles and the cinematographic shot. Penetration is the focus, and to film that, hands can't obstruct the view. The performers' bodies need to be positioned so that you can see between them. One of the best aspects of sex for a lot of people is the skin-to-skin, body-to-body sensuality of another person through your connection (even if just physical) and expression. In reality, there are so many ways to explore sexuality with someone that are pleasurable, fun, and intimate, and don't include penetration. Sexual activities that many people consider foreplay are a part of arousal and setting up for pleasurable penetration.

- Usually the physical space or environment in porn is forbidden or contrived. In reality, environments in which people have sex should be taken into consideration to maximize pleasure. The privacy, comfort, and safety of the setting is important so that both people feel as comfortable as possible. Being uncomfortable or worrying about privacy or safety can put the brakes on pleasure.

- At least half of all porn videos feature anal sex, and women are usually the ones receiving it. In reality, some women like anal and some do not. If both parties consent to anal sex, it requires thoughtful prepa-ration. Because there are voluntary and involuntary muscles in the anus, a person cannot relax their rectum like they would a vagina. Preparation and lubricant are essential to prevent pain and promote pleasure during anal sex. Along with thoughtful consent, anal sex (like all forms of intercourse) requires protection. Unprotected anal sex carries the highest risk for STDs of any sexual activity.

- In porn, sex is always intense and severe. Porn performers quickly get to penetration. In fact, sex can take on all kinds of different feels and intensities, and shouldn't be rushed. Foreplay is a process that involves anticipation and imagination. What sexually arouses or turns someone on is very individual, and discovering what excites your partner can be the biggest turn-on of all. Sex isn't just about arousal; it's about a relationship and how a couple interacts and treats each other, and how that connects to their sexual activity. Penetration is part of sex, but it doesn't have to be central: sex can be erotic in many different ways, and some of the best sex incorporates sensual-ity, love, vulnerability, and intimacy.

- The response in porn sex is consistently exaggerated. In reality, some people, if they are truly having an amazing sexual experience, will respond this way. Some people may respond to pleasure qui-etly, some somewhat vocally, some with body language only. The responses are as diverse as individual people are. What's important is being engaged and communicative so that you actually know how much a person is enjoying the experience with you. Any sexual expe-rience can be the ultimate. It depends on who you are, who you're with, and the connection you have.

PARENT–TEEN CONVERSATION STARTERS

It's important to emphasize with teenagers that a sexual relationship is an interpersonal one that can include both emotional and physical intimacy; the connection usually includes romantic interest and sexual attraction. Too often in American culture, sexuality is discussed with sexist, exclusive, impersonal, unemotional, and one-sided language that involves "scoring." Think about the euphemism of "getting to third base." This doesn't result in healthy sexual development. Encourage your teen to define manhood and womanhood for themselves, to consider what it means to be nonbinary and embrace a third gender, to avoid letting stereotypes shape their actions, and to be sober and brave in social and sexual situations. Remind them that sexual discovery should be good, exciting, and fun for both partners.

- What does gender mean to you?
- What does it mean to be a boy? What does it mean to be a man?
- What does it mean to be a girl? A woman?
- What does it mean to be nonbinary, gender-nonconforming, or transgender?
- What are the cultural norms specific to your gender? Which of those may get in the way of healthy, authentic connection?
- What are some of the commonly used slang words used to describe sexuality? Who and what does it value and devalue?
- Are the ways men are represented in media different from the male role models you look up to?
- Are the ways women are represented in media different from the female role models you look up to?
- How are peer attitudes influential? How does this relate to gender and relationship dynamics?

When discussing music in particular:

- Do you think this song is about attraction, infatuation, or a meaningful and loving relationship? How do you know?
- Do you think people think about the words as much as the music?
- What about the song is misogynistic? Objectifying?
- Does the song represent what's real in healthy sexual relationships?
- What does the song value or devalue about sex?

When discussing film or video:

- How did you know the characters were attracted to each other?
- Were there any other factors influencing them getting together?
- Do you think they both wanted and desired what they did together?
- Do you think they were ready?
- How did they communicate what they wanted or didn't want?
- Sexual exploration can be awkward sometimes. Did you notice any awkward moments? If so, how did the couple deal with it?
- How was consent explicitly asked for? Did the question allow for yes or no? When and how should it have been asked for?
- Did both people show care and respect for each other? Specifically, in what ways?
- If they didn't, what could have been done differently?
- Did you see or hear any coercion?
- Do you think the scene was an accurate representation of what real-life sexual exploration is like?
- Was the sexual exploration safe and responsible? If not, what got in the way of it being so?
- Did you see any gender stereotypes?
- Was there a social power dynamic?

- Did both people walk away from the experience with their dignity intact?

- What was the impact of the sexual exploration on their relationship?

Resources

Amaze.org: An online free resource that encourages and empowers parenting adults to communicate openly and honestly about puberty, reproduction, relationships, sex, and sexuality. A video about how to talk to your kids about porn is also included.

Videos

Reshma Saujani TED Talk: Teach Girls Bravery Not Perfection: https://www.ted.com/talks/reshma_saujani_teach_girls_bravery_not_perfection

Justin Baldoni TED Talk: Why I'm Done Trying to Be "Man Enough": https://www.ted.com/talks/justin_baldoni_why_i_m_done_trying_to_be_man_enough?language=en

John Oliver: Transgender Rights: https://www.youtube.com/watch?v=hmoAX9f6MOc

Emily Nagoski: The Truth about Unwanted Arousal: https://www.ted.com/talks/emily_nagoski_the_truth_about_unwanted_arousal?language=en

Gary Wilson TED Talk: The Great Porn Experiment: https://www.youtube.com/watch?v=wSF82AwSDiU

Articles

"When Did Porn Become Sex Ed?" by Peggy Orenstein, *New York Times*, March 19, 2016

"What Teenagers Are Learning From Online Porn" by Maggie Jones, https://longform.org/posts/what-teenagers-are-learning-from-online-porn

Books

A Guide to Gender (2nd edition): The Social Justice Advocate's Handbook by Sam Killermann

Enough as She Is: How to Help Girls Move Beyond Impossible Standards of Success to Live, Happy, Healthy and Fulfilling Lives by Rachel Simmons

Girls & Sex: Navigating the Complicated New Landscape by Peggy Orenstein

Masterminds & Wingmen: Helping Our Boys Cope with Schoolyard Power, Locker-Room Tests, Girlfriends, and the New Rules of Boy World by Rosalind Wiseman

Sexploitation: Helping Kids Develop Healthy Sexuality in a Porn-Driven World by Cindy Pierce

STRAIGHT ANSWERS TO TEEN QUESTIONS

Are media images of sex true to life?

Nope. A lot of the sexual exploration that is portrayed in the media is unrealistic, especially scenes involving casual sex in which the couple doesn't know each other very well or it's their first time being sexually intimate. Someone has to know what gives them pleasure to be able to communicate it, and if a couple is discovering that together, it takes time and communication to know someone's body and what makes them feel good. A lot of the media images we see of sexual intimacy are a producer's vision of what will appeal to the audience and what's going to be perceived as "hot." A minutes-long sex scene can take hours to film, and there are people directing the characters, as well as body doubles substituting for the actors. If something doesn't go exactly how the director wants, they'll just reshoot. After the actual filming, there is a ton of editing to create the perfect representation that the film company wants their audience to see and hear. Meanwhile, real life gets awkward, including during sex, with no opportunity to reshoot. Some people, if they've been sexually intimate with a partner over time, will have the opportunity to talk about, guide, and "retake" what they're going for sexually. In that case, it could be easy and smooth. For some people that may just happen, but that's rare, especially if someone doesn't have a lot of experience and understanding of how sex and intimacy works. Figuring this out is what sexual experience is all about, and if you have a partner you trust and with whom you can communicate openly, such exploration can be playful and gratifying— and very sexy.

People in porn films are always moaning and groaning—do all people act that way when they're getting off?

Some do, some don't. Pleasurable sounds are a form of sexual communication. As discussed above, media images are intended to provoke a response from its audience, a way to let the audience know that the sex is good is to emphasize the audio part of the scene. Porn stars are directed to have exaggerated responses. In real life, some people react this way during sex. Others respond quietly, some vocally, some with body language only, and some in a combination of these. What's important is being engaged and communicative so you know how much a person is enjoying the experience with you. You can ask or say, "How did that feel?" "Is there something you're interested in trying?" "What makes you feel good?" or "I want this to feel good for both of us."

How long does sex actually take?

It depends on what you're going for and varies from couple to couple. If we are talking about a broader definition of sex that includes any kind of sexual activity, it could be a few moments or several hours. For instance, two people may embrace exploring their sensuality together by making out for an hour while they are feeling each other's bodies over and under clothes. Or they might be looking for a quick release of sexual tension and make each other orgasm in a few minutes.

This question, however, is usually asking how long sexual intercourse *should* last. There are only a few times when I use the word *should* when talking about sexual activity: it *should* be consensual, it *should* be safe, it *should* be good (satisfying) for both people. I believe the question about how long sexual intercourse should last results from the cultural pressure to perform during sexual activity. Teenagers want to know if they're normal, so they want to measure themselves relative to a cultural standard. But when they do so, they are allowing external criteria to determine whether their performance is "good" and enjoyable. The irony is that pressure of this kind may actually inhibit pleasure. The reality is that satisfaction should be determined by the internal, felt experience of the people involved.

When teens ask this question, I always ask, "What are you going for?" Hopefully, the answer to this question includes what both people want. To know this requires some communication. To experience the full potential of a couple's pleasure, I encourage young people to:

1. Think of their individual sense of readiness, so they know what level of intimacy they are good with;

2. Be open to the many different kinds of sexual activity there are to experience;

3. Suspend judgment of yourself and your partner, and be flexible with what you do together (as long as it is consensual, of course).

This requires two people to be close enough that they can talk honestly with each other. This is one of the benefits of knowing your partner well. This way, sexual activity is really an exploration and both participants are free to discover what feels good for themselves and each other, which ultimately is what sex should be.

Now, for what my students *really* want to know. (I make them listen to the above before handing over the following information.) A study published in the *Journal of Sexual Medicine* is often cited to answer how long intravaginal "ejaculatory latencies" (or how long an erect penis in a vagina during intercourse stays hard before ejaculation) should last. It found that for each couple in the study the range was 33 seconds to 44 minutes, for an average of 5.4 minutes. In a study from 2008 titled "Canadian and American Sex Therapists' Perceptions of Normal and Abnormal Ejaculatory Latencies: How Long Should Intercourse Last?" the findings state that "normative" intravaginal intercourse lasts three to thirteen minutes. So pretty much any amount of time is normal. Of course, this is a heteronormative statistic—I wish I could offer one that is more inclusive. What's important though is that the sexual activity is pleasurable overall for everyone involved and not to focus on performance versus felt experience!

Why do guys do that aggressive pounding thing when having sex?

Unfortunately, the majority of young people in the United States don't receive comprehensive sexuality education that includes information on pleasurable and fulfilling sexual relationships. We also live in a sex-negative culture that includes a lot of over-sexualization, sex stigma, and body-shaming, so there are few positive and pleasurable representations of sexuality for young people. Many young people are curious about sex and how it works. As a result, many young people turn to the internet and end up looking at porn to figure it out. That's like watching *The Fast and the Furious* to learn how to drive. Porn is not a realistic representation of healthy, pleasurable, communicative, and responsible sex. The majority of porn is contractual, not consensual. It's all about the "smash" and represents imbalanced power dynamics. It's more about one person dominating over another than genuine mutual pleasure.

Because many teens get their ideas about sex from pornography, many think that harsh, aggressive, pounding sex, a porn staple, is normal and what every partner wants. Because pounding sex is so prevalent in porn, teens may also have the mistaken impression that it is the best way to stimulate their partner to orgasm. Sure, some people like aggressive sex and get off on it, but many do not; for many women, in fact, rough pounding isn't stimulating at all.

If you are engaging in sex with someone else, both partners need to be sensitive to what turns the other on, and if something doesn't feel good to you, it's important to speak up. Tell your partner what does feel good, and if you're not sure, take time to explore that together. You can say, "How would you feel about me guiding your hand?" or "I'm not sure what I like. Can we figure that out together?" or "What feels good?" or "Let's talk about what we want."

How different is porn from actual sex?

It depends on the type of porn you're watching. There is so-called feminist and ethical porn that is available for a fee, but most of the young people I talk to watch mainstream porn that is available for free on the internet. Mainstream porn features actors performing and doesn't present either natural bodies or healthy sex. This material doesn't present safe sexuality practices such as asking for consent, communicating about desires and limitations, or negotiating protection from unwanted pregnancy and STDs. It's intended to entertain people and gain maximum viewership to make money, so everything is intense and exaggerated. It doesn't present relationships that are equitable or reciprocal, where partners respect and care about each other in a sexual experience that prioritizes both partners' pleasure.

Why do some people like fetishes and kinky sex?

Emily Nagoski, one of my favorite sex educators, puts it like this: we aren't born with fetishes. Our brains learn what is sexually relevant as we grow and develop. So from the time we're born, our brains start to link sexual sensations with external stimuli (for example, the sensation of our genitals against our hands, the sights and smells around us, etc.). We are conditioned to associate arousal with our environment. People with sexual fetishes usually remember the fetish as beginning very early in their lives. Sometimes fetishes develop because there's sexual stimulation happening somewhere in a person's brain while they are affected by external stimuli.[18]

"Kinky" sex has to do with what people's brains perceive as sexually stimulating and desirable. There is huge range of behaviors that people may refer to as kinky. Sometimes people are referring to sexual preferences that seem outside the socially acceptable norm, and other times people are referring to the huge range of *bondage, dominance, submission, sadomasochism*—or BDSM—practices. In BDSM culture, people derive erotic pleasure from engaging in sexual behaviors that often include restraints and constrictions, and imbalanced interpersonal and social power dynamics, and also from inflicting or receiving pain. Because porn and books like *Fifty Shades of Grey* have become mainstream, many teenagers have been exposed to BDSM sexuality. What's important to understand is that not all media representations of kinky sex are true to the BDSM culture and community, and that people who practice true BDSM sex should be consenting adults who are well practiced in managing the physical and emotional safety of the sex to ensure that it is consensual. This requires a certain level of maturity and capacity for sexual communication. I encourage my students who are curious about this type of sex to learn, explore, and practice the basics of sexual communication until they are confident in their ability to engage in consensual, ethical, and good sex within a variety of contexts. They can look forward to exploring BDSM sexuality once they have more experience and a much deeper understanding of how sex works.

What's the effect of media on sexuality and relationships?

Each year, teenagers are exposed to over fourteen thousand sexual images through media. That's a lot! In 2017, Common Sense Media published a major study on the impact on teens by media depictions of gender (TV and film). The study found that young people may internalize the gender stereotypes they see in media, and that it can shape their behavior. As it relates to sexuality, the research showed that:

- Media reinforce the idea that masculine traits and behaviors are more valued than feminine traits and behaviors, and boys who consume these media messages are more likely to show masculine behaviors and beliefs.

- Media promote the notion that girls should be concerned about their appearance and should treat their bodies as sexual objects for others' consumption.

- In adolescence, media use is associated with more tolerant views of sexual harassment and more support for the belief that women are at least partially responsible for their own sexual assaults.

- The TV programs and films that young people watch reinforce traditional gender stereotypes.

- Youth of color may be particularly vulnerable to the effects of media use on gender-role development.

- As children enter teenage years, media provide lessons on how they are expected to behave in romantic and sexual situations, and these lessons are strongly gendered.

A lot of traditional gender roles reinforce each other and perpetuate traditional gendered beliefs in what I call the "gender paradigm." Those gender roles of masculinity as superior and femininity as inferior, as well as men being strong, hard, emotionless, and applauded for sexual conquests, and women being passive, overly emotional, deferential, and limited in their right to pleasure, get in the way of authentic connection and communication, and building a foundation for healthy, high-quality relationships.

Adults can help teens question the stereotypes they see in the media and steer them toward healthier depictions of gender roles, sex, and intimacy.

How come people always say they want to go out with someone who is nice, but it's the assholes who get all of the attention?

This is *such* a good question. There is a cultural idea, perpetuated in the media, that being "bad" (aggressive, edgy, unkind, even bullying) is somehow dashing and desirable. Some people think they can change or even "save" a so-called bad person, and they romanticize or excuse the bad behavior. Some people grow up with a similar dynamic in their homes, and it's what they are familiar with and attracted to. Cindy Pierce's book *Sexploitation* and Rosalind Wiseman's book *Masterminds and Wingmen* describe what they call "asshole tickets" or "asshole passes." These are passes that our culture grants "special" people in our culture, particularly men who rely on their privilege and take advantage of their power and entitlement. If a guy is handsome, athletic, smart, and rich, he is granted a large stack of asshole passes: no matter how badly he acts, women want to date him, people want to be his friend, he gets most of the jobs he applies for. How often and how long he can get away with it correlates with how special he is perceived to be. Many people in our society, including adults, accept the currency of asshole tickets.[19]

In my experience, teenagers are often attracted to and impressed by aggressive, brash, daring, yet charismatic personalities. Teens with these qualities are considered hot and often get a lot of romantic attention—even if they're arrogant and mean. Quieter, more thoughtful teens are often not as popular (which can be different from being well liked), and they get less social affirmation for being kind and compassionate. But in the long run, maintaining your values, being vulnerable, and treating people with respect will carry its own benefits (and you'll feel better about yourself if you act with integrity). For most people, it only takes a few relationships with assholes to realize the value of someone who may not be as flashy but has integrity and treats others well. Although it may be hard to believe when you're in high school, in my experience, kindness and respect win in the end.

My friends who are girls totally slut-shame other girls and each other. How do I get them to stop?

If you hear your friends slut-shaming—judging someone negatively for their sexual expression—a friend or acquaintance, try asking them questions to help them realize what they're doing. Don't use the word *why*, which connotes judgment and can put people on the defensive. Find out where they got their information and ask questions like "Do you know what is going on with her?" or "What do you think it feels like for her to be in that situation?" or "What do you mean by that?" You can also not participate in the conversation at all. If your friends ask why you're quiet, you can say, "I don't think it's any of my business" or "I don't think it's cool to judge her—I've been judged before and it doesn't feel good" or "My mom has been talking to me a lot about how judging other women is hurtful to all women, so I can't go there." You can also be completely straightforward and say, "Hey, I don't feel right judging her. It doesn't do anything good for any of us, and it isn't fair. When we make it OK to judge her by doing it ourselves, we make it OK for other people to do it to us."

How much is too much porn? Can you masturbate too much? Is it bad for you?

First, masturbation is a healthy human activity. It is normal to masturbate (it's also perfectly normal not to masturbate), and masturbation does not physically hurt you. Masturbation done privately and from fantasies of your own imagination is healthy. Can you masturbate too much? Like any behavior, if you are masturbating to the point that it impacts the regular, healthy functioning of your life, then it may be too much. Masturbation can bring you pleasure and satisfaction without negatively impacting your life, but if it starts to get in the way of other activities, that's an indication that you may be overdoing it.

It is optimal to masturbate in a variety of contexts and to a variety of stimuli, so your sexual response cycle can be triggered by different things and you don't require hyped-up and exaggerated sexual images to experience sexual pleasure. Some people masturbate to porn, some do not. You may be watching too much porn if it is influencing your ideas of what healthy sexuality and relationships should be. This can be a problem for young people who don't have real-life sexual experiences to help keep porn in perspective. A teen brain is still under construction, and teens are still forming their sexual identity and patterns of behavior.

To date, research on pornography and its effects on behavior hasn't been definitive. The problem with mainstream porn (the free stuff you find on sites like Pornhub, YouTube, or Redtube) is that it presents someone else's sexual fantasies versus using your own imagination. The majority of the sex represented on these sites is violent, objectifying, and nonreciprocal. This can influence your overall understanding of sex. Some boys who watch lots of porn report starting to think about girls in different and concerning ways.

If I don't want to be judged as a prude, and I don't want to be judged as a slut, how am I supposed to act?

This spectrum of prude-shaming and slut-shaming (slut is a negative and damaging word for someone who chooses to be sexually active, and prude is a negative and damaging word for someone who chooses to not be sexually active) is negative all around. Neither end of this spectrum is positive, affirming, or empowering. Shame pushes and pulls people apart. It is not constructive or healthy for any of us. I encourage you to reflect upon who you are, what you value, what you want and need, and act accordingly. Be aware of social dynamics, keep them in perspective, and choose friends with whom you can be yourself and who encourage you to live your truth in healthy ways. People may still judge you, but if you are true to yourself, you can more easily ignore their judgments. And do your best not to judge others, either!

Why shouldn't I send nudes?
I'm proud of my body and want to share it.

Body pride is beautiful, and if you want to share your body with someone you trust and feel safe with, that's positive. However, taking and sending nudes under the age of eighteen is a federal offense and can carry severe consequences. The federal government considers taking, sending, and forwarding nudes as trafficking in child pornography, even if you are taking and sending pictures of yourself. States have created teen sexting laws that address this because federal law can be severe in how it impacts a young person. Those sexting laws vary from state to state.

Even if you are eighteen or older, there is a privacy issue at stake.

It is important to think of the digital space as an extension of your personal space. A smartphone with a camera is different than a regular camera. A digital image sent out into cyberspace has the potential to become the billboard of your life. It is also important to remember that there is a false sense of security when sending anything over social media. Have you read the terms and conditions of the Snapchat or Instagram accounts you set up? Nothing that you send belongs to you. And once you send a picture of yourself, it can be screenshot, forwarded, posted, or exploited in many other ways. Autonomy is an important aspect of healthy sexuality. It means you get to control your narrative. When you lose that control, your image becomes objectified.

If you are considering sending out a nude, stop and ask yourself, *Would I want a college admissions person to see this? My future partner? My future boss? My future in-laws?* Once you send something out into the digital space, you lose control and ownership of it. If you feel empowered with body pride and want to own that, keep it for yourself and those you choose to share it with in person.

CHAPTER FIVE

Love, Pleasure, and Good Sex

We all want the young people we care about to be happy and to grow up to have honest, fulfilling emotional and sexual partnerships. But to get there will take practice, like most things in life, and there is real value in the romantic bonds our children form as teens and young adults. Parents and other adults often label youthful relationships with condescending terms like "puppy love" or "schoolgirl crush," but this minimizes the power and intimacy of many teen relationships. A former student, Clara, wrote in an assignment, "How can adults expect us to take our relationships seriously if they don't?" This is the essential first step for all of us—to affirm that teenagers can have romantic and sexual feelings and relationships that are important to them. We can do this in a way that is not intrusive or overbearing, but with an appropriate balance of caution and calm, prudence and encouragement.

The more teens understand themselves and what it takes to be in a healthy relationship, the greater success they will have with relationships throughout their lives.

Experiencing authentic connection with someone in a healthy relationship can be fun, positive, joyful, and enriching. It's an opportunity to practice care and communication, and to maintain a sense of individuality within a relationship—to learn what feels good for both partners and to express feelings. Healthy relationships take practice, and learning what doesn't work can be as valuable as understanding what does. The more teens understand themselves and what it takes to be in a healthy relationship, the greater success they will have with relationships throughout their lives. Experiences—good and bad—can help our children understand the difference between mature love and other intense forms of attraction, show them how to move beyond hookups to real connection, and teach them how to start and build relationships that include reciprocity, trust, safety, and joy.

I find that the majority of my students believe the way to initiate a relationship is to physically hookup with another person. A hookup lets them know if they're compatible, and if they are, something might develop between them. I suggest that starting a relationship by being sexual (whether it's ephemeral and purely physical, or romantic and going to last two years) runs the risk of the other person viewing the relationship as primarily sexual. You're being physically intimate before you've had a chance to establish trust and effective communication–elements that take time to build. When teenagers get together physically first, how do they know what the other person's intentions are and whether they align with their own? Even if they've heard from friends that the other person likes them, how can they be sure of this information or what "like" means in this context? Trust is built through the shared experience of feeling safe in moments of vulnerability. When we trust someone, we have confidence that their behavior aligns with who they profess to be and that they have the capacity to follow through with what they say they'll do. How can we know all of this if our first experience is strictly physical?

It's important to note that some adults may have the capacity to engage in purely physical experiences for their own sexual gratification without the context of a relationship. But despite the celebration of hookups among today's young people, I find that the majority of the teens I talk to long for connection and relationships. Many don't think that this is an option for them, or fear that they will be vulnerable and experience rejection, or they believe the only way to someone's heart is through their genitals. Many are convinced that no one else wants an intimate connection because the myth of hookup culture reigns supreme.

Teens are also figuring out who they are and what they want. (Ideally this becomes clearer with adulthood, and should adults engage in impersonal sexual activity, it's because they want to and it's on their own terms.) It's essential that adults help teens understand the value of romantic and committed sexual relationships and show respect for these relationships in teens' lives.

Several years ago, I was teaching a class about the different types of relationships people engage in—from hookups, to friends with benefits, to exclusive dating, and so on. At one point, Joe, a sophomore boy, raised his hand and said, "We're talking about what all of these different relationships are like once we're in them, but how do we start one? I mean, I know how to ask someone to hookup. I learned that a long time ago, but what about asking someone out for real?"

An excellent and humbling question. It reminded me of how unique and challenging the experience of moving from childhood into young adulthood is. Even teenagers who look, talk, and act like they are experienced and worldly are constantly being bombarded by contradictory information about sex and relationships through media and their friends, with no real way to interpret it. Joe's question inspired a deeper conversation about the glorification of hookup culture in the media and the hypersexualized adult American culture that many teens try to emulate in their quest to make it through the gauntlet of adolescence. We also discussed the fact that many teens learn about impersonal sex through TV, movies, music, and all the media they consume through their phones and computers—including internet porn.

In 2017, Making Caring Common at the Harvard Graduate School of Education released a report, "The Talk: How Adults Can Promote Young People's Healthy Relationships and Prevent Misogyny and Sexual Harassment." The report found that both teens and adults "greatly overestimate the size of the 'hookup culture,' and these misconceptions can be detrimental to young people."

The myth that everyone is having constant hookups puts pressure on teens to keep up.

The report reflects my observations as a sex educator. The myth that everyone is having constant hookups puts pressure on teens to keep up, because they are developmentally and neurologically programmed to seek the acceptance of their peers. Also, the hookups that *are* happening are more likely to be shared at school on Monday morning, since these encounters are assumed to be public and are irresistible gossip fodder. Teens are far less likely to hear about the substantive, caring, and joyful experiences of teen couples in exclusive relationships. So, if teens are exposed to a steady diet of pop culture, their peers are all talking about hookups, and they aren't hearing much from parents and other adults about healthy relationships (a reality confirmed by the Making Caring Common researchers) it's no surprise that many are confused about how to form and maintain caring, mutually respectful, and fulfilling romantic connections.

Based on my own observations, which have since been bolstered by the Making Caring Common study, I restructured my class. The curricula of the six-week class now follows the arc of a romantic relationship, an idea I got from a phenomenal colleague, Ivy Chen, who teaches human sexuality at San Francisco State University. (I make it clear to my students that the class is organized this way to facilitate learning: in real life, of course, relationships develop along different timelines.)

Week one is "Sexuality and Self." During this week, we talk about the fact that people need to have a certain level of self-awareness to engage in a healthy relationship—physically and romantically. I emphasize that the capacity to consider and care about another person is an essential element in all relationships, and that a teen who lacks that capacity isn't ready for a sexual or romantic relationship.

Empathy and respect for another is central as we approach our lesson on how to ask someone out.

Kamalah and Noah have a couple of classes together and catch each other's eyes from time to time, but quickly look away. Once, Noah held Kamalah's gaze for a while until she broke it with a smile and looked up at the teacher, trying to refocus. Whenever the desk next to Kamalah's is open, Noah sits in it. If there is a partner activity, they choose each other. When Kamalah talks to her friends about Noah, they always say, "It is *so* obvious. He is *so* into you." Noah also asked Kamalah's friend for her Instagram and "likes" everything she posts.

One day, Kamalah and Noah are sitting next to each other in English class. During a break between class periods, students often run out to grab snacks and drinks. Kamalah asks Noah, "Hey, you want to go up to the corner store with me?" They walk up to the mini-market and grab something to eat. As they're walking back to campus, close enough to each other that their arms brush, Noah asks, "Hey, what are you doing later? You want to go to the park and kick it?" A smile spreads across Kamalah's face, "Yeah, I'll meet you in the student center at three and we can go from there."

Making eyes at each other, the smiles, the open body language, the subtle angling to sit next to each other, and then the more obvious expression of interest by seeking out each other on Instagram and Snapchat, are all social indicators of attraction. The feelings of nervous anticipation and excitement could be caused by certain hormones and regions of the brain that are involved in emotions, sexual attraction, and attachment.

There were some small gestures that indicated interest before Noah directly made the ask. Kamalah's invitation to go to the store "with me" communicated interest more personal than a platonic "hey, let's get some food." There was some friend-sourcing as well: Kamalah's friends reassure her that her interest in Noah seems to be reciprocated. Both Kamalah and Noah's questions about doing something together are consensual in that they allow for a yes or no response. There's some privacy to their interaction, and Noah has come up with something specific to do. He could have made a suggestion based on what he knows about Kamalah's preferences. For example, if she mentioned a specific movie, he could have asked if she wanted to see it together, or he could have simply asked her, "What do you want to do together?" Their exchanges and moments of vulnerability were balanced, and they treated each other with respect.

What if either Noah or Kamalah didn't have an interest in the other and wanted to decline the invitation? How do you treat each other with respect (that is, in a way that recognizes the other person's value) in those circumstances, and why is that important? If someone appropriately and respectfully asks you out, they've paid you a compliment and made themselves vulnerable because they think you're worth that risk. At the very least, they deserve an honest answer and to be treated with respect too. Students know that kindness in the face of vulnerability goes a long way, and that honesty is important—if often awkward and difficult.

A simple but direct response is almost always the best: "I appreciate your asking, but no thanks" is the way to go. In my classes there is almost always a student who talks about consideration and cautions against creating false hope (e.g., saying something like "Not right now, maybe later"). Being vague because you don't want to feel bad about rejecting someone may be easier on you, but it's harder on the other person. The same can be true of the common response "I don't think of you that way. Let's just be friends." This may seem softer than a direct no, but it is actually diminishing to hear if you're on the receiving end.

Hearing no when you ask someone out is hard. In the words of my students, "It sucks!" and can be uncomfortable, painful, and tough on one's self-esteem. However, most students (and many adults) say they would rather the other person be honest than give an ambivalent response when no is actually what they mean.

I caution students to avoid negativity and to practice positive relationship skills instead. That means respectfully saying no and not exploiting that person's vulnerability afterward with gossip (which is different from respectful sharing) about the incident with friends and others. We want to inspire positivity and promote a culture of dignity, so that everyone can be their true self and feel comfortable taking risks.

More importantly, how young people handle such situations helps them develop morality. Morality is built across the developmental stages in the form of appreciation (the ability to know and value other people), [20] gratitude (the capability to be thankful, which includes humility, humanity, and the capacity to act with kindness), and empathy (the ability to put yourself in the other person's position and understand and care about how they feel).

In our relationship with our teenagers, we should emphasize and reflect the morals we want them to express in their own lives, including honesty, kindness, loyalty, generosity, a commitment to justice, the capacity to think through moral dilemmas, and the ability to sacrifice for important principles. [21] These habits of paying attention to and caring for others and the social emotional skills needed to treat people are separate from happiness or self-esteem. We can cultivate them in our children, not only by talking about them, but also by modeling them ourselves. [22] In the long term, the empowerment of living a life of integrity is what leads to overall well-being—which may very well include happiness and success.

Developing a relationship with another person is also about consent. Consent, which is detailed in chapters 1 and 3, starts even before two people are together in a physically intimate moment. When we ask someone for something and they say no, how do we respond? I find my students are intrigued by the exercise of reflecting on their own response to adversity or challenge. They welcome the opportunity to learn how to be more resilient when they are immersed in a culture that applauds effortless perfection, supports entitlement, and pressures us to be constantly happy. Discussing how to manage one's own desires, how to communicate them, and how to listen for a partner's limits and desires, contributes to a teen's self-awareness and understanding of empathy and consent.

It is helpful for adults to discuss the differences between various types of intense feelings with the teens in their life. Explore with teenagers the distinction among attraction, infatuation, sexual and romantic caring, and love. Attraction can be hard to describe or quantify because it's so personal, but it's possible to guide our teenagers to greater awareness of what qualities attract them to another person. Are they attracted to the other person's intellect, honesty, kindness, or sense of humor? Or are they attracted to someone because they are elusive, or considered hot or popular or unattainable? Are they attracted to someone solely on the basis of physical appearance? These questions can help teens understand what they are looking for in a relationship, and the elements that go into a healthy human connection.

Acting on an attraction and developing relationship skills are two different things. Relationship-building requires courage, time, reflection, patience, persistence, and attention. Like most worthwhile things in life, relationships require an element of hard work. Not only do relationships have the potential to enrich our lives with companionship, steady support, and real-time joy, but also the practical practice of relationships, no matter how they end, can help us get better at them and to understand who we are, what we need, and how to be a caring partner. Relationships contribute to our capacity to love and be loved.

The foundation of a healthy relationship is effective communication, the ability to actively listen to another, to be present and empathetic.

The foundation of a healthy relationship is effective communication, the ability to actively listen to another, to be present and empathetic. With practice, we learn to be aware of our body language, suspend judgment, and respond with our partner in mind before shifting to how we are impacted. We also learn to effectively express our own needs and desires with clarity and authenticity in a reciprocal exchange of who, what, and how we are with each other. Sooner or later all relationships get bumpy. It's not the obstacles but the way we overcome them that makes the difference. Relationships are an exercise in true commitment.

Patrick and Kelsey have been in an exclusive sexual relationship for a year. One day, they make plans to watch the sunset at the beach after Patrick's late-afternoon lacrosse practice. The start of practice is delayed and then, after practice, some guys and the coach get to talking. By the time Patrick looks at his watch, he realizes how late it is. He looks on his phone and sees several texts from Kelsey: "where r u?" "r we going?" "hello????" and a missed call. Patrick calls Kelsey and says, "I'm so sorry, I had no idea how late it got. Please meet me at my house." Kelsey responds, "Fine. Whatever. It's OK." Patrick can hear annoyance in her voice.

Patrick is pulling clothes on after his shower when Kelsey gets there. Patrick can tell she's mad. He's learned that he has to push her to talk about her feelings to get to the root of a problem. "How are you really feeling?" he asks her. "Can we talk, like, more about this?" Kelsey is mad that Patrick messed up their plans, not that he was playing lacrosse—she is supportive of that—but the lack of communication.

Patrick tells her, "I know I made a mistake. I can't fix it right now. How can I do better in the future?" Kelsey tells him she understands how he could get caught up with his friends and asks that he make more of an effort to communicate in the future. Patrick commits to doing this. The vibe is a bit awkward and they aren't as affectionate with each other at first, but they slowly warm up as the evening goes on.

In this example, Kelsey and Patrick are accountable to their relationship. Even though Kelsey is mad, she still shows up to be with Patrick. Since Patrick made the mistake, he makes an effort to reach out and talk about it. Both of them take responsibility and remain open to one another, instead of being reactive or defensive.

It may feel easier to be passive when things get tough in a relationship, and to shut down and avoid difficult discussions and feelings, but in the end this can lead to a fraught and unfulfilling partnership. Sex educator Emily Nagoski says that feelings are like a tunnel: you have to go through them (and their darkness) to get to the light on the other side. Ignoring or brushing off moments like this can lead to a backup. The backup can make us stuck and cause a smaller moment that takes a relatively small amount of effort to process to grow bigger and become more difficult to manage. Dealing with issues sooner rather than later will lead over time to better communication and a stronger relationship.

Kelsey and Patrick care about each other. Sometimes we can be angry or disappointed with people we care about. We can have those feelings at the same time. Patrick feels badly for disappointing Kelsey. He urges her to tell him what's really going on, is accountable for his mistake, and asks for suggestions to improve. Kelsey is understanding, expresses what would work better for her, and asks for what she needs. Patrick commits to do better and meet that need. Kelsey is open and forgiving.

Both Kelsey and Patrick are willing to work together toward a solution. Neither of them is vehement and confrontational. There isn't unnecessary judgment and drama. When there has been contention in a relationship, it's normal for things to feel uncomfortable for a while, but Kelsey and Patrick see their plans through and spend time together, which reassures them of their connection and serves to smooth things out. It will be important for Patrick to follow through with his commitment and for Kelsey to do the same when issues she needs to work on come up. It is also helpful to talk about why an issue like lack of communication may persist. It could stem from different cultural values, how either of them grew up, or something deeper that isn't about their relationship. Everyone brings baggage to a relationship. It can be helpful to explore this with a partner in an effort to understand and solve the problem. If, however, despite talking things through and professing to do better, the lack of communication continues or another issue persists, it's time to think about whether the relationship should continue. People in healthy relationships are able to make these changes and should share more good times than bad.

All of this can feel easier said than done. There is a lot that can get in the way of our aspirations to be effective communicators and caring partners. Teenagers are new to all of this, steeped in a culture (adult culture as well as their own) that doesn't encourage healthy vulnerability; they also have many expectations, competing influences, and pressures that they're dealing with. It is helpful for all of us to think about what gets in the way of our relationship aspirations, including fear of rejection, insecurity, complacency, and other factors, and to come up with strategies to overcome these obstacles. This is when friends can be a supportive resource. Trusted friends and adults can help teens examine healthy and unhealthy dynamics, and explore the values we want them to uphold in their relationships. Discussion with supportive friends can also hold teenagers accountable, provide perspective, and help them figure out their own readiness when it comes to intimacy and sexual activity.

As a relationship progresses, the question of when to have sex or how far it should go usually comes up. Not only is consent essential, but also both partners' well-being should be paramount as well. In my classroom, when we discuss ethical sexual decision-making, the assumption is that it will be, at the very least, legal and consensual. But I encourage my students to go beyond this minimum standard and strive for interactions that are ethical, and take their partner's well-being into consideration every step of the way. This means striving for sexual connections that are pleasurable and satisfying for both partners and that enrich the relationship. My students have generated a great list of questions to ask themselves and others when considering how far to go sexually:

- Will you be clearheaded?
- Do you have perspective on whether your intentions and your partner's are real?
- Are you considerate of each other?
- Is the relationship balanced? Is there mutual respect (treating each other how you want to be treated)?
- Do you feel genuine desire for what you want to do?
- Do you feel like you can ask for what you want?
- Are you prepared? (contraception and STD protection)
- Will you be in a safe environment?
- Are you comfortable with your own and your partner's body?
- Is sex a big deal to you? Will it make you feel more emotionally intimate?
- Have you asked if your partner wants to?
- Have you thought about the physical and emotional consequences?
- Is there anything influencing your decision (from substances to peer pressure to parents' wishes)?

- Do you trust and respect them?
- Do you feel safe with them?
- Do you feel like you could comfortably say no? Will what you do together be appropriately private?
- Is your relationship consensual so far?
- Do they care as much about your experiences as theirs?
- What do you really want? To be closer physically? To express how much you care? To make someone feel good? To get off? To make someone jealous? To be able to participate in the conversations your friends have about sex?

These questions will help teens think through their reasons for having sex, and perhaps give them pause if they're feeling pressured by their partner, their peers, or both. The answers to these questions will provide teens with information about potential consequences of the sexual activity. Ultimately, the decision to go for it is up to both partners and will be based on intuition, which is why the probability for a positive experience is higher if you discuss these questions with your partner (and consider them yourself) beforehand. This requires bravery, communication skills, and trust. It's also true that in relationships, the most difficult conversations are often the ones that are most important to have. If you and your partner don't feel close and trusting enough to talk about these issues, you may not be ready for the vulnerability of sexual intimacy.

Blake and Clay have been hanging out for several months. Blake identifies as gay and is out at school and to his family, and Clay is questioning but assumed straight by his friends and family. Blake and Clay go to different high schools. They met through mutual friends and got to know each other at a couple of parties and hangouts. Their time together is fun and the flow of their conversation natural, spanning everything from classes and shared interests to families and fears.

As their friendship deepens, so does their affection for each other. In private, there is a physical closeness that is not quite cuddling, but feels intimate nonetheless. In between episodes while binge-watching *Shameless*, Blake turns to Clay and asks, "Hey, I don't want to freak you out, but I kinda feel connected to you as more than just a friend." Clay freezes for a moment and says, "Do you think I'm gay?"

"It doesn't matter what I think," Blake replies. "Only you really know. Either way, you can trust me. I know it can be a scary thing to figure out alone."

Clay is quiet and pensive, then says, "Yeah, I don't know. I have to admit I've thought about it. But I just don't know."

"OK, well, just know that I'm here to talk about it." Blake responds. Clay nods and thanks him.

They watch two more episodes of the show, then Clay moves closer to Blake with his eyes averted. Their foreheads touch. Blake whispers, "You OK?" Clay nods his head yes and lifts his chin so they can kiss.

"How do you want this to go? I mean, between the two of us," Blake asks.

Clay says, "I'm down for being together but I'm not ready for anyone to know anything yet."

"OK."

Blake and Clay have an authentic and intimate connection. Their interaction is caring, empathetic, and consensual, and they're willing to have a challenging conversation about what their intentions are and how they understand their sexual identities. They have agreed to take things slow and be in it together. This is ethical sexual activity. Blake and Clay are tending to each other and the context (the external circumstances and their internal states of mind and emotions) in which their dynamic is happening. Blake honors Clay's personal process of discovery, as well as his need for privacy in a world that is still largely homophobic.

How this works out between Blake and Clay will depend on their ability to maintain open communication about what they need and want from the relationship as it progresses. There are all kinds of aspects of our identities that can impact our relationships, including religion, gender, size, ability, language, and ethnicity, to name a few. What matters is how a couple deals with these factors and maintains a sense of dignity while they figure out how it influences the dynamic of their partnership. For some, challenges like these deepen their connection.

Ash identifies as gender-nonconforming, and Roan identifies as female-to-male (FTM) transgender. Ash and Roan have been friends since middle school and romantically together for six months. Their communication has been open and honest from the beginning. They have expressed their love for each other and have decided that they're ready to have sex. It's the weekend and Roan's parents are gone for the day, so they are alone at his house, in Roan's bed. Having already discussed safe sex and made the necessary purchases, there is an excited anticipation between them, which is expressed through hushed whispers and giggling.

Usually, when they are together, Roan keeps his breast binder on because of some body dysphoria. He wants Ash to see him as he sees himself, and he is able to be more comfortable and experience more pleasure this way. While Ash and Roan are exploring each other sexually, they pause during intimate moments, their foreheads together, and ask "OK?" of each other. Roan decides to take his binder off. They turn the lights off and while he removes it, they hold each other's gaze and come back together in a kiss. The transition is slightly awkward, so they keep kissing until they both feel comfortable again. Ash moves a hand up Roan's back and hints toward his chest, looks into Roan's eyes with a questioning look. Roan shakes his head no, so Ash continues with touching that is pleasurable for both of them, then Ash asks Roan to guide them.

Roan and Ash's relationship is built on trust, respect, and compassion. Not only is it consensual in that they ask each other what they want and how they feel about sexual intimacy before they engage in it, but also it is kind and safe. Kindness comes from the heart and feels caring—it shows that the other person sees and honors who you are. There is generosity in how Roan and Ash are vulnerable with each other. Their pleasure comes from the full expression of their desire to be physically intimate and their ability to trust each other, which will deepen their connection.

I often tell my students, "Sex is a dialogue. It is an expression, a conversation that involves communication and listening." Then I ask the class to name qualities of a good conversation. Everyone can contribute to this activity—they have all had a quality conversation in their lives. They identify the importance of focused attention and being present (no distractions like looking at a phone), each person's body language is open and receptive to a reciprocal and balanced exchange, there's an awareness of whether humor or seriousness is appropriate, pauses are OK when they happen, there's no judgment but a feeling of safety because they can trust each other to respect what they're sharing and any vulnerability, both people aspire to genuinely understand the other, and both are honest, patient, and care about what's shared.

After we've written these attributes on the board, I ask, "How does a good conversation leave you feeling?" This list is consistent with each class: "thoughtful," "like I've grown," "inspired," and "satisfied, and like I'd want to do it again."

Sophie and Jackson have known each other since they were nine. Their families are friends and spend a lot of time together over summers at the shore. They live in different states during the school year and keep in touch through Instagram, Snapchat, and FaceTime. When they reached eighth grade, Sophie and Jackson's emotional intimate relationship started to include physical intimacy too. Always quick to fall back into their natural connection, summers are fun and easy. Sometimes Sophie and Jackson share hours of quiet time together and other times their adventures are exciting and joyful. What they love the most are the long conversations they share, talking about what they want for the future, what it's like for Sophie when her parents fight, and how much Jackson misses his brother, who went to college, while lazing on the dock between swims in the ocean.

They've always been physically affectionate, and as they get older their sexual exploration becomes more adventurous and they start having conversations about the possibility of intercourse. They talk about how to be safe, what they want the experience to be like, and their own sense of readiness. They ask each other questions like

"Are you nervous about anything?" "What if we start and it doesn't feel right?" and "What will make it feel good?"

One rainy day when their families have gone sightseeing, they're in bed and Sophie goes down on Jackson. After a couple of minutes, he gently lifts her chin and asks, "Do you want to have sex?" Sophie says yes. As Jackson gets a condom, he asks, "You sure?" and Sophie replies, "Definitely." They fumble a bit and have fun working through the awkwardness with giggles. Their intercourse is slow and intimate, and they kiss passionately and gaze into each other's eyes. When they're done, they are comfortable being quiet and together. They talk about the sex a little—enough to know that they both enjoyed it—that it was what they both wanted and that they're looking forward to doing it again. They are excited and grounded at the same time.

Sophie and Jackson are fully and equally invested in having "good" sex. It is consensual. Both have contributed to conversations about readiness and what they want. In the moment, through nonverbal communication and asking, each knows that the activity they're engaged in is what the other person genuinely wants too. There are no substances, age differentials, or other factors that might skew their understanding of consent. Their activity is ethical. They care about each other's well-being and have talked about safety. An important note: they did not use protection during oral sex, which put them at risk for oral STDs. They have discussed sexual communication and how their sexual experience can include the intimacy and joy of their friendship. Their previous shared sexual experiences serve as context and understanding for their conversations. The sex is also good, and both partners are satisfied. Their shared values of trust, safety, communication, and pleasure are all in practice. The experience deepens their intimacy, physically feels really great, and is satisfying. They're looking forward to more. It's a positive sexual experience. True to their effective sexual communication, they also discuss where their relationship stands and what they need from each other when they part after summer is over.

It's important to many of my students that I acknowledge that some teens can have good sex outside of the context of a relationship. I find that those teenagers have a certain level of experience and confidence when it comes to communication. They know their limits and can communicate their boundaries. They know their own pleasure so they can tell someone what feels good. And they know what it's like to feel safe so they know what they can share and what they should hold on to. This also requires a strong sense of self-awareness and the capacity to listen for, respect, and consider their partner's needs and well-being. These teens understand that good sex is a shared experience between partners whose sexual values and intentions align.

The discovery of sexuality with a dedicated partner with whom you can explore, experiment, share, and grow is a gift.

The majority of the teenagers I work with aren't yet at a place in terms of their experience and level of maturity where they can have impersonal good sex. In fact, a lot of my adult friends talk about how challenging this is. The trust, care, and sense of physical and emotional safety that is built through a healthy and established relationship allows for exploration and learning. The discovery of sexuality with a dedicated partner with whom you can explore, experiment, share, and grow is a gift. It is to a teen's benefit to know the difference between something meaningful and something insubstantial. Many of my students confuse infatuation and sexual attraction with deeper feelings.

Hugh and Rose were set up by a mutual friend a couple of months ago and have been on a couple of dates since: dinner, the movies, a couple of walks in the park. Their time together is nice enough, although their conversations can feel a bit forced and superficial, and Rose realizes they don't have that much to talk about. Rose sneaks over to Hugh's house from time to time to hook up, which is always intense and hot. The progression of their exploration is always super smooth—much more than their conversations. Each time they are together now, they go straight for a bedroom to mess around, which usually ends with Rose giving Hugh a blow job.

One day, Rose gets a Snap from Hugh: "my parents took off wanna come over?" When Rose arrives, the two don't even talk but go straight for Hugh's bed. Hugh is sitting on the edge and Rose is straddling him. They are intensely making out, which feels really good to both of them, then they take each other's shirts off. From the outside, it may appear that what is happening between them is hot, but from the inside, Rose doesn't feel that way. It's like she's watching herself from above, and not feeling much.

When Hugh asks, "How do you want me to fuck you?" Rose responds by kissing him harder and pushing him down on the bed. Then Hugh puts on a condom, and Rose guides him to intercourse. Rose moves in and out of feeling engaged, and periodically looks down at what is happening as if from a distance. After Hugh orgasms, they talk in bed for about ten minutes and then it's time for Rose to go.

Rose and Hugh are physically attracted to each other, but there isn't much of an emotional connection. Their conversations are superficial and the time they spend together doesn't seem to strengthen their bond. They are both into their sexual connection, but it isn't reciprocal since it usually ends with Rose getting Hugh off. Hugh doesn't seem to be aware of or particularly interested in Rose's sexual pleasure, and he never asks if and how he could make intercourse more satisfying for her.

Neither Rose nor Hugh has brought their families, the people who care about them most, into each other's lives, and there is a lot of sneaking around and secrecy. Their sexual encounters are like a performance of what they see in the media, rather than an engaged and felt experience. There isn't much emotional intimacy or investment in each other's experience or lives outside the sexual connection.

Rose and Hugh are more infatuated with each other than anything else. Is their sexual relationship consensual? When we talked about it, Rose told me that it was consensual through wordless communication. Was it ethical? Just because a sexual connection is legal doesn't mean it's right. In Rose's mind it was fine—not regrettable yet "meh"—and kind of a waste of time, especially since she is now engaged in a relationship with plenty of good sex, so she has something to compare it to. Hugh may have felt differently, but for sex to be truly good it needs to be good for both partners.

Sometimes it's hard to tell if the sexual aspect of a relationship is infatuation or the result of an authentic connection that has led to sexual desire. Many students come to my office to talk about the feelings they've developed for a friend, or they're in a "friends with benefits" (FWB) relationship that has become complicated. One person has developed feelings, or their partner is distancing themselves, or an FWB hooked up with someone else and their initial partner is upset, even though their relationship is supposed to be open.

These relationships often start off casually and with the best of intentions. A person cares about their friend and trusts them, so the addition of sexual activity seems like a good idea. In many cases, however, one of the friends develops feelings, and things quickly become awkward and complicated, and in many cases the friendship is lost.

Of course, this isn't always the case. Friendships can often turn into intimate and authentic relationships that are all the stronger because they are built on mutual trust and longstanding affection. In fact, whenever my class asks me what the definition of love is, I reference author and sex editor Al Vernacchio, who says that love includes the qualities of best friendship plus romantic and/or sexual desire. But I always make a distinction between a friendship that turns into a committed relationship and an FWB situation. I point out that FWB is a way to avoid being accountable to the responsibilities of a relationship while reaping the benefits of companionship, trust, care, and sexual gratification. (To be clear, there is nothing wrong with this as long as both parties are honest about their expectations.)

Taylor and Morgan have been best friends since the first day of freshman year. They had an immediate connection and have been inseparable ever since. Through shared experiences with each other and their other friends, they have built trust over time. They know the other will always have their back and be supportive when things get tough. Their time together is always fun, but they can also be serious and talk about real stuff.

It's the summer between sophomore and junior years. After a day of hanging out at the beach, dinner with Morgan's family, and a movie, Taylor decides to crash at Morgan's house. While listening to music on Morgan's bed, Taylor slowly moves in to kiss Morgan. Morgan pulls away just enough so that Taylor stops.

Morgan says, with kindness in her voice, "Whoa, what's up?" Taylor doesn't respond right away, then says, "I don't know, I just thought...that maybe we could hook up or take our friendship to another level."

Morgan is surprised but calm and admits that the possibility has crossed her mind, too, but she worries that if it doesn't work out, their friendship will never be the same again. Morgan suggests they could hook up but keep it quiet; an FWB sort of situation that they'll keep open in case either one wants to hook up with other people as well. If it doesn't feel right, they'll just take the physical part out of it and go back to being friends.

If the sexual desire between Morgan and Taylor is something they both genuinely feel and are interested in exploring within the context of their relationship, it's possible that a romantic dimension won't be ephemeral but meaningful and long-lasting. Of course, there is always risk to a friendship when sexual activity is introduced, mostly because sex is a bonding behavior and there are real biochemical responses to engaging in it that will compound the platonic intimacy with sexual intimacy. This leads to vulnerability. Vulnerability requires courage; it also leads to deeper connection. The more we care, the more exposed we are, so if the relationship turns out to be one-sided or not work out, the fallout can be devastating. All of the intertwined pieces of friendship and sexuality can be challenging to navigate and deal with. Such relationships are a test of resilience and getting through it will build strength. Still, if it doesn't work between them, Morgan and Taylor may need to take time away from each other before they can come back together and redefine their friendship without the sexual and romantic intimacy that they experienced.

All of the intertwined pieces of friendship and sexuality can be challenging to navigate and deal with.

I would counsel against Morgan's suggestion of keeping their relationship quiet. Many students tell me that this is a way to protect their experiment because if it doesn't work out, the public knowledge would make it even harder to get over and would make both parties feel even more exposed. I say if you're going to have a relationship, stand up for it entirely. Be accountable and honor what you've decided to do together by allowing it to be real to the people who care about you. Secrecy and a partial commitment won't inspire the attention and investment a relationship deserves. Yes, being open about your relationship requires more risk, but those feelings of vulnerability will still be there between Taylor and Morgan no matter how public or secret their decision is. Privacy is an important aspect of a healthy relationship, but that's not what is behind Morgan's proposal. Morgan seems to be tentative about doing something that could make her friendship with Taylor different, and she is scared to feel rejection in the moment or down the line. In the end, it will be to Morgan and Taylor's benefit to be real with each other and decide how much healthy risk they're willing to take.

Relationships can be especially complicated for adolescents when there is a social power dynamic, especially if the adolescent is a young adult (over eighteen), and their partner is significantly older or more experienced. I caution my students about the emotional safety of these relationships, since they rarely mean the same thing to both people. This can be hard for teens to see because the perceived confidence and success of someone more experienced is seductive and the added infatuation may cloud their judgment.

Gracie just graduated from high school and has her first summer job that isn't with peers but adults. She is looking forward to working with Melinda, the older manager of the restaurant where she's waiting tables. Gracie is both intimidated and intrigued by Melinda and her abrasive confidence; she exudes experience and maturity. It's seductive and intoxicating—Gracie thinks, *I want to be that way.*

Melinda is openly gay and has a girlfriend who also works at the restaurant. Melinda often talks about women she's been with in a conquest-oriented and objectifying way, always mentioning their physical attributes. Gracie is just discovering her attraction to women and over time develops a crush on Melinda. The older woman begins routinely inviting Gracie for drinks at the bar across the street after work. Melinda always buys the drinks since Gracie is underage.

One night after drinks and flirting, Melinda invites Gracie over to her place, reassuring her that her girlfriend is OK with it. At her apartment, Melinda shares that she's sick of being a phase in people's lives and wants something more. Gracie thinks Melinda wouldn't be a phase in *her* life but stays quiet because she knows Melinda has a girlfriend, and after chatting for a while, she leaves. Gracie is in a taxi heading home when she gets a text from Melinda saying that she's never felt about anyone the way she does about Gracie. Stunned that Melinda could be attracted to her when she could be with so many older, more experienced women, Gracie is flattered. A few weeks later, when Melinda breaks up with her girlfriend, she and Gracie start going out together.

The affair is intense and includes furtive exchanges in the restaurant linen closet. But soon after the relationship starts, Melinda abruptly breaks up with Gracie, who is devastated.

A few weeks after the breakup, Gracie starts college and is distracted by her new environment and experiences. Out of the blue, she receives a text from Melinda requesting a nude photo. Gracie isn't comfortable with that and says so. But Melinda badgers her, writing things like "I thought you cared about me" and "After everything we've been through, how could you not trust me?"

Gracie's attraction goes beyond infatuation. She is drawn to Melinda's seemingly empowered sexual identity as she is tentatively figuring out her own. Gracie looks up to Melinda because she feels special that someone who has so many choices for sexual partnership would focus on her. The draw of Melinda's attention is powerful, especially as Gracie is charting unfamiliar territory and looking for firm ground. The unequal dynamic compromises Gracie's ability to make rational decisions. Melinda's request for nude pics reveals the true nature of the relationship between them. Melinda uses guilt and shame to try to coerce Gracie; if she really cared about Gracie, she wouldn't treat her that way.

Gracie shared this story with me and told me that being away at school helped give her perspective. She asserted herself with Melinda and refused to send nude photos. She also showed her text threads to a friend who noticed the dysfunction of the dynamic, which then led to Gracie blocking Melinda on social media. Self-reflection followed for Gracie, and her retrospective clarity and learning helped inform her subsequent decision-making. Her hope is that this story will help other young people recognize and avoid imbalanced personal power dynamics.

For adults hoping to prepare teenagers for the sexual experiences ahead of them, it's valuable to discuss all of the possibilities for relationships, good and bad. It's understandable that we want to protect teens we care about from dangerous and painful situations, but we must also give them the respect and autonomy to make their own mistakes. Meanwhile, it's essential to provide positive messages about intimacy, sex, and love, as well as cautionary ones, and to emphasize the many wonderful and life-affirming benefits of emotional and sexual intimacy.

PARENT–TEEN CONVERSATION STARTERS

For teenagers to understand what healthy romantic and sexual relationships look, sound, and feel like, they need to understand how all relationships in their lives may influence them. Most students can distinguish between the different types of relationships in their lives and talk about them; however, understanding the significance and meaning of relationships can be challenging. For students to discover who they are in relationships, they will need to reflect upon the dynamics of their existing relationships with friends, family, teachers, peers, coaches, and others.

It's important for students to understand that relationships require varying levels of work to reap rewards, and that practice and reflection in their relationships will help them develop greater self-awareness in romantic relationships as well. Because we live in such a hypersexualized culture, students are often challenged to know what a healthy romantic relationship looks like (many adults are too). The following questions will help provide teens with essential information as they explore and experience relationships.

- What physical, emotional, and psychological qualities do you find attractive in another person?
- What does it feel like to really like someone?
- What does it mean to have an authentic connection?
- If you were interested in asking someone out, how would you go about it?
- What's the value in treating someone with respect?
- What's the difference between attraction, infatuation, like, and love?
- How do you know when you're ready for certain levels of intimacy?
- What are the strongest messages you've gotten about gender roles? Do they impact your relationships in any way?
- Does everybody have the same definition of *hot*? Where does that come from?
- What do you do if you think someone is hot and your friends don't?
- What do people do when their sexuality doesn't fit into traditional boxes?
- How do we understand and construct sexual identity?
- How do people decide whether to date?
- Who are the datable people? Who are the people you want to hook up with?
- Are the people you want to hook up with different from the dateable people? What characterizes the difference?
- How much does public awareness or public knowledge of your dating or sexual behavior shape who you initiate dating or hooking up with? Does it impact your public confidence?
- How does this factor into your self-image and personal values? Your own sense of love and being loved?
- What does social media have to do with it?

- How would you characterize a healthy relationship? An unhealthy one? What if a relationship has elements of both? What are the deal breakers? Which aspects can be worked on and to what point?
- What are some of the benefits of a healthy dating relationship?
- How do you see love portrayed in the media? In movies, TV, music, literature? Is it consistent or are there variations?
- How is familial love different from platonic love different from romantic love?
- What examples of love have you seen in real life? How would you characterize it? Did you notice any common aspects of those relationships? Did you notice any differences?
- How do you think people know when they're ready for sexual intimacy?
- What are the ways in which people express love?
- How do you think love builds and deepens between people?
- How do you think romantic love connects to pleasure and desire?
- What are the biggest challenges of love and relationships?
- What is the difference between healthy love and unhealthy love?
- What can you do if love isn't reciprocated?
- What can you do if you are in romantic love and the relationship is in trouble or ends?
- How does love contribute to our growth as people?

Resources

Making Caring Common is a website with many parent resources, such as "For Families: 5 Tips for Guiding Teens and Young Adults in Developing Healthy Romantic Relationships," and "For Families: 6 Tips for Reducing and Preventing Misogyny and Sexual Harassment among Teens and Young Adults." https://mcc.gse.harvard.edu/resources-for-families

San Francisco Sex Information is an organization with a website that provides free, confidential, medically accurate, nonjudgmental information about sex. https://www.sfsi.org/

Queer Sex Ed is an organization with a website that is a queer-positive, sex-positive platform for open, honest, and direct communication about sex and relationships. https://www.queersexed.org/

Scarleteen provides inclusive, comprehensive, supportive sexuality and relationship information for teenagers and emerging adults. http://www.scarleteen.com/

Video

Robert Waldinger TED Talk: What Makes a Good Life: Lessons from the Longest Study on Happiness: https://www.ted.com/talks/robert_waldinger_what_makes_a_good_life_lessons_from_the_longest_study_on_happiness?

Peggy Orenstein TED Talk: What Young Women Believe About Their Own Sexual Pleasure: https://www.ted.com/talks/peggy_orenstein_what_young_women_believe_about_their_own_sexual_pleasure

Articles

"Good Genes are Nice, but Joy is Better" by Liz Mineo, *The Harvard Gazette*, April 11, 2017

"Six Ways Parents and Schools Can Teach Teens About Love" by Phyllis L. Fagell, *Sacramento Bee*, December 23, 2016

Books

S.E.X.: The All-You-Need-To-Know Guide to Get You Through Your Teens and Twenties by Heather Corinna

STRAIGHT ANSWERS TO TEEN QUESTIONS

I've only ever hooked up with people...
How do I ask someone out?

There are a few things you can think about to try to set yourself up for success. Pay attention to the person you are interested in and notice what they like to do. Approach them at an appropriate time and in an appropriate place—for instance, not during finals or when they are rushing somewhere, but when there's some time and a certain level of privacy. Express your interest in a way that allows for yes or no. Be prepared for either. Have something in mind that you can do together. Use language that communicates your interest, like "Wanna hang at the mall with me?" If you are more comfortable easing into things, you can ask them to hang out with you and your friends. Just remember, if you want to establish an authentic connection, ask the person yourself. This is more meaningful than friend-sourcing.

Asking someone is challenging because most of us worry about awkward moments or being rejected. Be courageous and sincere with a little vulnerability. Pace yourself. Trust and the ability to open up to someone else takes time and must be earned by spending meaningful time together. If they say no, maintain your composure, allowing both of you to keep your dignity. If you are the person being asked out, empathize with the fact that the other person is making themselves vulnerable. If you decline, be honest and respectful. Treat people how you would like to be treated while staying true to yourself.

Is it possible to have sex for the first
time and not have it hurt?

Yes, but it depends on the individual as well as how they are feeling and thinking about their first time. It is important for people to pace themselves when exploring their sexuality, especially when it comes to first-time experiences. Understand that just because you may have done something with one person, that doesn't mean that it will be the same kind of experience with someone else. Consider the context, the person, your state of being and theirs; these are all factors of a sexual experience. These are variables that can make each sexual experience different, even if you've had previous experiences.

People have different definitions of sex. For two girls, sex for the first time may be the first time they experience oral together or the first time they orgasm with each other. For two boys it may involve just being with someone they feel complete with relative to their sexual orientation, or it may be anal intercourse. For an opposite cisgender (people whose gender identity aligns with the sex they were assigned at birth) couple, it may be a more traditional notion of losing virginity through vaginal-penile intercourse. A lot of anyone's experience with sex has to do with how they *feel* about the situation. For an experience to be pleasurable and not painful, it's important to pay attention to how safe someone feels, and how sure they are that they want to do it. If they are ready for the experience and they are able to relax and not worry about getting pregnant, contracting an STD, or being slut-shamed, it's going to be better. It's important to communicate about how to lower the risk and what your limits and boundaries are. Then you can introduce discussion about using foreplay and lubricant to massage and relax muscles, making penetration easier and more pleasurable.

Before having sex, both people should know what feels good to themselves and each other, as well as how to practice consent. Someone with a vulva should know where her clitoris is, and both partners should be invested in each other's pleasure as well as safety. If two people are communicative, participating for the right reasons, able to ask for and give enthusiastic consent, and mature enough to support each other's pleasure and use things like lube and condoms, the probability of a first-time experience without pain is higher. It's also true that even while paying attention to all of this, there may be some discomfort. As long as the experience is safe, consensual, and desired, and the discomfort is minimal, it probably won't outweigh the positive aspects of the experience.

It's not like someone I'd have a relationship with now will be the person I marry. Why would I even want to have a committed relationship? What would I get out of it besides a sad breakup?

Real-time joy. Experiencing authentic connection and exploring your sexuality with someone in a healthy relationship can be a positive, fun, and enriching experience. Even though you may not marry that other person, your experience will help you learn about yourself and who you are in relationships. Healthy relationships provide you with the opportunity to practice care and communication, as well as how to maintain a sense of individuality while creating a bond with someone else. Eventually, you may want to choose a life partner. The more you understand about yourself and what it takes to be in a healthy relationship, the greater success you are likely to have in your relationships. Healthy, committed relationships can feel safer than random hookups because you and your partner can build trust and feel the rewards of being cared for and respected. Exploring sexuality with someone you care for can lead to a deeper understanding of what feels good for you and for another person, which can lead to better sexual experiences. Expressing your feelings for someone sexually adds a new dimension to the pleasures of physical sexual experiences. These kinds of skills take practice, and depending on how your earlier relationships end, you may keep mean-ingful friendships. Getting through a breakup can build resilience and con-tribute to understanding the importance of dignity. Knowing what doesn't work for you in a relationship can be as valuable as knowing what does.

How do I know what someone likes sexually?

The only way to know is to ask and pay attention to the answer. Body language and pleasurable sounds provide a good indication but can be misinterpreted. Everyone experiences pleasure in different ways, which depends on their individual body, their desire, and the context of the situation. Sure, there are some common erogenous zones (areas on the body that are sexually sensitive and responsive to stimulation), but even those can vary from person to person and situation to situation. Pace yourselves, be engaged, pay attention, and explore while practicing con-sent. You can ask, "How does this feel?" or "Are you comfortable showing me what you like?" or "Are you up for trying this?" or "Is this OK, does it feel good?" Showing you care about someone's experience and being respectful while you do it is being a generous lover—and it's sexy too. It can be a total turn-on to discover what feels good for both of you together. If you figure it out, your sexual activity is going to feel how it's supposed to—good!

How do I make someone orgasm?

First, people have orgasms themselves. You can support that process, but people don't "give" other people orgasms. The person you're with has to allow it to happen for them. You can help someone get there, but it ultimately comes from within. All orgasms are a release of sexual tension, and how that feels depends on the situation. Most people need desire (wanting), a positive context (feeling good and comfortable with the situation and setting), and sustained, rhythmic stimulation of their most sexually sensitive spot in that moment for pleasure (for some people that's their clitoris, and for some it's the head of the penis, or it could be a different erogenous zone). Some people orgasm without any of that, and sometimes orgasms happen without intention. Sometimes they can happen while you are dreaming.

To support someone else in allowing an orgasm to happen, communication is important. Your partner's desire to engage in the sexual activity with you is important, as is their comfort with the situation. Concerns can get in the way of someone's orgasm; for instance, worrying about readiness, getting pregnant, an STD, or a parent walking in on you. Talk any concerns through and take action to resolve them. Finally, talk about how the rhythm and sustained stimulation (of their erogenous zone) feels best. That stimulation can be with hands, mouths, pelvises rubbing together, or genitals. Sometimes orgasms come easily and quickly, and sometimes they take time, patience, and practice. Try not to have expectations and put pressure on yourselves. That can get in the way of pleasure.

Notice that I haven't mentioned intercourse. People don't need to have intercourse to orgasm. In fact, how you see orgasm represented most of the time in the media (two people having simultaneous orgasms after a very brief period of intercourse) is not realistic, and not all people orgasm with intercourse. Only 33 percent of adult people with vaginas reliably orgasm with intercourse.[23] Paying attention to what feels good for your partner (not just physically) and communication are key.

At this age is it OK to not want or crave sex?

Absolutely. Everyone has an individual sense of readiness when it comes to exploring sexuality. Sex is actually not a "drive" like many people think, but rather an *incentive motivation system*. Biologically, instead of feeling pushed by an uncomfortable internal experience like hunger, which drives you to eat, incentive motivation systems are about being pulled by an attractive external stimulus. It's a curiosity. How sensitive and attracted we are to external stimuli depends on our brain. Your brain is your biggest sex organ. Your brain is learning what's sexually relevant, which is what leads to a genital response like an erection or a wet vulva. That's called *arousal*. Arousal within sexual context is sexual desire. The part of your brain that governs your desire may not be fully developed, or it may not be sensitive to sexual stimuli at this time. Or there may be other things that are putting the brakes on your curiosity. What is most important for you to understand is that it's completely normal to not want or crave sex at this age, and for some folks, ever. There are people who don't experience sexual desire, or who just feel romantic desire, and identify as asexual. If you are concerned about how you're feeling, you may want to discuss this with someone you trust.

What does a healthy sexual relationship look like?

A healthy relationship is supportive, kind, balanced, and respectful. The people in it enjoy their time together, support each other's personal growth, and are able to work through their challenges and adversity in constructive ways. The following is a list of qualities and behaviors characteristic of healthy and unhealthy relationships.

In a healthy relationship, both people:

- Treat each other with respect.
- Maintain individuality.
- Have their own friends who they spend time with, both with and without their partner.

- Are able to deal with and resolve conflicts productively.

- Are supportive of each other.

- Can trust each other.

- Are interested in each other's lives.

- Feel safe and comfortable.

- Maintain a balance of power.

- Communicate clearly with open honesty.

- Feel heard when they express feelings.

- Celebrate each other's accomplishments.

- Maintain an appropriate level of privacy.

- Are able to say no and respect each other's boundaries.

- Do not abuse technology or social media to constantly check on each other.

- Do not work through issues in the relationship through technology, but do so in person.

- Are sexually intimate by choice and consistently respect the concept of consent.

- Are honest about their sexual history.

- Make healthy decisions about substance use.

In an unhealthy relationship, one or both people:

- Are controlling and manipulative of each other.

- Say hurtful things even if they say they're joking or just teasing, and call their partners "too sensitive" if they express not liking it.

- Cover or make excuses for their partner's negative behavior.

- Curse at, name call, or place blame on the other person if something goes wrong.

- Expect their partner to ask permission to go places and do things.

- Discourage their partner's independence and private time with friends and family.
- Criticize their partner's friends or family.
- Ignore their partner when they are speaking.
- Are overly possessive or jealous about ordinary behavior and relationships.
- Control their partner's money or other belongings.
- Continue to pressure their partner after they've said no.
- Lie to their partner.
- Are violent in any way (pushing, grabbing, hitting, punching) or are verbally abusive (yelling, screaming, mocking, criticizing, belittling).
- Dictate what their partner wears.
- Are nervous or scared around their partner.
- Cringe or move away from their partner when they are angry.
- Express their anger by name-calling or using put-downs.
- Blame their own or their partner's negative behavior on alcohol or drugs.

This list, which is adapted from the very helpful, authoritative online resource *Go Ask Alice!* (https://goaskalice.columbia.edu), identifies qualities in isolation from each other, and characterizes them as healthy or unhealthy. Some relationships will have varying degrees of different characteristics from both lists. Of course, some qualities are deal breakers, like abusive, controlling, and violent behavior. Some qualities on the negative list can be worked on, like encouraging more independence or being direct and honest when asking for what one needs. What's important is that the relationship has more qualities from the healthy list, and that any negative behaviors are addressed and changes are made for the better. If this isn't the case and negative behaviors recur, you should reconsider the relationship.

How do I tell my partner what I want from them sexually, without offending them or sounding aggressive?

This response assumes you are both practicing consent with your sexual exploration, and that whenever you introduce another level of intimacy, you ask each other if you're OK with what's happening or about to happen.

Effective communication is a cornerstone of every healthy relationship. Context is important too. That means you have to consider where, when, and how you talk about a sensitive topic in addition to what you're actually asking. Try approaching the conversation when you're not actually participating in sexual activity. Make sure you have privacy, a safe setting, and enough time to talk the issue through.

If you're hooking up with someone and not in a committed relationship, your sexual activity should be consensual and legal, and your approach ethical. If this is the case, initiating a dialogue about sexual preferences and desires is completely appropriate.

In either type of situation, you can check in and ask, "Are you comfortable with everything we've done so far?" If you get positive feedback, you can ask, "How would you feel about trying some new stuff?" If there's some hesitation or it doesn't seem like everything you've been doing so far is 100 percent OK, continue to discuss it, but do not try to talk your partner into anything. You can ask follow-up questions like, "What are the things that feel good to you?" "What's the stuff that doesn't feel right?" "Has there ever been a time when you felt pressured or obligated?" "Is there anything I can do to be more supportive or communicative?"

In moments of vulnerability, we all appreciate sincere reassurance. You can share what you appreciate about your relationship and express that you care about your partner's experience and want your sexual activity to reflect that. It's important to pay attention to both your impact and your intentions. If you and your partner feel good about what's taken place between you so far, you can introduce what you want sexually. You can also ask if there is anything they'd like to try. Be sure to listen carefully to what your partner is saying, and if there are things your partner isn't into, adjust your behavior accordingly and be willing to accept a no if your partner isn't ready for something you'd like to try.

If you treat each other with respect, your ask shouldn't come across as offensive or aggressive. And the way someone receives an ask (which should allow for yes or no or additional conversation) is very individual. This is one of the reasons knowing and trusting your partner can lead to better sex. It creates a foundation of trust, safety, and acceptance that allows for curiosity and exploration. Introduce the idea, see how it goes, then add a little more. Sex is a dialogue. Some people need time to think through and process it as it's happening, some people know exactly what they want, when, and how, and there are many variations in between. So get your communication skills on and start talking. If you come from a place of care and treat your partner with respect, the dialogue will increase the trust between you.

What should you do if you feel like you're in a dependent relationship?

Talk your situation through with a friend or trusted adult. Ask if they've observed some dependence in your relationship dynamic. It may be time to have a direct, open, and honest conversation with your partner about how you're feeling and what you believe is motivating your dependence. It will be important to talk through your intentions for supporting the relationship by exercising more independence. Then make a point of spending more time with friends and family, and engaging in the activities you care about. Encourage your partner to do the same. If your partner objects or tries to guilt-trip you about taking time apart, you should consider this as a red flag. Be gentle and considerate, but insist on having more space and independence.

Think about the reasons you are in the relationship. What attracted you to your partner in the first place? What keeps you together? Were you able to appreciate and love yourself without a romantic partner? Do you bring out the best in each other? How does your partner respond to your dependence? Do they see and experience the relationship in the same way? As you engage in self-reflection, find a trusted adult to talk it over with you and figure out if the relationship is healthy and whether it should continue.

When do I know when to say "I love you"?

Love is a physiological and neurological process. It is also highly subjective. It is a word that's used to describe intense feelings that are generated by that process. Leo Tolstoy said, "If it is true that there are as many minds as there are heads, then there are as many kinds of love as there are hearts." Love, what it means to us, and how we express it, is in many ways informed by our own experience of it. Do you have positive associations with the word love? Is it a word easily used to express feeling in your family or among friends? Or is it rarely used and saved for moments of more serious, intimate expression?

Saying you love something like "I love ice cream" expresses how intense your enthusiasm for eating it is. Someone's love for ice cream is relatively inconsequential. When someone says "I love you" to another person, they are professing feelings about a relationship that may be of consequence, depending on the nature of the connection. This is when the other person's experience with the word in their own lives may inform how they hear what's being expressed and what sort of interpretation or meaning they assign it. It could be serious or lighthearted. It could be a huge deal in the case of a long-term relationship that is built on many shared experiences, trust, loyalty, deep care, emotional closeness, support, and time, and said by someone who takes the word seriously and describes a mature connection. Or it could be more friendly and describe intense but possibly ephemeral feelings of passion, or be mistaken for infatuation by someone who's been surrounded by people who use it casually. To really know, you'd have to know something about the person saying it. It also requires communication to understand what the other person means when they use the word.

Does having sex with someone create some type of bond with that person?

Yes. In fact, if someone says, "I can have sex without feelings," their statement is scientifically incorrect. Sex is an expression of feelings, sometimes physical, sometimes emotional, sometimes a combination of both. Sex is a bonding behavior, and there are hormones that are released while it's happening that encourage connection. During adolescence, there are certain hormones and regions of the brain that are involved in emotions, sexual attraction, excitement, attachment, and desire, and while scientists still don't know exactly how these areas and hormones interact and develop, we are learning more about them all the time. In fact, there can be overlap between sexual desire and emotional love. Both activate a section of the same part of the brain, so transitions from lust to love and vice versa can happen. This reality is the reason it's important for two people to be clear about what the sexual activity they participate in means to them. If they have different conceptions of this, one person is likely to get hurt. Communication is key for responsible and ethical sexual behavior.

What's the difference between sexual and romantic attraction?

There are some subtle distinctions between the two because sexual and romantic attraction are often intertwined. Sexual attraction is a desire for sexual, physical intimacy. Romantic attraction tends to focus on building emotional intimacy, not just having sex, although it usually includes sexual attraction. It is also possible for romantic attraction to grow out of sexual attraction or to be deepened by it. Based on my research, this varies from person to person. To know what you and your partner are feeling requires some self-awareness, self-reflection, and lots of communication.

I think I might be close to starting a relationship; how do I make sure that I don't screw it up so I can find love?

Remember that relationship skills and love are two different things that are often intertwined, so it's important to be mindful of both. To create a loving relationship, the connection between two people should be genuine. This means that both people need to be their true selves and honest about their feelings. Trying too hard and forcing feelings can backfire. It's important to cultivate authentic connection through meaningful experiences together.

Love involves care and trust, which is built over time. Part of what makes it special is that it can't be forced, and falling in love is a unique and personal process. Prioritize honest communication, patience, respect, empathy, and fun. Pace yourself, be yourself, and stay open to the experience, however it unfolds. If it doesn't happen, call on your resilience and embrace the support and love of your family and friends while you process the disappointment. If it does...jump for joy and celebrate with gratitude.

What is sex-positive sex?

Let's say two people are sexually active within the context of a consensual and ethical relationship, and that their culture values all wanted sexual relationships. Both people have received informative, meaningful education about safe sexuality practices and all of the joys and bummers that are a part of sexual experiences. They've been encouraged to develop and embrace a sense of personal desire, readiness, and sexual agency, and have had the opportunity to develop a positive self-awareness and body image that affirms their capacity for pleasure.

The sex-positive sex itself is intense and sweet, all at once. When it's tender, it's not a Hallmark card, but a cookie fresh out of the oven—yummy, delectable, and melt-in-your-mouth. When it's fiery, it's because the energy and strong unity of shared desire feel so urgent and wanted that both partners want the other, like hungry people who've just been served a delicious meal.

By the time either person gets near the other's genitals, they are receptive and aroused. Both partners are equally nervous and fearless. Words are used to express affection and specify desires and are often integrated in the unique sexual language of pleasurable sounds and laughter. Whose hands are whose hands, whose limbs are whose limbs, is tough to tell if someone was watching. If one sexual activity lasts only a few minutes, no one cares, because they just slide into another, craving all of it; this dance continues with fluidity from one rhythm into another with feelings only of floating, not failure. If and when something hurts or is uncomfortable, voicing that is easy because both partners trust each other to seek contact that not only doesn't hurt, but also feels super good.

There is no embarrassment or shame about normal body functions and fluids. After all, sex is about embracing another's full self and humanity—physical as well as spiritual. Someone, at some point, may do something that is completely instinctive and really sexy. Someone will laugh out loud. No one will be stressed over how long it'll go on, because minutes feel like hours and vice versa.

Everyone gets off, whether through orgasm, having a hand in someone else's pleasure, being that close to someone you adore or are attached to, or whatever unique expression of diverse sexuality turns each person on. Neither partner has to ask the other if they got off or not—it has been clearly demonstrated, and if either partner does not feel satisfied, they say so because they know their partner wants to give and receive pleasure mutually.

The sex doesn't just feel OK, nor is it good because it was painless. This sex feels freaking awesome. Sometimes it's thrilling like riding a roller coaster and at other times comforting and fulfilling like cruising on the couch after a long day.

Afterward, beyond the affirming love and care, both partners are reduced to smiles and vague expressions of satisfaction, gratitude, and wonder. Great sex isn't just about deep emotional intimacy; it is also about desire and the full expression of that desire within the context of safety, equality, and joy.

Note: This answer is adapted from Heather Corinna's essay, "An Immodest Proposal"; check out her sex-positive resource book for teenagers (it's the textbook for my class), *S.E.X.: The All-You-Need-To-Know Sexuality Guide to Get You Through Your Teens and Twenties*.

CHAPTER SIX

Bystander Intervention

What We Can All Do to Prevent Sexual Harassment and Assault

> Harrison, Dominic, and Jack are in the locker room after baseball practice. Jack is talking about the new junior transfer, Jules, who is in his social studies class. He says, "Damn, dude, she's hella fine." Harrison is quiet and looks straight ahead. Dominic responds, "Yeah, she's a dime. Stacked too. You gotta tap that. I dare you." Harrison is uncomfortable and anxious as he thinks about his resolve to stand up to sexist talk, so he doesn't say anything. Jack comes back with, "This weekend, I'll get Laney to invite her to Kyle's." Dominic says, "For sure, bro, I'm your wingman. Get her wasted."

Harrison knows that trying to get someone drunk for a hookup is non-consensual and predatory. He wants to say something to his friends about what they're saying but fears judgment, ridicule, and possibly rejection. Dominic and Jack start talking about other things, and it seems Harrison has lost his opportunity to speak up. Relieved to find an excuse for not questioning his friends' behavior, Harrison still feels guilty for not stepping up and telling his friends that calculating to have a nonconsensual hookup is wrong. Jules cannot give consent while incapacitated, so any sexual activity within that context could be assault.

A growing body of research shows that bystander intervention is an important element in preventing sexual assault.

A growing body of research shows that bystander intervention (when anyone who isn't a perpetrator or victim in any given situation intervenes to prevent or interrupt sexual harassment or sexual assault) is an important element in preventing sexual assault. Bystanders are in a position to discourage, prevent, or interrupt an assault before it happens. Bystander intervention doesn't have to jeopardize the safety of the bystander. A complement to other sexual assault prevention approaches, bystander intervention helps foster and support culture that is intolerant to abusive behavior and encourages leadership by speaking up in opposition to negative and inappropriate behavior.

The majority of the teenagers I teach want to be allies and bring an end to sexual harassment and assault. They also share that this can be difficult, as Harrison found when he considered confronting his friends in the locker room. Teens are developmentally and neurologically programmed to seek the acceptance of their peers. It is important to acknowledge that the obstacles they feel get in the way of their ability to intervene in challenging situations. Standing up to and for someone requires a certain level of confidence. Teenagers need the proper tools and practice to do this. Teenagers are also steeped in a culture that encourages entitlement, objectification, misogyny, and sexual conquest, and normalizes coercive behavior. All these factors may complicate their resolve to act.

We can give our children the tools they need to help themselves and their friends to be safe and look out for one another.

Teenagers need guidance on what to say as a bystander and how and when to say it. In my classes, students embrace the opportunity to share with each other ideas for how to maintain their social standing and stick up for others when people are engaged in risky, inappropriate, or aggressive behavior. As adults, we can give our children the tools they need to help themselves and their friends be safe and look out for each other.

Intervention can range from telling a friend that their sexist language is not OK, to putting an arm around someone who is being targeted and getting them back to their friends, to calling the police if you are witness to a violent assault taking place.

Once adolescents understand the importance of consent, most are able to identify potentially compromising situations. When I ask students if they have been witness to or experienced harassment or nonconsensual situations, the majority of them admit that they have, and are able to deepen their understanding of the significance of harassment and assault through in-depth discussions. It's important to discuss gender dynamics, cultural norms surrounding sexuality, and how teen culture normalizes coercive behavior in many aspects of adolescent life.

Celia is at a party where all of her friends are drinking and smoking weed. Not interested in getting wasted, she is nursing her cup of beer and hanging out with her friend Brianna in the corner of the room. Their other friends are playing drinking games at the kitchen table. Every now and then, Drake comes over with a bottle of hard alcohol and encourages shots. One friend wants to capture the scene on social media and says, "C'mon, c'mon, everyone get in, everyone get in." They notice Celia and Brianna and say, "Hey! C'mon, get in, but you have to take a shot." Celia says, "Nah, we're good, you go for it." Not listening, Drake hands them shots. Celia and Brianna reluctantly take the shots and rally their best photo poses. After the picture is taken, several people throw back their drinks and chant, "Shot! Shot!" to encourage Celia and Brianna to drink theirs too.

When I discuss the above scenario in my classes, students typically don't acknowledge it as a coercive situation at first. The intention, they insist, is to have fun, include all friends in that fun, and document the experience through an image posted on social media. Most of my students insist that Drake's intentions are good—and they're right, given the cultural normalization of drinking among young people today. The problem is the impact.

We need to remind teenagers that whatever the intention, the impact of their behavior may be negative and detrimental. Young people feeling they can't say no because they don't want to be considered uncool or a bummer, or seen as rejecting their friend's efforts to include them, may get in the way of confidently saying "no thanks." And their friends glossing over the importance of consent when it comes to bodies and behavior, whether it be to drink, go do "stupid" stuff, or hook up with someone, is real. If that coercive peer pressure isn't checked, it can cross over into different aspects of the teen social dynamic as well.

Every situation is different and there is no single right way to intervene.

Every situation is different and there is no single right way to intervene. As adults, we have to remember that some kids don't feel like they're just saying no to the drug or the drink. They often feel as if they are rejecting the friend who is offering it—or even the friendship itself. Since most teens are very concerned about their relationships and how their actions may impact their social standing in their friend group or community, it's important to go through hypothetical scenarios and brainstorm possible strategies that will mitigate these social dynamics.

What would bystander intervention look like in the scenario above? In the moment, Brianna could reinforce Celia's no by interrupting the dynamic and offering to take the picture and directing people to pose without Celia, or say, "Nah, really, we're good" or "Actually, I gotta pee," and taking Celia by the arm to go find the bathroom. Another friend might notice the discomfort and intervene by telling the others, "They're good, leave 'em alone." Or she could distract the others by proposing another game or interrupting the dynamic by saying, "Hey, come check this out over here," providing at least a temporary out for Brianna and Celia.

When teenagers witness a potential assault, similar strategies for interrupting the dynamic can be effective. Most of the time, a friend saying something brief and to the point can be extremely effective, changing the mood and distracting the potential assailant.

> Jenny and Maya pregame with friends before going to a senior party. They check in with each other about whom they're going to see and what they're going to do. Maya is interested in Troy from math class and plans to meet him there. She and Jenny agree that it will be a chill night and that they won't let each other get too wasted. Maya

tells Jenny that she wants to just hang out with Troy—that she isn't down to hook up yet.

At the party, Maya and Jenny head down to the basement, where their friends have been hanging out. There is a keg and boxed wine. Liam encourages Jenny and Maya to get under the wine spout. Liam turns on the spout as Maya chugs. Soon all of the kids start cheering, "Go, go, go! Drink, drink, drink!" It's not until Maya waves an arm that Jenny asks him to turn it off. Maya comes up flushed and tipsy but pleased by all the cheering.

Jenny and Maya grab plastic cups full of beer and blend into the crowd. They spot Troy on the other side of the room. Jenny finds other friends so Maya and Troy can hang out. Soon Maya and Troy are dancing in the living room. Troy takes Maya's hand and pulls her toward the stairs; she stumbles a little as they pass Daniella. They also pass James, who is on his way down. After a while, Jenny realizes that she doesn't see Maya and Troy anymore. She figures they are somewhere close, but it's hard to tell because it's so crowded.

It's quieter upstairs, but Troy and Maya can still feel the beat of the music coming through the floor. Troy pulls Maya into a bedroom and kisses her against the door. Hands explore bodies as they make out. Troy pauses and looks at Maya while he starts to unbutton her shirt. She smiles, but sways. Troy takes her to the bed, where she flops down. Troy is heavy on top of Maya, who is struggling to say "wait" through her alcohol haze and Troy's mouth all over hers.

A short time later, Jenny heads upstairs with her friend Scott to look for Maya. They knock on doors and find the couple in one of the bedrooms. Jenny tells Maya, "C'mon, we gotta go. My curfew's up and you're with me." Troy tries to protest, but Scott says, "Hey, man, some of your buddies are looking for you downstairs. It seemed important." Jenny grabs Maya and they leave.

Who are the bystanders in this situation and what could they have done to help Maya? Daniella may have noticed Maya stumbling, which likely meant she was drunk and therefore couldn't consent. When Daniella saw Maya being led upstairs by Troy, she could have stopped the two of them on some pretext, saying, for example, "Hey, Maya, I think Jenny's looking for you" or "I have that tampon you were asking for earlier." She could have then edged Maya away from Troy.

James, who Maya and Troy passed on his way down the stairs, could have gone to find one of Maya's friends. Or he could have said, "Hey, you two have to come see something—follow me," and led them downstairs. He could even be direct, telling Troy, "Hey, man, looks like you could get yourself into some trouble. Let's go back downstairs" or "All the rooms are taken upstairs and there's a line for the bathroom."

In this scenario, Jenny proves to be someone who sticks with her friends. She knew Maya was drunk from the wine-box chug and that she only wanted to get to know Troy, not hook up with him. She noticed Maya was gone, recruited her friend Scott as backup, and went looking for her. Notice that she didn't berate Troy or cause an argument. Instead, she and Scott defused the situation with some harmless white lies (Jenny's curfew was not up, and Troy's friends weren't looking for him) and got Maya out of there. What made for an effective intervention in this case is that Jenny and Maya were together and watching out for each other.

If an assault situation is in an advanced stage, or involves a large number of people, bystanders may need to turn to others for help.

If an assault situation is in an advanced stage, or involves a large number of people, bystanders may need to turn to others for help.

> At a house party with a bunch of friends, Danny and Claire are in the hallway upstairs waiting for the bathroom when they see a young woman who appears to be passed out on a bed. Danny has a class with the girl but isn't sure who her friends are. They see a couple of guys enter the room and close the door. Danny whispers to Claire, "That's sketch." They decide to wait and see what's up. At least five minutes pass and everyone's still in the room. Then another guy goes into the room and closes the door.

In this case, Danny and Claire don't know the girl who is clearly in jeopardy. Even though it's intimidating and they don't know the people involved, it's important for Danny and Claire to respond in some way—and *quickly*. Because there are so many people involved in this case, Danny and Claire should probably track down another friend or two to help them interrupt the assault.

Invoking fictional backup is a good idea too. The duo might, for example, knock forcefully on the door, and say, "Hey, is [name] in there? Someone's called the cops—we gotta go. Not leaving without her." If the door is locked, they should be persistent. Once the door opens, bystanders should go to the girl and assist her out of the room. If you can, make a mental note of who is in the room. Then find the girl's friends and get her to safety. If she is conscious and has experienced trauma, ask her what she needs and provide options for support. (See Appendix B, "Assaulted: What You and Your Child Need to Know if They Are Assaulted," in the back of this book to find out what the options are.)

Don't forget that as parents, you may be bystanders too. It's important to know that alcohol being served to minors, whether we know about it or not, and any subsequent infractions that take place on our property, including assault, make us subject to state "social host" liability laws and vulnerable to lawsuits, fines, and jail time. Not only do we need to consider the legal consequences of underage substance use but also the impact it has on teen brain development, how it relates to one's capacity to provide affirmative consent, and the danger posed by drinking and driving. Even if you've never seen your teen drink alcohol, you should assume that he or she has at least been exposed to it. It's important to talk about alcohol-related issues with teens early and often, including accountability, values, and how to handle compromising situations.

> **Even if you've never seen your teen drink alcohol, you should assume that he or she has at the least been exposed to it.**

Sometimes sexual harassment and assault happens on school grounds. Many students talk about the inappropriate behavior they witness but don't know how to step in. Many say they don't want the negative attention to shift to them, fear being labeled a snitch, or don't believe speaking up will make a difference because the issue is so pervasive or because their school doesn't do anything about it. As parents, we can provide guidance; we can also talk to school administrators about addressing sexual harassment and assault.

Lizzy and Olivia have just changed into their uniforms for a soccer game and are in a hurry to meet the travel bus. They enter the back stairwell on the third floor of the school building and see David and Melanie on the second-floor landing, engaged in a heated argument. The couple is notorious for their volatile, dramatic relationship. Now, Melanie sounds defensive. "I swear, he was just asking me about the test on Thursday. He was not hitting on me!" David yells back, "Yeah, right, I'm sure you were into it. I saw you! Slut!" Melanie fires back, "Slut? What about you and Gina the other night?" David replies, "Don't try to turn this around. We're talking about you."

David shoves Melanie against the wall. Lizzy and Olivia quickly walk by with their eyes on the floor. Lizzy can't help but glance at David while they pass. David glares and says, "What are you looking at? Mind your own business, bitch." Olivia and Lizzy pick up their pace, get to the first floor, and exit the stairwell.

What should Olivia and Lizzy do in this situation? They may be tempted to remain silent, since they're rushing to get on the bus. Besides, neither of them are friends with David or Gina. Also, David has addressed them in a threatening way, so Lizzie and Olivia likely fear retaliation if they intervene.

Still, doing nothing risks allowing a dangerous situation to persist, while speaking up could make a big difference. Before they get on the bus, Lizzie and Olivia could, for example, tell an adult that there is an argument going on in the stairwell. Or the girls could seek Gina out later and acknowledge what they saw and suggest an adult who can help. They could go to a trusted adult to discuss the dating violence between David and Gina. If there were other people there, too, Lizzie and Olivia could have confronted David, saying something like "Hey, don't shove her," and asked Gina if she wanted to go with them. (For teen readers: Don't intervene in a situation if there is any risk of violence; if this is the case, you should always seek help from an adult. It's also important to practice self-care after the incident by talking to someone you trust to help you process any fear or distress triggered by the situation.)

A large proportion of harassment and assault incidents target people in the LGBTQQ+ community.

> Ty, a sophomore, is transgender. He recently tried out for the school play and landed one of the most sought-after roles. After the first rehearsal, Ty is on his way to the faculty bathroom, which he has permission to use because he has experienced bullying in the boys bathroom. In the hallway, Cheri and Dawn are sitting on floor, leaning against the lockers, doing their homework, while other students are milling around before going home. Near the bathroom door, a couple of juniors, Amari and Devin, who had tried out for the role Ty got, step in front of him and push him back. Amari says, loud enough to make a few heads turn, "You think you're pretty special, huh?" Devin follows with, "You even get your own toilet." Ty doesn't say anything and attempts to enter the bathroom again. He wants to escape inside because there's a lock on the door. Amari says, "What *are* you, anyway?" and starts poking at Ty and then grabs his crotch. Devin says, "Let's find out." He shoves Ty into the bathroom. Devin and Amari go in, too, and lock the door.

Cheri and Dawn have a few options: they can try to engage other bystanders to help them try to get the boys out of the bathroom. One of the students should immediately find an adult, someone with authority like a teacher or administrator who can immediately and directly address the situation. In the meantime, other kids can knock on the door just to let Ty and Devin know that people have observed what's going on.

Similar bullying dynamics are also pervasive online.

Brad sends Jordan and some others in a group text a nude that he got from his friend, Jim. It's a Snap of Jim's ex, Natalie. She sent it to Jim when they were exclusive and intended it to be private. Brad is always looking for nudes; he collects them and sells them to others. Brad knew Jim had a bunch from Natalie, so he bugged him to screenshot a few and forward them. Jim finally sent him a couple. Brad loves scrolling through the nudes when chilling with his buddies. It's fun when they recognize girls they've hooked up with or know from middle school.

Jordan has always had a crush on Natalie. They follow each other on Instagram. He always likes her photos and she likes his. A couple of his friends have been telling him he should try to hook up with her. The next time Natalie posts a sunset on her Snapchat Story, Jordan comments on it:

> Yo thats dope

> yeah haha

Jordan then Snaps a picture to Natalie. It's a half profile.

> what's up?

Natalie Snaps a picture of her feet, the TV on in the background.

> haha nothing wbu

Jordan Snaps back an image of his hand grabbing his pants at the crotch.

> in the mood for something, do you send nudes?

Natalie doesn't open the Snap for a while, then she Snaps just a photo of the wall.

> nah

Jordan Snaps the nude he got from Brad.

> cmon I know u do

Natalie Snaps an annoyed face.

> what

Jordan Snaps his jawline with a half-smile.

> nvm u down to hu tho?

Natalie Snaps a weirded-out expression

> hah idk

Jordan Snaps a dick pic.

> haha I know you want it

This is sexual harassment in cyberspace. My students tell me that there is a lot of it taking place on social media and over text. Since some people feel a sense of anonymity because there isn't anyone in their physical presence to see or hold them accountable for their behavior, they feel they have free reign to do things in the virtual world that they wouldn't in person.

Bystanders can make a positive difference in cyberharassment situations too. There is a group text that goes out with the nude. In addition, many people know that Brad collects nudes, which means he is gathering them from others. Taking, saving, sharing, and forwarding naked pictures is a federal crime. It's considered trafficking in child pornography when the subjects of the photo are younger than eighteen years old. Anyone who knows Brad or is on any of his text chains could let him know or reinforce this; someone should warn Jim as well. Brad's friends could also refuse to send, share, or give his efforts any attention. They could say, for example, "You know you can get in a lot of trouble for that" or "Guys, chill with sending her stuff in the chat. It's none of our business if she didn't send it to us."

Natalie could ask an adult she trusts to hold Brad and Jim accountable for their actions and discourage further harassment through counseling and consequences. She could also talk to her friends about what's going on or to Jim about having violated her trust by forwarding the photo. Their support and intervention would also go a long way in preventing the same thing from happening to other girls.

PARENT–TEEN CONVERSATION STARTERS

As discussed earlier, teenagers are concrete thinkers, so the best way to get them thinking and problem-solving about bystander intervention is to watch a video or discuss hypothetical scenarios. Even better, if you hear about a real incident, sit down and discuss it with your teen. It is imperative to honor the social realities your teen faces and to directly address their concerns about social consequences. Don't forget to discuss values and to call upon and model empathy. Here are some basic guidelines to share with your teen for safely intervening in a potentially dangerous situation:

- Intervene early, before a problem becomes a crisis.
- Make safe choices about your level of intervention. Know your limits as a helper and act accordingly.
- Communicate clearly and be honest and direct. Try to be assertive, not inflammatory, and keep your voice calm and matter-of-fact.
- Consider distracting the potential victim and/or perpetrator. If you can, find an excuse to separate them to ensure the potential victim's safety.
- Consider recruiting friends and other bystanders.
- Consider reaching out to an authority figure. If you perceive the situation to be violent, this may include campus security or the police.
- Many fraternities and sororities now have members designated to watch out for potential sexual assault situations. If a situation seems potentially dangerous, find out who the member is and tell them what is going on.

Some questions to consider include:

1. What's the problem?
2. What are the risks?
3. Who is present and involved in the dynamic? Who is present or on the periphery who may not be integral to the dynamic?
4. Where do you see yourself in the scenario?
5. How might you directly address the negative behavior, distract the potential perpetrator, or delegate the responsibility?
6. How would you get the victim to safety and help them access support?

Resources

Videos

Stop Sexual Assaults in Schools (educational videos on sexual harassment and assault): http://stopsexualassaultinschools.org/videos/

Jackson Katz: Violence Against Women—It's a Men's Issue: https://www.ted.com/talks/jackson_katz_violence_against_women_it_s_a_men_s_issue

Who Are You?: https://www.youtube.com/watch?v=iUj2OHLAG3w

Step Up American University: https://www.youtube.com/watch?v=491e8Oku0Jw

Stop Street Harassment: http://www.stopstreetharassment.org/

Ten Hours of Walking in New York City: https://www.youtube.com/watch?v=iQBjhZtLtRk

STRAIGHT ANSWERS TO TEEN QUESTIONS

What if the sketchy person is my friend?

There are a few things you can do in this situation.

1. Speak directly to your friend. Wait until you are alone to avoid publicly humiliating your friend. It is often easier to talk when engaged in an activity like playing video games or getting ready to go out. You could say, "Hey, remember how you were hitting on [name] pretty hard last time? You know that you can get in trouble for that, and that if someone's been partying and is the slightest bit wasted, they can't give consent." If your friend is in a relationship and substances aren't involved, you could say, "Hey, is everything all right? The way you and [name] have been getting along doesn't seem right. You know, it's not OK to [be so controlling]."

2. If what's happening is within a partying context, you can distract

your friend if you witness them being inappropriate or aggressive. You could say, "Hey, help me out with something. I promised someone I'd meet them downstairs with drinks" or "Hey, I hear they have a drinking game going on downstairs. Let's go check it out."

3. Choose to abstain from illegal substance use and encourage your friend to do the same. Many nonconsensual sexual situations happen within the context of partying with substances. Teen brains are more vulnerable to toxicity and substances can impair someone's ability to communicate and interpret social sexual cues.

4. You can find the friends of the person your friend is trying to hook up with and let them know that things seem off; then come up with a plan together.

5. If your friend's behavior is hurting someone else and they aren't listening to you, find an adult you can talk to with the intention of getting your friend help. The adult can help you strategize about a way to intervene; they may even be able to discreetly and confidentially intervene for you. It's also important to take care of yourself. Make sure you yourself have someone to talk to because this kind of situation can weigh heavily on you.

Isn't this just snitching?

Many of my students say they would feel like a snitch if they told an adult or person in a position of authority about a compromising situation. But intervening as a bystander in a harmful situation by reporting to an adult is different from snitching. Intervening in this way is intended to right a wrong. Snitching is telling on another person with the intention of getting that person in trouble. If you are a bystander intervening to prevent harm and make the problem go away, then you are part of a solution. In addition, people who perpetrate assault need help and an intervention to change their behavior, so telling someone who can help your friend is a supportive move in the long run and could prevent them from getting in even worse trouble down the line.

What if I step in but get hurt because of it?

There are many ways to step in without confronting someone. You'll want to make sure you assess the safety of the situation before you step in, create a distraction, or call someone else to help. If the situation seems dangerous, is escalating, or doesn't look as if it will stop on its own, consider calling someone like campus security or the police instead of intervening. If you follow the guidelines for bystander intervention included in this book, the risk of you getting hurt goes down exponentially. If you do get hurt, do your best to get away from the situation and call for help. Ask others to assist you while someone else calls for an adult in authority, campus security, or the police. These folks should also help you get any medical attention you may need. Once at a medical facility, you can also acquire resources for counseling if you experienced the situation as traumatic.

What if I want to help but I don't want anyone to know?

If you are in high school, check with your school counselor about reporting policies and if you can report what you know while maintaining confidentiality. You can also tell an adult who can share the information for you. If you are on a college campus, you can speak to the campus Title IX coordinator. You can make an anonymous phone call to the police and campus security. If you call and they ask for your name, you can state that you wish to remain anonymous. A lot of my students are concerned about violating the teen code that one should never snitch. If you are concerned about snitching, remember that your intentions are to help someone and do the right thing, so you are reporting information for that purpose, not telling on someone to get them in trouble. If you are concerned that you may get in trouble for your own behavior, such as underage drinking, many schools have amnesty policies. An amnesty policy should state that the school will not take disciplinary action against individuals reporting in good faith, including witnesses for nonviolent code-of-conduct offenses that are related to the assault, including the use of intoxicating substances at or around the time of the reported incident.

How do I help when I see someone I don't know being sexually harassed on the street?

It's important to evaluate the situation and the source of the harassment. If someone is getting unwanted gender-based or sexual attention on the street—for instance, catcalling, making comments or gestures, or honking while following in a car—you can be an ally. Since you don't know the person, it's important to remember that they may or may not want your help. You can move within the proximity of the person but make sure you're not too close. Sometimes someone else's presence is enough to change the dynamic. You can also stop what you're doing and let the person see you. Let them know you see what's happening, so they can ask for your help.

If you feel confident that you can stay safe, you can also use your body to stand in front of the harasser and act as a shield. You can calmly and confidently tell the harasser to stop. Always focus on de-escalating, not inflaming or antagonizing the harasser. You can also enlist others to help.

If the harasser is your friend or someone you know, you can say any of the following depending on what you're comfortable with: "Please stop," "It's street harassment. It's not a compliment," "Really, man? C'mon cut it out," "You're giving us a bad name," "I don't care if you think she's hot, it's not OK," "Do you know how many women and girls get harassed every day? It's not funny," "What if that was your mom or sister?"

How do I help in a situation where it looks like someone is going to be or is being assaulted?

There is no single right way to help in a potential assault situation, and I've outlined some options earlier in this chapter. To make safe choices about how you respond, think about your capacity and limits as a helper and act based on the dynamic you see happening. If you decide to speak up, clearly communicate that what you see happening is wrong. Be honest and direct. Be assertive, not inflammatory. You may also consider distracting the potential victim and/or perpetrator. Think about how you may separate them. If you feel intimidated, consider recruiting friends and other bystanders. If you think it's best to have some distance from the interaction, you may tell someone in charge who will take action. The priority is to get the potential victim to safety and away from the potential perpetrator. If you accomplish this, make sure that the person you have helped is safe and has access to people and resources that will support them. If you have your own feelings about what happened, make sure you talk to someone to process your own experience as well.

What if my friends judge or make fun of me? What if I lose all my friends?

Most of us fear judgment and rejection. It is healthy to want to belong and have people we care about and who care about us in our lives. Bystander intervention is a matter of values, and what you chose to do (or not do) will honor or betray those values. If you know in your heart that something is wrong, it's important for you to stand up for what you believe in. Friends should try to encourage and bring out the best in each other. You have to ask yourself, *Is doing the right thing worth risking being made fun of by my friends? And if my friends judge me for what I believe to be important, are they really my friends?* It's important to know, too, that the right thing isn't always the easy thing. In fact, sometimes it's the most difficult.

What if I know my friend is being pressured into a hookup? How do I help them?

If your friend is being coerced over Snapchat, other social media, or sexting, and you are there and witness it, be direct and honest. You can say, "That doesn't sound right. [Name] is pressuring you with persuasive language and trying to play on the fact that you like them. [Name] is also working your insecurities, and the fact that [they're hot, you like them, they're older, they're popular, etc.]."

If this is a pattern and your friend tells you about it, express your concern. To set the two of you up for the best possible conversation, pick a time to bring it up when you have some time and privacy. You could say, "I noticed [Name] is always talking you into hooking up. That's not consensual. Does it feel that way?" ("Notice" is a good word because it doesn't come across as judgmental.) Continue with more questions that focus on how your friend feels about the hooking up and use "I" statements to express what you've observed. You could suggest that your friend talk to a trusted adult, like the school counselor. If your friend is not receptive or responsive to your help, go to a trusted adult to discuss what to do. It is also important to find support for yourself since it can feel frustrating and out of your control when you know something isn't right and you're not able to help.

Why should I step in and take a risk for someone else's bad decisions?

Harassment, sexual assault, and rape are never punishment for bad decisions. Sexual harassment and sexual assault are used to take away someone's power. It is a form of bullying. No one asks to be bullied, harassed, or assaulted. Gender violence and sexism is still acceptable in many sectors of our culture, and many people still consider women and members of other marginalized groups as inferior and not deserving of equality. When we step up to speak up for others, we are part of a movement that says all people are deserving of safety, dignity, and respect.

Where I come from, maintaining my masculinity is about survival. It's all I have. If I question my friends and what they're doing, they could turn on me. How am I supposed to protect myself on the streets if I don't have anyone?

This concern is real for many young people. In communities where survival is literally determined by someone being perceived as strong and powerful, and strength and power are culturally defined by acts that may be detrimental to someone's well-being, doing right or being perceived as soft can leave people publicly vulnerable or at risk. But being "hard" can get in the way of caring, respectful, and communicative relationships, so start with yourself. Do your best to be open and talk to your partner. Ask them how they want to be treated and share what's important to you. Be straight with them about the challenges you face and the conflict you experience with stepping up against the misogynist and disrespectful treatment of others. Standing up for the equal treatment of others is brave. If you are someone with social power, make it cool to respect yourself and each other. Make honoring people's gender and sexuality something to brag about.

If your friends are being masculine or hard in negative ways, it's all about how you question them. You can explain that you're trying to keep them out of trouble, or away from someone's cousin, brother, or parent. Sometimes we think that intervening means getting all "after-school special" on them, but in fact it just means challenging their thinking in a way they can hear and shows you care as a friend. Looking out for your friends is the ultimate sign of respect, and in many cultures, it's the ultimate way to show masculinity. The problem is, if we look out for friends in ways that hurt them, like allowing negative behavior, they may end up in real trouble—if not now, in the future. Nobody wants to be seen as a punk, so make sure your friend knows you are looking out for them. That's what friendship is all about.

CHAPTER SEVEN

"How Can I Stay Safe?"

Making the Best Choices in Difficult Situations

My daughter, who is seventeen, was walking home from the bus stop last spring when a man drove past. He pulled a quick 180-degree turn and drove slowly behind her. Whenever she looked over her shoulder to see if he was there, he made an obscene facial expression. After several drivers behind him began honking, he sped to the corner and turned. My daughter ran to our house. Once inside, she looked out the window and could see him driving past, looking for her. He finally drove away, and she immediately called me. The whole incident took just a few minutes but, to her, it felt like hours. She was terrified.

I frequently hear from my students about the catcalling they experience or witness while waiting for a bus, the inappropriate comments from passersby on the street, the ass-grabbing at music concerts, the leering that occurs when they're eating out, and the creepy comments from drivers when they use ride-sharing services. As teenagers venture beyond the safety of parental oversight and exercise developmentally appropriate independence, they will be exposed to more of the world's realities—positive and negative. Just as we taught our children to cross the street by first looking both ways, required them to wear a helmet while riding a bike, helped them memorize our phone numbers in case they got lost or lost their phones, and told them what to do if they were separated from us in an airport or other public place, it's essential that we talk with our teenagers about the risks and safety of their newfound independence.

Adolescent brains are still under construction, so even if a teenager knows certain information, how they may think about and apply it in any given situation may be different from the way an adult would. It's important that teens learn how to fail and call on their resilience to move through disappointment and pain. It is also important for them to be able to take healthy risks and to embrace the value of authentic success. It will likely take some trial and error, but it's essential that teens learn to distinguish between positive and negative risks. Granting them the independence to take positive risks will allow them to recognize what personal growth and earning success looks, sounds, and feels like.

Mark Twain said, "Good judgment is the result of experience and experience is the result of bad judgment." Still, there are plenty of experiences that we hope our children never have to go through, and wise counsel from caring adults or hearing someone else's story can help them avoid them. When it comes to risky behavior and bad choices, especially as they relate to sexuality, we need to be concrete and specific. This guidance needs to be part of an ongoing conversation about healthy sexuality that emphasizes that the experience of sexual exploration should be safe, respectful, and positive.

We must be clear that sexual assault is never a justifiable punishment for a perceived poor decision. At the same time, while it isn't fair, the fact is that women, some men, and people of marginalized sexual identities need to learn how to keep themselves safe to avoid harassment and assault whenever possible. At the same time, as a society we should be teaching men—who perpetrate 99 percent of the instances of sexual violence—that such behavior is never acceptable.

In an ideal world, of course, precautions against harassment and assault wouldn't be necessary. As long as they are, we would be remiss not to address issues of prevention and intervention. Research tells us that there are some decisions that can inadvertently cause us to present as a target to people who look for opportunities to exploit and abuse others, making us more vulnerable to assault.

The prevalence of sexual harassment and assault among teenagers is difficult to accurately assess because victims often do not report their experiences.

The prevalence of sexual harassment and assault among teenagers is difficult to accurately assess because victims often do not report their experiences; however, studies have shown that about 20 percent of girls and over 5 percent of boys are victims of sexual abuse. (This is only what's reported; most experts believe that the numbers are much higher.) In fact, 44 percent of attacks against teens take place before the victim is eighteen. Sexual assault is a national problem that threatens the safety of our schools and the productivity and development of our students. Consider these alarming statistics:

Sexual assault is a national problem that threatens the safety of our schools and the productivity and development of our students.

- Approximately 1.8 million adolescents in the United States have been victims of sexual assault.[24]

- 35.8 percent of sexual assaults occur when the victim is between ages twelve and seventeen.[25]

- Teens ages sixteen to nineteen were 3.5 times more likely than the general population to be victims of rape, attempted rape, or sexual assault.[26]

- In college, one in five women is sexually assaulted.[27]

- Assault is most common in a woman's freshman or sophomore year of college.[28]

- In the majority of cases (75 to 80 percent), the woman knows her attacker, whether an acquaintance, classmate, friend, or current or ex-boyfriend.[29]

- Many are survivors of "incapacitated" assault: they are sexually abused while drunk, drugged, passed out, or otherwise incapacitated.[30]

- 5 percent of college men report they are survivors of sexual assault.[31] It's thought that the number is actually higher due to gender norms that prevent men from coming forward.

- An American Academy of Pediatrics study of young adults who are victimized in adolescence shows increased rates of destructive behaviors, including substance abuse, depression, and suicidal ideation.[32]

In 2017, the Associated Press released an article written after months of research and federal data analysis about the prevalence of sexual violence in K–12 school districts across the country. Ranging from rape and sodomy to forced oral sex and fondling, the sexual misconduct that the AP tracked was often mischaracterized by schools as bullying, hazing, or consensual behavior. The sexual violence took place anywhere students were left unsupervised, which included buses, bathrooms, locker rooms, and hallways. The report made clear that no type of school is immune to sexual violence and that all types of children are vulnerable, whether it be an inner-city neighborhood, blue-collar farm town, or upper-class suburb.

No type of school is immune to sexual violence.

According to the AP's analysis of the federal incident-based crime data, of the assaults that were reported and accounted for in the study, unwanted fondling was the most common form of assault, but about one in five of the students assaulted were raped, sodomized, or penetrated with an object. And contrary to public perception, student sexual assaults by peers were far more common than those by teachers.

Those who perpetrate the assaults cannot be classified into one group. There is tremendous diversity of personalities and personal circumstances: offenders may be outgoing or reclusive, socially savvy or awkward, wealthy or poor. They may attend schools in urban settings, outer suburbs, or small towns. The one shared trait of perpetrators is a lack of empathy, and most, though not all, are boys.

In independent schools, the numbers are similar. In a survey conducted by Independent School Health Check for the National Association of Independent Schools, out of 3,500 students who are sexually active, one in ten girls and one in twenty boys had experienced forced intercourse or rape (the survey didn't consider other forms of sexual assault). Of those who experienced forced intercourse, three in ten identified as transgender. These trends and statistics continue into college.

According to the National Sexual Violence Resource Center, nearly two-thirds of college students experience sexual harassment, and 20 to 25 percent of women and 15 percent of men are victims of forced sex during their time in college. In the latest, most comprehensive report to date, the Association of American Colleges and Universities' *Campus Climate Survey on Sexual Assault and Misconduct* (revised October 20, 2017) found that a significant percentage of the incidents are associated with alcohol use. The presence of alcohol or inebriated people does not necessarily mean a sexual assault will occur, of course. But there is evidence that alcohol (which is also termed "the number one date-rape drug") and other so-called date-rape drugs (such as Rohypnol, Xanax, and GHB) often contribute to an individual's vulnerability to sexual assault. Alcohol can lower inhibitions and impair cognitive functioning so that someone may not seek, hear, or respect consent, thereby potentially leading to sexual assault.

Adolescence is a period of development that often includes increased risk-taking behavior.

Adolescence is a period of development that often includes increased risk-taking behavior. This may include experimentation with drugs and alcohol and exploration of sexual activity and relationships. The developing teenage brain is more vulnerable to the negative effects of alcohol and more sensitive to the sedative qualities of certain drugs. Before going to sleep or passing out, teens can experience greater cognitive impairment.

It is important to communicate that underage drinking is illegal. Students may perceive this as unfair; nevertheless, it's the law and carries consequences should it be broken. When we encourage students to pass, abstain, or just say no to alcohol or other substances, they are likely to believe that it isn't just the drug itself that they're rejecting, it's the person who is offering it to them too. This is an important distinction to explore and discuss. It is very different for a teenager to say no to their best friend or person they are interested in hanging out with, who is trying to support them (e.g., provide relief from stress) or offer a good time (e.g., "Come on, it'll be fun"), than to a random person on the street.

If a teen expresses stress over a big test, for example, and their friend offers a drug, saying, "Dude, just take this. It'll calm you down, make you feel better," they may feel like refusing would not only reject the drug, but also their friend, who is trying to provide support. Or consider a teenager who is romantically interested in another teen, and at a party that teen says, "Hey, I've been looking for you. Want to play quarters? It'll be fun." If the first teen says no, they'll be passing up an opportunity to spend time with their crush.

The risk of discussing sexual assault and alcohol and drug use is that it can sound like victim-blaming (i.e., if you drink or take drugs and you're assaulted, it is your fault). This isn't true, of course, and we can emphasize that, while also pointing out how substance abuse can make a person more vulnerable. We all love and care about our children, so are we interested not only in what's legal, but also what's ethical and good for their well-being. When we encourage critical thinking and awareness, resourcefulness and resilience, it can be extremely helpful to discuss the what-ifs.

In the classroom, I find teenagers may identify the possible worst-case scenario of a situation, as well as the ideal that we should all aspire to. I try to guide them to what's realistic given the context, priorities, and cognitive realities of who they are and the dynamics taking place. This exploration should be free of guilt, judgment, and shame, and include multiple possibilities as well as potential outcomes. The goal is to identify moments when a decision can be made to increase the probability of a positive outcome. I approach these scenarios not only from a legal and consensual perspective, but also how decisions and behaviors can affirm moral values and safety. I try to keep the discussion positive, affirming the importance of each participant's sense of readiness and well-being.

> Isabel and Natalie are at a party. It's a small group of high school sophomores. Isabel has been crushing on Leo big-time; he's at the gathering with his friend, Cameron, who's friends with Natalie. Natalie has been encouraging Isabel to get with Leo, but Isabel is self-conscious and not as experienced with boys as Natalie is. Natalie told Cameron before the party that Isabel's into Leo and would be down to hook up. Cameron said he would see what he could do. Everyone's been partying, and it's getting late. Isabel and Natalie are out on the back porch with Leo and Cameron. Leo says to Isabel, "Hey, you want to go for a walk, sober up a bit?" Isabel hesitates and says she's all right to just hang where they are. Natalie nudges her and says, "Go on, have some fun. Go with him." Isabel pauses, then stands, steadies herself, and goes with Leo. Natalie says to Cameron, "He's cool, right? He won't be a jerk, right?" Cameron says, "He's cool. He'll show her a good time." Natalie says, "He likes her, right?" Cameron replies, "Yeah, he likes her. Likes her for tonight."

Friend-sourcing happens a lot among teenagers. This sharing of information and benevolent support in brokering a hookup or potential relationship is a way of bonding. Vulnerability can be scary, so a friend's inquiry can soften rejection or any awkward interaction. It also provides opportunity for friends to show loyalty and affirm their connection with others. This negotiation involved in bringing people together can feel socially powerful. Some teens see parties as an opportunity to casually connect and alcohol as a form of liquid courage, or an excuse if a hookup ends badly. The potential problem with this is that intentions may be misunderstood or lost in translation, and someone cannot legally consent to sexual activity if they are under the influence of substances.

Natalie's intention is to support Isabel's attraction and desire to connect with Leo. She is unintentionally pressuring Isabel, who is somewhat insecure and not as confident as Natalie when it comes to boys and sexual exploration. Among teenagers, there is tremendous pressure to be sexually experienced, and many teens, especially young women, often define their worth by the sexual attention they receive. When Leo asks Isabel if she wants to go for a walk and she hesitates, her intuition is telling her that it's a bad idea and that she should remain in the safety of the group. Natalie's encouragement quiets Isabel's instinct, and although it's well-meaning, it is not in Isabel's best interest. Isabel is clearly incapacitated. The fact that Isabel likes Leo and her friends are encouraging her makes it hard for her to assert herself. She may fear being perceived as uptight, a tease, or even, in some circles, a bitch.

After Isabel and Leo walk off, Natalie second-guesses her role. She knows that just because Leo may want to hook up doesn't mean he is interested in or wants to go out with Isabel. Isabel likes Leo and is interested in being more than just friends or a hookup. The way Cameron confirms Leo's physical interest and talks about it in an objectifying way indicates that authentic connection isn't Leo's priority. What should Natalie do now to help her friend?

Ideally, Leo will treat Isabel with respect and listen to what she wants, taking into account that she has been drinking. Ideally, Isabel has the wherewithal to set boundaries with Leo and express what she wants. Natalie could also say to Cameron, "That doesn't sound like what Isabel wants. I don't want them getting into trouble. Let's bring them back." And if Cameron isn't agreeable, she could go on her own or with other friends to find the couple and intervene in the hookup.

When I talk to students, we discuss these guidelines:

1. Stick with your friends. Do not allow isolation.
2. Support friends, following your intuition.
3. Know your limits and avoid drunk hookups. Make sure intentions are aligned and clear before moving toward intimacy, even with someone you think you know.

Sometimes, we end up in situations where someone we don't know sees our exposure as an opportunity to exert their influence.

Tammy is a junior who is looking at colleges. She goes to visit her older brother and some alums from her high school who attend a well-known university. Not wanting to hang out with her brother the entire night, Tammy makes plans to meet up with high school alum friends Blake and Trey. When Tammy gets to their dorm, they've already eaten and want to go to another friend's dorm suite to pre-game. Tammy didn't have dinner but forgets about her hunger as they meet a bunch of people in a dorm, where she does a few shots.

Next, they head to a concert, but stop at a party on the way, and Tammy consumes mixed drinks and beer. The concert is packed and Tammy is disoriented. She can't quite keep up with friends, and after about two songs, she feels sick and makes her way to the outskirts of the campus quad. She goes behind a clump of trees and throws up. A couple of boys come across her on their way into the crowd. One elbows his friend, and says, "Hey, check this out." He lifts Tammy's skirt. Another boy says, "You lost?" He grabs her from behind and pushes her into the first boy, who wraps his arms around her and presses his pelvis up against her. A couple of other boys see what's happening and approach, saying, "Hey, knock it off, man." The harassers laugh, say "whatever," and disappear into the crowd. The guys who intervened ask if she's OK. Since Tammy can barely stand, they wave over campus security, who shuttle her to student health services, where it's determined Tammy needs to go to the ER to be treated for alcohol poisoning.

What happened during the course of the evening that led to Tammy's exposure? Tammy made plans independent of her older brother, who likely would have looked out for her in this unfamiliar territory. Tammy decided to hang out with two people she knew, but not well. Tammy didn't eat dinner, and an empty stomach makes a person much more prone to intoxication. The amount of alcohol Tammy consumed wasn't within her limits, and she ended up alone. As a result of a series of seemingly innocuous decisions, Tammy found herself at risk for a whole host of problems from sexual assault to alcohol poisoning. Fortunately, thanks to the intervention of some bystanders, Tammy got the help she needed before anything serious occurred.

Drugs, especially alcohol, may motivate some teenagers to take risks without thinking through the physical and ethical implications. In many ways our society normalizes teen objectification and sexualization, as well as substance use. My students observe that they're trained by society not to think of sexual objectification as a big deal and may even feel flattered by it, as if it affirms their attractiveness and desirability. This makes them more likely to participate in activities they don't want or aren't ready for. Many grown women experience the same confusion, so it's no surprise that teenagers do too. As parents, we have a responsibility to understand and work through these issues and help our daughters do so.

> Sally and Fiona are both sixteen and at an outdoor music festival with a bunch of their friends. Because they're underage, their tickets didn't include a wristband that provides access to alcohol. The group is having fun but bemoaning the fact that they don't have beer or weed. Sally pulls Fiona aside and says, "Hey, how about we 'do it' for the beer.'" Fiona says, "Yeah, I bet we could score some weed too." Sally nods her head toward the back of the crowd where a couple of older guys are drinking and vaping dabs. The girls approach the men and start dancing with them. The guys are enthusiastically entertained by their attention, and the one Sally is dancing with moves in real close. She can smell his breath and see into his glassy eyes. "Can I borrow your wristband? Maybe a hit of your rig? I'll make it worth your while." The guy pauses, looking into her face as if he's contemplating something, and says, "Sure, why the fuck not? Back here." He and Sally disappear behind a line of portable toilets for a five-minute blow job. When they come back out, Sally has on the wristband and the man gets his friend to give them each a hit of the rig.

I heard about the above scenario from a friend of the girls, Diana, because "it just didn't seem right." Diana didn't say anything at the time because Sally and Fiona didn't question what they were doing and felt accomplished in acquiring what they wanted: to drink and get high. Still, Diana felt uneasy. Even if Sally is able to articulate why, she was taking risks. Not only was she drinking and using drugs, the sexual activity wasn't legally consensual because the man is an adult and she was a minor. She put herself at risk of contracting sexually transmitted infections as well.

These aspects of the situation were clear to Diana; it was the bartering part she was wrestling with. She was scared for what could have happened. Sally went out of view with someone she didn't know or trust who could have hurt her. What if he expected more than Sally was willing to give? What if he got angry if she didn't? What if he hurt her, or even pushed her into a car and drove away? These possibilities are scary to consider when you imagine them happening to someone you care about. And what if any those things happened, and Diana and Fiona tried to help, but couldn't? What would that feel like?

When Diana brought this up to Sally and Fiona, they brushed it off. It was fine, they said. They got what they wanted the way they wanted it. They actually felt proud of themselves and the way they had achieved their goal. They said they felt empowered.

Diana was left with the question *What is sexual empowerment?*

Empowerment is an active process by which we personally grow and become stronger and more confident in claiming our rights.

Empowerment is an active process by which we personally grow and become stronger and more confident in claiming our rights—a practice of autonomy and agency. Usually it is a collection of experiences and events that take place over time and contribute toward greater self-awareness, self-actualization, and esteem. We gain confidence in knowing what we're doing is right. Within the context of sexuality, this means exploring sex on our own terms in partnership, whether physical or emotional or both, with another person. Sexuality is about our identity—who we are and how we connect with others. People respond to us based on how they see us value our sexuality. Sexual acts are bonding behaviors that involve hormones and our brains. They mean something. They matter.

Empowered, healthy sexuality cannot happen when there are certain power differentials.

With teenagers in particular, empowered, healthy sexuality cannot happen when there are certain power differentials. Sexual behavior is an expression of feelings. For it to be enriching, it should mean the same thing to the people involved, whether it's just for physical gratification or something more. When there is an age gap like the one between Fiona and the man at the music festival, the interaction is imbalanced, which is why we have age of consent laws. Agency comes from controlling our own narrative. Going for a goal like getting high and using sex as the currency to acquire a material substance and ephemeral high, within the context of so much risk, does not contribute to personal growth. Sally's sexuality is devalued by the man who takes advantage of her desire to get something from him.

Within a party context, it is important for teenagers to surround themselves with people they can trust and depend on to look out for them. There is positive and negative groupthink that takes place among them as well. Would Sally have approached the man and made the offer by herself? Was Fiona's support a catalyst? What if Diana said something in the moment? Different friends will have clarity at different times, which is what makes our conversations about these issues with our teens so important. Diana might have intervened and said, "What if they're creepy or sketch? C'mon, we're fine, let's move up closer to the stage." Sometimes that's all it takes. Other times it's not. But having insight into a dynamic and the tools and practice to manage it creates the possibility that friends can have a positive influence on one another.

Whenever I ask my students what they value in their relationships, trust is consistently at the top of the list. Trust provides safety because it's built over time and across shared experiences through which we learn that we can depend on someone to understand and honor who we are. When teenagers choose to explore sex in an impersonal way, it's important to highlight the absence of trust. Sex is intimate, whether it's physical or emotional, so there is a level of vulnerability that's important to consider when it comes to how much we trust someone.

Kami goes out with friends to a "rager" that's happening at a friend of a friend's house. It's an open party and tons of kids from multiple schools are there. Kami starts dancing with a guy; they're obviously attracted to each other and having a lot of fun. Soon they're making out and grinding. The music is loud—people can't hear each other. After dancing for a while, the couple leaves to find a room downstairs. People are all over each other and hooking up. They go into a room and shut and lock the door. There's a couch they immediately fall onto and begin taking each other's clothes off. As the guy works to pull Kami's pants off, he says, "You all right? We doing this?" Kami responds, "Yeah, I'm into it, only if you have a condom, though." He pulls one out of his pocket. After he puts it on, Kami guides him to intercourse. At one point he says, "Let's switch it up" and turns her over so that he can enter from behind. When they are finished, Kami notices that the condom is on the floor. "Did you take it off?" she demands. "Did you come inside me?" He says, "Don't worry about it. I wasn't feeling it. It'll be all right."

In this scenario, the sexual activity is consensual up to a point. Kami and her partner are not incapacitated and there is a direct ask about intercourse. However, the situation is no longer consensual when Kami experiences *stealthing*, or birth control sabotage, which can be considered a form of assault. Since consent was given with the agreement that a condom would be used and it wasn't, Kami's consent is no longer valid. The practice of purposefully removing a condom or pushing it past the head and shaft of the penis to the base so it doesn't provide coverage, without consent, takes away the other person's autonomy regarding their sexual health and well-being. Kami is now at risk for sexually transmitted infections and pregnancy. She has also been disrespected. One of the benefits of knowing your partner is that there is a certain level of trust (at least in healthy relationships). The more impersonal a sexual experience, the more explicit about expectations one should be.

We want to believe that people are good and trustworthy; however, assuming someone is honest without really knowing them can carry high-stake risks. It can be especially difficult to tell if someone is trustworthy when we meet them online. Approximately one in seven youth internet users receive unwanted sexual solicitations, and in 27 percent of the incidents, solicitors asked youth for online photographs of themselves. Online sexual solicitation of young people may not be as prevalent as people think, but it happens enough that we should exercise caution and raise the awareness of our teenagers.

Malia, who is fifteen, likes to check out popular online hangouts; she meets Dylan in a random online chat room. Dylan says that he is older and engages Malia in chatting about their similar music tastes and activities. Dylan happens to be from the same general neighborhood, so the two connect over their favorite restaurants, stores, and places to skateboard. The tone of Malia's chat is flirty, and Dylan flirts back. They chat online a few more times and during one chat, Dylan asks for a picture of Malia's bare breasts. Malia hesitates, but he is quick to assure her that these are just for him and will keep him excited for when they actually get to meet in person someday. Malia sends a picture and Dylan tells her how hot she is and asks for more. Malia sends a few more. Next, Dylan wants Malia to masturbate for him in a video. Malia says no, and Dylan responds with a threat: "I have pictures of you, and if you don't want these to be sent to all of your [social channel] friends or posted publicly, you're going to do this for me."

Dylan is actually thirty and found Malia through a social media platform that publicly share someone's location. He manipulates her by appearing to know her neighborhood, so she feels a sense of familiarity and begins to trust him. As he grooms her further through positive attention and a sense of connection, she becomes willing to give more and more of herself. To please him and keep the connection, she sends naked photos. Once he coerces that leverage from her, he is able to exploit her vulnerability and fear to acquire more. Using naked images to extort additional exploitive sexual photos and video to control and abuse someone through social media is a predatory act known as *sextortion*. It's important to note that the University of New Hampshire's Crimes Against Children

Research Center reports that kids are more likely than adults to pressure other kids to send or post sexual content. No matter the age of the perpetrator, it's important to make sure our teenagers understand the risks of trusting strangers online.

Kids are more likely than adults to pressure other kids to send or post sexual content.

For parents, teenagers' relationship with technology can be difficult to understand. The majority of us are not digital natives, so it is challenging to understand how young people relate to and navigate cyberspace. Many young people see technology as a way to get to know a wide range of people. Cyberspace is a place they can go while being accounted for at home; they can also curate how they represent themselves, in a way that they can't in real life, to hide any awkwardness or insecurity.

There is a false sense of security that we all feel when moving through cyberspace from the comfort of our home or another familiar place. I always encourage my students to think of the digital space as an extension of their personal space. If someone a teenager doesn't know were to knock on their bedroom door, would they throw it open and invite them in? What would it take for someone to gain their trust in person, and how is it different when they meet a person online? It's important for teens to understand the risks of meeting people online and to be as wary of digital strangers as they would be if they met the person in real life. How some teens use the internet makes them an easy target for predators looking to exercise their power and control through sex. We want to encourage teenagers to tell us if they encounter a suspicious person online. If our teens do find themselves in a situation like that described above, it is important that we notify authorities and do everything we can to shut down the abusive behavior. In many cases, a sexual predator isn't interested in sextortion but in an exploitive in-person relationship.

How some teens use the internet makes them an easy target for predators looking to exercise their power and control through sex.

Scott identifies as gay and is looking for sexual or romantic connection, but there aren't many other kids who are out at his school, so he lies about his age to open a Grindr account. There are actually a lot of gay kids on Grindr, since high schools aren't always supportive environments for openly gay teens. Scott likes the app because he can block creepy people and can usually tell by someone's picture how old they are. Scott starts to chat with Tommy and initiates the first message:

> whats up

> whats up

> got a face pic?

> yep

After receiving the picture, Scott thinks, *He's hot enough*.

> are you actually 18? how old are you?

> in high school

> what brings you onto grindr?

> meeting people

> what are you into?

> music and hanging with my friends

> what's your snap?

Transition to Snapchat later:

> hey

> hey

> what are you doing

> just got out of the shower

Even though it's three in the afternoon, and Tommy includes a picture of his abs.

> hot

> do you have any pics?

Scott Snaps a torso pic in the mirror and sends it.

Later in the evening, Tommy Snaps Scott a dick pic.

> you want to meet up?

Scott and Tommy agree to meet. Two days later, when Scott walks into the cafe, there is only one man sitting alone, watching the door. Tommy looks like he's about forty years old. Their eyes meet, and Scott feels like he can't just walk out. Tommy waves him over. Scott is uneasy and isn't sure what he should do. This is his first Grindr meeting. Finding the courage to leave feels overwhelming, so he decides to at least say hello and sit down briefly.

Tommy is friendly and starts the conversation with a lot of questions. Scott doesn't know how to extract himself from the dialogue and leave. The rapid-fire questions are all about Scott's age: "How is it being in high school?" "Are there a lot of girls after you? How do you tell them you're not interested?" "What's your curfew?" "How do you manage to party without getting caught?" Scott's phone vibrates and he sees a text from his mom and has an idea. "Whoa, I totally forgot I told my mom I'd help her with something at home. I gotta go. Thanks. Bye." Tommy tries to protest, but Scott quickly leaves. Once out the door, he bolts down the street and hops on a bus.

Ideally, upon seeing Tommy's age and realizing deceit, Scott would immediately leave the cafe and block Tommy on his social accounts and phone. But this can be challenging for teenagers for many reasons: older–younger power dynamics, feeling they owe the other person something, the intimacy of eye contact and feeling trapped, the internal pressure to follow through with something that was brokered through an app that so many people use.

As adults, we may tell our teen that we don't want them using dating apps. Still, as many of my students tell me, it's likely going to happen anyway. It is reasonable to communicate your concern and tell your teenager not to use dating apps while under the age of eighteen, *and* to give them strategies for minimizing risk if they choose to exercise their will and do so anyway. Each parent has to decide how strict to be with their rules.

Former students who have learned through experience on these apps suggest the following: if two people are communicating via an app, request a photo immediately of the other person doing something specific that you've requested (e.g., give a thumbs-up). This can lower the risk of someone drawing from a bank of younger pictures to falsely represent themselves. Reinforce autonomy by reminding your teenager that if they aren't connecting with someone, they don't owe that person anything or need to engage in any way at all, and that it's OK to block them. In the above scenario, not only is Tommy dishonest and therefore not to be trusted, but also he asked a lot of questions that seemed to fetishize Scott's age and inexperience, rather than expressing any interest in him as a person.

Encourage your teen to trust their intuition and to slow down so they can pay attention to it. It is easy to bend the truth online to elicit a specific response or portray a certain image. Stress the importance of honesty in how your teenager represents themselves and their intentions. A relationship based on deception isn't worth much.

If your teen decides to meet an online connection in person, they should meet in a public place and tell a trusted friend.

If your teen decides to meet an online connection in person, they should meet in a public place and tell a trusted friend in advance who they're with and where they're meeting. While they are with that person, they can check their phone and say, "Sorry, just a sec, I need to tell my friend where I am." You can also encourage your teenager to take a friend along to the meeting. The friend can sit in a different part of the cafe during the meeting. Emphasize that they can end the meeting at any time and seek their friends' or your support.

Similar strategies are recommended for teens who engage in the currently popular practice of "seeking arrangements."

Julia is a young eighteen-year-old who just started her freshman year in college. After a couple months of socializing and making new friends, she realizes that money doesn't go as far as she thought it would. She hears from her suitemate, Lydia, that she can "seek arrangements" as a "sugar baby" with a sugar daddy or sugar mama on the internet. Apparently a few of the girls at school get two hundred dollars a date and all they have to do is let their "daddy" wine and dine them. Lydia warns Julia not to mention money at all while chatting on the site because it will automatically shut her account down. If the daddies want sex, they will tell her at the first meeting and she can take it or leave it. Julia looks at a few sites and decides on one that has a category called "College-Bound Sugar Baby" for students who want to graduate from college debt-free and build a professional network by spending time with someone willing to pay.

Julia curates a profile that makes her just a little older with a few nuanced changes to her interests and identity. She is chatting with a daddy who wants to meet. She shows him to her roommate, Cheri. Cheri expresses concern and tells Lydia this is a form of prostitution. "No it's not," Julia insists. "I'm not going to have sex with him." She agrees to meet the man.

The terms *sugar baby* and *sugar daddy*, especially when the "baby" is college-bound, reveal the inappropriate power dynamic of an "arrangement," even if Julia is technically an adult. Julia's suitemate is right that selling sexuality for money and personal gain is a form of prostitution. It can be seductive for a young person (and an adult too) to be the prized focus of someone's attention, particularly if that person comes across as more experienced and established. The attention and lure of monetary reward is enticing.

Arrangement also connotes consent—that there is a mutual understanding and negotiation that takes place to come to an agreement. However, the potential for being compromised is high. Meetings usually happen without the baby's friends or allies around, and there will be private moments even if it's agreed that there will be no physical intimacy. As we saw earlier, the more impersonal a connection, the less you can trust that the other person will care about your well-being or respect your boundaries and limitations, especially when money is involved and the person thinks you owe them something. Teenagers need to ask themselves *What am I going for? Is this how I want to value my sexuality? Is this a healthy or unhealthy risk? What does this ultimately lead to?* and *Is this worth the negative risks?* These are always good questions to ask oneself whenever engaging in precarious behavior.

A former student of mine, after the fall of her freshman year, shared that she saw all of the social dynamics and behavior we had discussed in health class her first weekend in college. The wisdom she shared was this: "You can talk about what to expect and think through all kinds of scenarios and the decisions you'll make, but the value isn't knowing what to do in that specific scenario, but knowing how to think about it and make a decision in the moment because things will always come up that you can't anticipate."

Another young woman in college told me, "Who you are at the beginning of the night, and the middle of the night, and later in the night, can change if you're partying." These observations highlight the importance of thinking ahead, practice, and ongoing dialogue with both friends and trusted adults. Life is fast-paced for our teenagers. The skills and tools they need to manage the ever-evolving dynamics of their social lives are crucial to their well-being. These tools include relevant information, physical and spiritual (religious or secular) self-awareness, resilience, and positive, authentic relationships, and they are all components of healthy sexuality.

PARENT–TEEN CONVERSATION STARTERS

- What's your understanding of healthy risks versus unhealthy risks? How does each contribute to or detract from your personal growth and well-being?

- What is your relationship with risk? Are you drawn to risky behavior or risk-averse?

- What is intuition? What are some things that might get in the way of you listening to your intuition? What are some strategies for getting around those obstacles?

- What's the difference between being excited and anxious because something is new and challenging, and being scared and anxious because something is unsafe?

- What is your orientation to adversity? When things get difficult or scary, how do you respond?

- What are some strategies for dealing with those situations when they come up?

- Who are the people you trust to look out for you? Who are you comfortable looking out for?

- What's your plan for times when you feel unsafe? Would that approach also work in different contexts?

- What is important to remember if you're caught by surprise? Or separated from people you can count on to watch out for you?

Resources

The U.S. Department of Justice's Raising Awareness about Sexual Abuse: Facts and Statistics": https://www.nsopw.gov/en-US/Education/FactsStatistics.

Facts on underage drinking and the associated risks: https://www.cdc.gov/ alcohol/fact-sheets/underage-drinking.htm.

Coverage of the Associated Press's reporting and data analysis of teenage assault: "Student on Student Sexual Assault is More Common Than We Thought" by the PBS Newshour: https://www.pbs.org/newshour/show/ student-student-sexual-assault-common-thought.

"Hidden Horror of School Sex Assaults Revealed by AP" by Robin McDowell, Reese Dunklin, Emily Schmall, and Justin Pritchard: https://www.ap.org/ explore/schoolhouse-sex-assault/hidden-horror-of-school-sex-assaults -revealed-by-ap.html.

"What Research Says and Doesn't Say about Student Sex Assault" by Reese Dunklin: https://www.apnews.com/5490c7a588f64bbcbd22c6778e7b86c8.

Common Sense Media's advice about online predators for parents: "The Facts About Online Predators Every Parent Should Know" by Christine Elgersma: https://www.commonsensemedia.org/blog/ the-facts-about-online-predators-every-parent-should-know.

National Sexual Violence Resource Center's resource on Title IX and staying safe in school: "10 Facts Everyone Should Know about Title IX" by Laura Palumbo: https://www.nsvrc.org/blogs/10-facts-everyone-should-know-about-title-ix.

Association of American Colleges and Universities: "Report on the AAU Campus Climate Survey on Sexual Assault and Sexual Misconduct" by David Cantor, Bonnie Fisher, Susan Chibnall, Reanne Townsend, Hyunshik Lee, Carol Bruce, and Gail Thomas.

American College Health Association's resource page on campus safety: "Campus and Sexual Violence" By American College Health Association: https://www.acha.org/ACHA/Resources/Topics/Violence.aspx.

Documentary Film

The Hunting Ground, produced by Amy Ziering; directed by Kirby Dick.

Audrie & Daisy, produced by Bonni Cohen, Sara Dosa, and Richard Berge; directed by Bonni Cohen and Jon Shenk.

STRAIGHT ANSWERS TO TEEN QUESTIONS
How do I avoid assault?

These guidelines are not included to imply that preventing sexual violence is the responsibility of the target or victim. They are included to promote safety while we as a society work to bring an end to sexual violence.

- When going out, always tell someone where you are going and with whom, and take a fully charged phone and money for emergency transportation.
- Plan for transportation and think about alternative transport should your plan fall through.
- If you go out with a group of people, make sure you have a friend you know well and trust. Before going out, discuss and commit to looking out for each other.
- Do not leave a party, concert, game, or other social event with someone you just met or do not know very well.
- Check out a first date or blind date with your friends. Insist on meeting the person in a public place like the movies, a mall, or a restaurant.
- If someone is aggressively hitting on you, be assertive and firmly say no. Do not be polite or apologetic. Don't smile or be concerned about hurting the other person's feelings. Get away from them and stick to your friends.
- If you take a cab or ride share by yourself, call someone at the

beginning of the ride, so the driver can hear you, to say where you're going and when you'll arrive.

- Do not let someone isolate you at a party. Common lines they may use include: "It's loud in here, do you want to go outside to talk?" or "It's crowded, want to go outside and get some air?" or "Let's go somewhere so we can talk. Upstairs is quiet."

- If walking at night or in quiet places, have a friend walk with you.

- When walking alone, walk with purpose and a sense of where you're going, and avoid distractions such as listening to music through earbuds.

- Understand the concept of consent and what you can do and say to make your intentions and limitations clearly known.

- If sexual assault commences, be explicit with your protest. Most perpetrators do not see their actions as rape. Use the word *rape*. For instance, say, "If you continue, you will be raping me" or "You are raping me," or scream "Rape!" If you are in public and someone is harassing or assaulting you, yell "Fire!" More people will respond to this than they will to "Help!"

- Speak up and out if you hear talk or see behavior that condones or encourages sexual assault.

- Encourage bystander awareness and action.

- Put emergency phone numbers into your phone. Those include campus security, emergency transportation options, friends with whom you've committed to helping and vice versa, the closest emergency room, and emergency hotlines. Consider downloading an app designed to connect you with your friends in a discreet way to stay safe. There are also apps, like Circle of 6 or Guardly, that allow you to locate friends' whereabouts.

- Join the movement against sexual assault. Find out how other people on your campus are taking action; gather ideas about what to do on websites like Futures Without Violence, Know Your IX, Culture of Respect, and The American Association of University Women. Organize and support what others are doing through organizations like Take Back the Night, The Clothesline Project, Carry That Weight, Party With Consent, End Rape on Campus, and The Monument Quilt. Men can find information on sites like Men Can Stop Rape.

- Trans, gender-nonconforming, and gender-nonbinary people can find safe dating tips at FORGESafe Dating Tips: https://forge -forward.org/wp-content/docs/Safe-Dating-Tips-FINAL.pdf.
- In college, join organizations that support survivors and work for change at your school.

If you choose to drink alcohol or take other drugs, in addition to the above tips:

- Know your limits.
- Avoid drugs and excessive alcohol use (binge drinking and drinking games, for example). Take into account others' substance use, and if someone attempts to persuade you to drink or take drugs, consider this a red flag.
- Make sure you have a trustworthy friend in your group who will keep an eye on everyone and uphold these safety tips. Rotate this respon- sibility and be accountable to each other.
- Do not put your friends into a cab alone if they are incapacitated. This applies to you too.
- Never accept an open drink from someone you do not completely trust or know.

- Keep your hand over your drink if you're at a table or bar.
- Never continue to drink a beverage that seems off or tastes different than you're used to.
- Do not mix substances.
- Do not drink from a punch bowl or take anything from a "fish bowl" (a bowl filled with a mix of prescription drugs).

How do I help a friend who's been assaulted?

- Believe them. The most simple but overlooked thing one can do is to believe the survivor confiding in you. Validate their feelings about the assault and be mindful of your tone. If you sound doubtful, your friend will feel unsupported.
- Put them at ease. Let them know that you are there for them and receptive to what they are sharing with you.
- Tell your friend that what happened to them was not their fault and that they didn't deserve it.
- Provide resources. You can suggest looking up your school's sexual assault policies and resource centers. You can help them find your school's advocate services as well. You can also suggest the resources below and help them figure out what they'd like to do. Each one has information for how to help a friend who has been assaulted, as well as information for survivors and their options:
  - » Promoting Awareness, Victim Empowerment (PAVE)
  - » End Rape on Campus
  - » Culture of Respect
  - » Rape, Abuse & Incest National Network (RAINN)

» Know Your IX

» National Sexual Violence Resource Center

» Sexual Assault Hotline: 1-800-656-HOPE

- Empower them. Let your friend know they are in complete control over any next steps. How they proceed is entirely up to them.

- Accompany them. Offer to go with your friend or give them a ride to where they'd like to go. Ask if they need somewhere to stay or any other emotional support. If someone has just been assaulted, it is not recommended that they be left alone.

- Offer to help them find your school's victim advocate services. In high school, this may be a trusted teacher, school counselor, dean, or Title IX coordinator. In college, this may be the same, or your school may have a resource center specifically for survivors of assault.

- Express admiration for their courage and recognize how difficult this must be for them.

- Continue to show support and care for your friend. This may mean listening to them talk about their experience or spending time together and engaging in activities that are enjoyable and not related to the assault. Make sure you respond to their needs. Remember that you don't have to do this alone; seek support for yourself as well as your friend.

- Be strong and take care of yourself as well.

(Adapted from Know Your IX and Culture of Respect)

- You can also tell them about a few books that may be helpful:

» *The Sexual Healing Journey: A Guide for Survivors of Sexual Abuse* by Wendy Maltz

» *Hope, Healing and Happiness: Going Inward to Transform Your Life* by Angela Rose, PAVE

» *Healing Sex: A Mind-Body Approach to Healing Sexual Trauma* by Staci Haines

What if no one believes me?

This is a common fear and gets in the way of people reporting sexual assault. There are people who will believe you. If your friends or family don't believe you, there are survivor advocacy and support groups that you can call for support. The federal government requires that public schools and college campuses have a Title IX coordinator. They will listen to your story and provide support. In a public high school, you can ask the front office who the Title IX coordinator is and they are required to tell you. If you are in college, look on your school's website under student support services or student health services. These offices should support you in getting the help you need. If you go to an independent or parochial school, the support person in these situations is usually the dean of students or administrator who handles discipline. For additional help, see the resource list in Appendix B of this book, and call the National Sexual Assault Hotline (800–656-HOPE) for resources outside of school.

How do I say no to a drink or drug without making the person who is offering feel like I'm rejecting them?

If this is a good friend, a simple "I'm OK, no thanks" or "I'm not drinking tonight" should be enough. If it isn't and your friend coerces or pressures you into taking the substance, it's time to reconsider your friendship. If you don't know them well, you can make up an excuse or lie. I talk a lot about the importance of honesty in this book, which I stand by; however,

I believe that in some circumstances a less-than-truthful excuse can be a way to protect your higher truth and well-being. So you could say "I have a game tomorrow—I promised Coach I wouldn't drink" or "I'm the designated driver tonight, but thanks" or "I've had a lot already, I'm good." Whatever your reason, make it about you, not them. If they persist and push, don't worry about saving any potential friendship or relationship and assertively say, "No. I don't want any."

How am I supposed to find someone to go out with if I don't use dating apps?

Get involved in activities that you like or are open to trying, which is a good way to meet people. You can friend-source too. If you see or meet someone you're interested in, discreetly ask around and see if any of your friends, or friends of friends, know them and when you might be able to meet them. In chapter 5, I discuss how to ask someone out in person if you're wondering about that.

If I want to use a dating app, what's the safest way?

Dating apps have a minimum age use policy; however, if you choose to use a dating app like Tinder, it's *how* you use it that makes the difference. It can be a way to establish initial contact, but getting to know that person should happen in person and through public shared experiences until you start to build trust. As you do that, think about everything discussed in this book and if the person you are getting to know understands and puts into practice the qualities of healthy relationship-building. They should be respectful of you from initial contact and vice versa; remember, consent starts before two people are together in a sexually physical way.

What do I do if the person I am attracted to only wants to hang out on the weekends at parties because that's how they feel less awkward?

This is OK for the first couple of times while you are getting to know each other; however, if this person is dependent on a party context or alcohol or drugs to be comfortable with you, then it won't be a healthy relationship. If you're OK with your time together being exclusive to a party scene then you could continue, but it doesn't sound like that's what you really want. Being with people when they're intoxicated isn't being with them in an authentic way. The substance gets in the way of that. In the end, that kind of relationship doesn't last and isn't meaningful. So have a conversation with them about what you notice and if you can try something different together. If they go for it, great. If not, it's time to move on, as hard as that may be.

How can I get to know someone at a party if it's not a good idea to ask them to go somewhere quieter?

You can try to find a spot to hang out that is still somewhat public but not quite central to what's going on. Or you can ask a couple of friends to hang out with you somewhere quieter. Or you can muster up the courage to express your interest and ask for their Instagram or Snapchat as well as the opportunity to hang out sometime. See chapter 4 for how to do that. I know it can feel like a party context in the moment is the only opportunity you'll have, but it isn't. Anything worthwhile will require some effort, a healthy risk, and time to get it right.

CHAPTER EIGHT

Strong Voices

An Anthology of Survivor Stories

This chapter is a collection of authentic survivor expressions I have collected for this book. The purpose is to build empathy, humanize the issue of sexual assault, cultivate connection and healing, and inspire action—not only to bring an end to sexual assault, but also so that you may become more open, willing, and able to deal with similar situations if they arise with your teen. Many of the tools to do this are discussed in earlier chapters of this book.

Thirteen survivors have opened themselves up to share their stories and truth with you in a way that has meaning for them. All of the authors are connected to the national nonprofit PAVE (Promoting Awareness, Victim Empowerment).

PAVE's mission is to "shatter the silence of sexual violence" through social advocacy, education, and survivor support. PAVE is an invaluable resource for survivors and their families. Founder and Executive Director Angela Rose, who is a survivor, is a respected national leader with a positive and proactive approach to preventing sexual assault.

Before reading this chapter, please know that it includes explicit accounts of sexual harassment, sexual assault, and rape. If you or someone you know has experienced sexual harassment, assault, or rape, you are not alone. It's important to understand your options and how you can access support. There are resources and hotlines throughout this book, as well as in Appendix B in the back, for people who have experienced sexual violence. Please practice self-care and consider whether you are able to read this chapter, are comfortable doing so, and how you may support yourself.

DELANEY

At sixteen, I was sexually assaulted by two older boys who went to my high school. The assault was traumatizing, but the subsequent aftermath is what really took a toll on my healing process. Not only did I have to return to school with the two boys who assaulted me and all their friends, but also the online media frenzy that ensued during and after school caused me to lose hope and all the confidence I had left in myself. I was a little girl growing up at the height of social media and internet popularity. I truly felt that I had no voice, and with all of the harassment I received online, I felt like I was to blame for what had happened. Not only did I receive constant reminders of how scandalous the kids at school perceived me to be, but also I soon started to receive threatening messages telling me to keep my mouth shut or I would be hurt or, as they wrote, "beat up and spit on for being the slut she is."

It was hard for me to understand why people were spreading lies about me. It took me years to finally understand what they didn't get—that no matter how hard I tried to defend myself, they were going to believe the easiest scenario that worked for them. When I was sexually assaulted, I didn't even know what to call it because I was so young and immature, and didn't know anything about sexual violence. In my sixteen-year-old mind, "rape" happened to young women who were attacked in an alley at night on the way to their car. So for a long time after my assault, I would only refer to it as "the incident" and "when it happened." Nobody ever told me what "it" really was. This truly impacted how I viewed not only myself, but also the entire experience at such a young age.

Because of the incessant bullying I received on social media, it took me over eight months to report the assault. In May 2012, a month after I reported my rape to the police, I tried to take my own life because I truly believed what people were saying about me on the internet. I was hospitalized, dropped out of school a month before summer, and was forced to move a hundred miles away to hide, away from my family and in fear for my life. At this point, I had lost every friend I had ever known due to this experience. Kids didn't want to be outcast like I was, so to them, the safer option was to silently back away as I was thrown to the wolves.

For months, my parents forced me to go to therapy, but every time I would walk in, the new therapist would either cry or not know what to say to me. So after twenty-one therapists in less than three years, I finally found one that told me, even after all I'd been through, everything was going to be OK. I wasn't raised in a religious household, but I think my spirituality played a huge role in my healing process. I had to believe that everything happens for a reason and that karma does indeed exist.

It took me many years to rebuild my life after my assault because I've had to endure five court trials as a result. Only recently did I find the ability to learn about the importance of self-care and take time to heal without feeling like this experience had pushed back my life. I've always been an artist, so painting plays a huge role in my therapy and healing. I also just finished my 100,000-word book about my story, which I intend to publish. But the biggest part of my healing has been speaking out about what happened to me. I felt so silenced for so long; taking back my voice has given me the opportunity to find my strength and courage I felt I had lost. I've always felt like it is my responsibility to end the harassment and the sexual harassment and assaults happening in high schools.

I've met so many other survivors along the way. It has truly helped me realize that I am not, nor will I ever be, alone in this. I still have a lot to work on and miles to go in my healing process, but for the first time in over five years, I can see a future for myself. I don't feel blame for what happened to me anymore, and I don't feel like I am the one who should be feeling shame for what happened to me. Building relationships has been my biggest battle in all of this, but every day I feel like I am learning to trust again. Every day I feel like I am learning how to love my life again and even though I still wake up with nightmares and have trouble with intimacy, I can see the light at the end of the tunnel.

JEAN

Growing up, I was always different from other girls. I didn't have a father figure in my life, so I always wanted attention from a male. I was a tomboy growing up and loved to be around boys. I would rather play baseball or skate outside with my brother than partake in traditional female activities. I knew I was different, but I never knew my power would be taken from me by a boy at only sixteen years of age.

I had just recovered from an eating disorder and I was starting to heal. I started to date a popular, good-looking football player. It started off well since he gave me the love I longed for and I was able to mask my pain for a little while. The relationship then took a turn and he began to abuse me. It started off with him just touching me and then to occasionally abusing me physically. I felt like a puppet while he just prowled my body with his hands. I was very vocal that this was not the relationship I wanted, but he did not care. He would shower me with gifts after abusing me because he knew I would accept his insincere apologies.

January 4 is a day that will always stay in my memory. He took me downstairs and the same old pattern began, but this time it was different. He was different. He was more violent than before. The look in his eyes was sinister. I knew something wasn't right. We were watching *The Notebook,* and during the movie he raped me. He was a predator and I was his prey. To this day, I still can't watch that movie.

The moment I knew everything would change was the moment I looked into the mirror after my assault. I was used to looking at a broken girl, but something was different. I wasn't just broken, I was destroyed. I walked out in pain and knew from that moment that I would never be the same again. A week later, he called me to tell me he was a monster and that he could not do it anymore. I was furious. Why did he get the control to end it after he had already taken my power when he assaulted me? I remember screaming, "You're going to rape me and then break up with me?" I was happy to be out of the cycle of abuse, but nothing could prepare me for what happened next.

For the next few weeks following the phone call, I went through life, but I barely existed. I felt guilty for letting the abuse go on for so long. I was more broken than I had ever been and I continued to see him at school. He knew he had abused me, so why couldn't he own up to what he did?

I felt hopeless. I had always thought of rape as a random guy in an alley who attacked you, not someone I knew and trusted. I could not take the pain and guilt anymore. I tried to end my life many times. I wondered why I was here and what my purpose was, and I decided I had to do something. I thought the justice system would be on my side, but I could not have been more wrong. I decided to report it to the police. Throughout the process I was asked questions like "What were you wearing?" and "Why did you stay with him?" I began to feel like I was at fault and did not see much hope in the future.

Going back to school after reporting was a nightmare. The entire school knew and now thought of me as a girl who lied about being raped. I was called all sorts of names, ranging from "slut" to "pathetic liar." Reporting made everything so much worse. No one believed me and I felt so alone. I had no one by my side. My friends abandoned me, and I was left with nothing.

I went back to the police station, where they told me that my assault was consensual. I was in shock and disbelief. I knew what had happened to me, and the fact that no one believed me tore me apart. The police barely investigated and decided to just sweep it under the rug. I had to try to forget how much that moment broke me—I was denied justice.

The torment at school went on for a year and a half. The school did nothing to protect me. My life was threatened, and I was even threatened to be raped again. I even had a classmate stand in front of the class and rally a group to tell me to kill myself. I would hide in the library, too afraid to go anywhere. The school told me everything was a misunderstanding. I couldn't take it anymore; I was so sick of feeling destroyed. I knew I needed to do something.

I started to speak with an advocate who inspired me to fight for my rights. She set me up with another survivor named Delaney Henderson. It meant everything to finally have someone believe and support me. The first thing she said to me was "From this moment on, you will never feel alone again." Together with Angela Rose, the founder of PAVE, she helped me fight for my rights. I was homeschooled for the last two months of my senior year of high school. I was finally able to heal and now I have an amazing support system by my side. I recently started working closely with PAVE and have found my purpose. The key to my healing has been sharing my story and being a beacon of hope to other survivors. The journey of surviving a sexual assault and the aftermath is tough to take on, but the moment we start speaking up, we inspire others to shatter the silence too.

I am now a freshman in college with a criminology major and hope to continue to heal by becoming a voice for those who feel they have been forced into silence. I find solace through poetry and often write about my assault to acknowledge my emotions and express them in a healthy way. I find it healing to not only accept what happened to me, but also to use it for a purpose. If I had been connected to another survivor like Delaney earlier, it would have changed my whole process. It is important for survivors to know they are not alone and that when they reach out, they have a whole world waiting for them.

ANONYMOUS

I was assaulted my junior year of high school by a close friend of mine. He was somebody I really trusted, so I felt confused, hurt, and manipulated. Because of the prevalence of victim-blaming in American culture, I had convinced myself that the interaction was consensual. I dismissed the anxiety and fear I felt with him as butterflies, and the nausea after the fact as puppy love. And honestly, I thought that my feelings of regret were normal. After a few months, I began to realize that those feelings were not normal for a healthy relationship, and I spoke to a licensed professional. I began to pursue therapy as well as a legal process. I thought that this would lead to an instantaneous sense of peace with the assault;

that was not realistic. The healing process definitely took time, energy, and support from others.

Arguably the most influential support system of my healing process has been the national organization PAVE. During the summer between my junior and senior years, I decided that I wanted to start a chapter of PAVE at my high school. I saw a great need for education and support in the student body. At our first meeting, we had three attendees. After a little nagging and a lot of hard work, we ended the year with fourteen committed, regular members at the chapter meetings. Our group was able to bring two campuswide campaign events to the school—the #ConsentIs campaign, as well as the What She Was Wearing? campaign. The overwhelming amount of support and participation we saw from the student body still astounds me to this day. My ability to support other survivors and advocate for sexual assault awareness was a crucial part of coming to terms with my story.

One thing that stands out to me about my story is something I told my therapist a few weeks ago. I told her that in the beginning of my journey, I felt like everything around me was a trigger, but now I feel like the world is full of possibilities. My faith has been a crucial part of getting me to this point. Instead of seeing a trigger multiple times a day, I now see my favorite Bible quote multiple times a day. That is something that truly amazes me—once my outlook on life changed, positivity began making its way into my daily life again.

A couple days ago, I described my story as a path. At first, the road was bumpy and full of dark, stormy nights. After enduring this challenging journey for some time, I began to see a clearing in the distance. I could see this wonderful world ahead of me full of sunshine, clear skies, and joy. Although I was still in the midst of the storm, I had hope for what was ahead of me. Now that I am through that clearing, I am thoroughly enjoying my life. That doesn't mean that I never think about the assault or that I am completely healed, but I am at a place where I am truly happy. I am able to be grateful for the rocky road that got me here because it allows me to appreciate where I am now.

ANONYMOUS

The last thing I remember was our argument. Hot, salty tears stained my cheeks. I couldn't breathe. I woke up, stripped of my clothes and my choice. Coincidentally, an officer pulled his car over without reason. That was my chance to say something, to seek justice legally, but I couldn't, and that's completely OK. This is my justice. Sharing my story on my terms, first through my most recent tattoo—a flower blossoming out of a butterfly, beautifully done by David Sugihara—and now, through writing.

I get to live in this beautiful yet corrupt world. A place flooded with love and joy but sprinkled with hate and pain. I get to feel happy. I get to feel sad. And I get to feel overjoyed. I don't *have* to be anything I don't want to be. I don't have to tell my story, but I have the privilege and voice to. I have the courage to say #MeToo; I don't have to say that I am a victim; I get to say that I am a survivor.

I started dating a boy my sophomore year of high school, and in the beginning, I thought it was really great. We agreed on mundane things like our hatred of pickles and disagreed on things like our preference for dogs versus cats. Over time, our disagreements grew divisive, and his jokes grew dark, like the time he and his "squad" faked his own stabbing death in front of me on April Fools' Day, or joked about rape. Then he started lying to me about small things. He lied to me for a year about his religion, making me think that we shared a common faith when we didn't. He was controlling and manipulative. He didn't want me to wear anything that was tight or in any way revealing, like leggings. He especially did not approve of tattoos, which I did not have at the time. After that, the manipulation progressed and any argument we had ended up being my fault. Our arguments were so toxic that I wasn't able to breathe, and I would cry to the point of fainting. This didn't matter though. He still pursued his goal, even though he knew I was *not conscious* and *not consenting*. When I brought it up to him, he denied everything. He told me that he did nothing wrong and "reassured" me that everything was fine.

At that point, I stopped caring. I stopped caring for myself and for anything that happened to me. I didn't tell my friends or my family. I didn't know how to because of the constant lies he fed me and the lies that he told his friends. I tried to push it out of my head, but I kept blaming myself for everything that happened. Days went by when strangers, friends, and even teachers would pass me by in the hall and I would either be on the verge of tears, sobbing, or dead silent. I wasn't *me* anymore, I didn't know how to be. I was empty, and I just let the time pass by.

I ended the relationship during the summer after junior year. He made sure to get the word out that he ended things first. As always, I was the "crazy one" or whatever picture he painted for his friends, who misconstrued it in their own way to the rest of the grade. In the end, none of that mattered. We had half our classes together senior year. He wasn't going anywhere.

At the start of senior year, I thought that it would be easy to ignore him. We ended up seated near each other in most classes, so I requested seat changes in each class. Only two teachers moved me. I also couldn't avoid group projects and of course we ended up paired together. At that point, our toxic relationship was rekindled and he treated me like a girlfriend, yet he didn't want to label it. Yet again keeping secrets. I was extremely naive and gave him a million too many chances that he did not deserve. The end of senior year was prom season. We had not been talking for weeks because he had lied to me about drugs and hooking up with a girl at a party that he went to after I was supporting him at his dance performance that same night. He bragged to his boys about it, told them not to tell me after they said they wanted to tell me, and of course they followed through by not telling me because of the "bro code."

I ended things completely after that night thanks to some encouragement I got from a good friend after she saw how badly he treated me. But, despite everything, he still expected me to go to prom with him because I had promised while we were dating. In retrospect, I think I was absolutely insane for going with him, but he was scary manipulative— physically and emotionally—and had the power of his squad to create any number of social consequences and rumors. I was afraid. So, I laid out the rules and told him that we could go together for pictures only, but that he couldn't touch me. Of course, after this conversation he went and told his friends—who are known to spread any gossip throughout the grade—that he didn't want to go to prom with me and that he only wanted to go with me for the pictures.

At prom, I hung out with my friends, which he was not happy about. I tried to have fun on my own, but he confronted me and told me that he could think of five other girls who were better dates than I was. He was angry the whole night and screamed at me in front of students and teachers. Nobody did anything. They just watched and let him yell at me. He blamed me for anything he could. I left with a guy friend. After that night, he made every effort to make my life a living hell.

He constantly texted me that I was a slut, a whore—pretty much any derogatory term that you could think of. He and his squad spread rumors to everybody in the grade, all variations of his lies. Girls in his group posted on social media, word for word, "She's a piece of shit and I hope karma bites her in the ass," and that I cheated on him—which is impossible considering we were completely broken up—with my guy friend that I left with after prom because he was kind enough to keep me company after I had been screamed at the whole night. They claimed I was doing this because I was trying to get back at him when, in reality, I wanted nothing to do with him. I just wanted to get away from him. I had people in the halls who I hadn't talked to since elementary school come up to me and tell me that they were hearing about me. Everyone was talking.

I stopped responding to him and his squad's harassment. They did not deserve any responses, and I just waited things out until graduation. His squad was spreading rumors and harassing me into the summer in any way they could that would hurt me the most. Of course, none of these people know what actually happened between us. Nobody in their group cared enough to know, cared enough to seek out another perspective. Even if they did know, I'm not convinced they would've condemned him and his actions. I guess it's their actions that speak louder than words. No matter how many lies they told, the rumors would never define me or taint who I am. I couldn't hold my story in any longer, so I decided to tell my friends and family what really happened. I told them the truth about his toxicity: the rape, sexual assault, harassment, and the bullying.

Rape can happen to anyone, regardless of gender, sexuality, or what they're wearing (if you recall, he didn't want me to wear anything classified as showy), regardless of the location or background a person comes from, or even how long you know the person. It can happen. It could be somebody who you deeply trust and care for, even someone you dated for a few years like I did. *Nobody* fits the mold of a sexual assault victim; there is no such thing.

I could've chosen to ignore this for the rest of my life, but he is an expired part of my past and he did things to me that cannot be ignored. This does not define me. I am not who my abuser was, and I never will be. I am sharing this story with you today because I am trying to give justice to the woman I didn't know I would become four years ago. I am living proof that I am "fearfully and wonderfully made" (Psalm 139:14). I want to empower the women and men out there who have had these experiences to address them in their own time, in their own way. I want people who have heard of other people's experiences, including mine, to help educate others about this topic; to talk about it. I want to encourage everyone not to be a passive bystander and stand up for those around you; are we really any better than the abuser if we don't help the person hurting?

I was the person hurting for so long, and honestly, sometimes I still am. But I am resilient and I will persist. Nobody else gets to define who I am. I didn't think that my story would make a difference to anyone, but the Sprinkle of Jesus app on my phone that sends little words of wisdom throughout the day tells me otherwise. It says, "Someone's breakthrough is locked up in the testimony that you're ashamed to tell." After reading that, I realized it was time to speak up and be braver than I thought I could be. I am not ashamed of my testimony; it deserves to be heard. I want to share this not to get even, but to step forward in my healing process and spread awareness to others. I've been put on this earth for a reason just like every single person is. And like the flower in my tattoo, I am living, breathing evidence that something beautiful and strong can grow out of ugly circumstances, regardless of how difficult it is. Beauty, acceptance, and an abundance of faith has come out of the freedom that

I've felt through sharing my story. I am beyond blessed to be here and to grow a strong army of women and men, supporters and survivors, along the way who will not stand for silence.

ANONYMOUS

I was sexually assaulted when I was fourteen, during my freshman year. All three of my remaining grandparents were nearing the end of their lives and my family was spread thin. It took me awhile to finally reach out for help. My first resources were close friends, who after a year, finally persuaded me to tell my parents. I did not start acting on my fears until senior year, when I was able to tackle my problems head on with activism. I organized a day of sexual violence education for my whole high school. I will remember my peers' responses and love for the rest of my life.

I am now heading into my freshman year of college and I am scared the cycle will only repeat itself. Except now I possess important tools that I lacked before: I know to surround myself with people I trust, to keep survivor/victim resources at my fingertips, and to be the ally I wish that I had when I was raped. I also know that although it was not my fault, society sucks, and it is only smart to prepare myself: walk with a buddy at night, keep a self-defense mechanism in my purse, and don't provoke possible predators.

After my assault, I had a hard time touching men, although I quickly learned to disguise that fear since I had not told my family, and I wanted desperately to be able to hug my baby brother. It took me another two years to feel sexual pleasure. Once my mom knew what kind of trouble I was having, she quickly became my superhero. She skipped all the awkwardness and bought me vibrators and lube to encourage my sexual abilities. She wanted me to be able to pleasure myself before having another sexual experience. It took awhile and my sex toy collection is embarrass-ingly large, but I finally did it. In terms of mental self-care, I learned to ask for help—something I was too scared to do before. I never sought out a therapist, but I leaned on great friends, adult mentors, and my amazing parents. Looking back, my fear of asking for help came from not wanting to burden the people I loved. But in reality, I hurt them more by not trusting them in the first place.

I have yet to tackle sex again after my assault, which is something I am working up to. I still consider myself a virgin when talking with friends, although technically I am not. For me, the fear of a "first time" has increased tenfold. I want to have experience and to be good in bed (like any eighteen-year-old), but I have a huge fence to jump first—or rather a fifty-foot wall. I am in college now, so my old support systems are miles away. I am hoping to build new connections before jumping into the deep end. First and foremost, I know my boundaries. I only hope that when I share them with my partner that they will respect them.

Today, I am confident in myself. I have spent years arming myself with tools—weapons even—to combat the sexist society we live in. I know that nothing that happened or that might happen in the future was or is my fault. I even know how to recognize symptoms in my friends in case I can provide support to them. I also know that some things are just out of my control. I love myself and my body. I worship the journey that got me to this point of healing. I have come so far. It would be disrespectful to my younger self to look down upon my experience. Now I am better prepared. I am a warrior.

ANONYMOUS

When I was fifteen, my best friend's on-again, off-again boyfriend sexually assaulted me at a party. Heavy drinking was involved, and I could barely function. I told him no and to stop but he didn't listen. As he forced himself on top of me, I tried to yell, but I was so intoxicated I don't think I could; it seemed more like a whisper. I tried pushing him off, but I wasn't strong enough; my whole body felt limp.

After it happened, I passed out, woke up the next morning, and left as soon as possible. I decided I wasn't going to tell anyone; I was afraid of the effects it could have, of everyone in my small town knowing, my family, let alone my best friend. In some ways I even tried to cover it up. I'm not sure what I was thinking because nobody really knew anyways. Time passed and I had mostly moved on with my life. I accepted what had happened to me and even opened up to a few people.

Until the day, about a year later, I got a text from him, saying he thinks "we should tell [my best friend] about how we hooked up that one night. She's your best friend and deserves to know." *Hooked up!? Are you kidding me?!* I responded by saying that's not what happened at all, that he forced it, and it was sexual assault. He then called me multiple different names. My best friend found out two different stories, his and mine. She was devastated and wanted time to think, but I truly believed deep down she would have my back.

She later told me she didn't know who to believe and would just forgive both of us. I was probably one of the most difficult days of my life, to hear her say that. She still to this day (six years later) will bring him up, just occasional random chitchat, and it literally makes me hate her. After that, more people found out and would call me a lying whore or slut, etc. I, for the most part, have come to terms with everything that happened, but one of the few regrets I have is not reporting it and letting him walk away from what he did to me with no repercussions.

I'm *so* thankful for all the high school survivors speaking out. We need this to end, for girls to feel safe about reporting sexual assaults and having the community support them, not tear them down.

RICH

My molestation took place back in spring of 1970, the year I graduated from grammar school and started high school. By that fall, I discovered that smoking marijuana allowed me to sleep. The next few years are a blur. I did some crazy drugs all through high school and even overdosed on heroin. I continued my drug use even through my time in the military. There's a book I'd like to write. I finally sobered myself up at "the turn of the century." (I've always wanted to use that expression.)

Upon sobering up and discovering social media, I began to have memories creep back. What he did was wrong. Was I alone? I sure felt like I was. I didn't pursue it much. I started working at my father-in-law's restaurant in Hollywood. Ask me sometime and I'll show you the pictures.

On my way to work, driving up Los Feliz, I would always listen to the news. It seemed for a while that every day I would hear a story of how a teacher, coach, priest, or whoever was arrested for molesting a child. This one particular day, I was at a light when I started to hear another story of molestation. I got mad. I hit the wheel and yelled that someone has to stop this. From the back seat and into my right ear, I clearly heard, "Why not you?" It was so clear that I turned to look who was back there even though I knew I was alone. I got to work and kept quiet.

One of my customers was a priest who was very nice. He came in that night and of course we started some small talk when he asked me if I had heard of all the molestations on the news. He must have sensed from my reaction because he looked at me more seriously and asked, "You?" I didn't say much, but he gave me a contact number for the church. It took me a month before I actually called, but once I did, the ball started rolling.

The church seemed very interested in my story and once they got me to sign my statement, I no longer heard from them. I felt like once again, I had been taken advantage of. Things kept happening that told me that what I was trying to do was the right path, such as meeting a friend from Facebook in person only to find out she was a counselor who specializes in post-traumatic stress disorder (PTSD), something many survivors experience. I asked her to become my counselor; she did and we later became very good friends. Another instance was when I called the Chicago Police Department and was connected to the one officer who actually knew my perpetrator; seriously, what are the odds?

I tried going after the church financially since it seemed that money was what they were most concerned about. All I originally wanted was to stop my molester from doing it again and to help any other child he may have hurt. The church seemed only interested in their liability. It was difficult to find a lawyer willing to help, and in the process I lost my family and wife. My brother at one point said to me that I was complicit in my molestation, that I was looking for a father figure and now I was looking for a payday. I haven't spoken to him since.

Once I was living in Colorado, I started going to the VA hospital and started PTSD counseling in earnest. I was alone except for my daughters and their families. I found a lawyer willing to help, and through another friend, got a job and some self-respect back. I quit smoking and started exercising and tried to get healthy. It was a year or more of talking with lawyers going against the church. I finally settled for a small amount and felt that I was done. But I wasn't done.

I made contact with Angela Rose and decided I wanted to meet her and tell her my story, to find out what I could do to really help someone. I was lucky enough to meet Angela in San Diego in August 2017. On that trip I also spent a little time with a friend I had known for years, now my fiancée, my dearest Jackie. I found I could not love another until I loved myself first. I had to start my healing and my self-acceptance in order to find the love of my life. If there is anyone who needs help, please reach out, there is a hand just waiting to grab on to help you shatter the silence.

TAMMY

You are not alone. You should never feel ashamed. My best advice is to forgive. That day of judgment will come for everyone. If you are a survivor, my story is somewhat similar to yours and I would like to share it with you. The first time I was raped was when I was eight years old. A distant cousin in my family who was fifteen decided to take something so very precious from me. At the time, I did not know what sex was or what rape was and so it happened. I knew deep down that it was something wrong, but I did not know what. After he was done, I remember getting up and finding his mom, my aunt, and telling her what just happened. She called me a filthy little liar and that I better never say another word about it to anyone for fear of something bad happening. At the age of eight, so many things went through my mind. I remember going home and seeing my mom and all I could think was, *Wow, I did something wrong*. But what did I do that was wrong? So I chose to say nothing. That memory was repressed all the way until I was twelve years old when sex became something I knew more about. Those memories flooded my mind and it finally hit me. *Wow, I was raped*. Still, I did not tell anyone other than my best friend. I mean how do you bring something like that up four years after it happened? I was still full of shame. My outlet had become alcohol and drugs, and it progressed faster and faster as the years passed.

The second time I was raped, I was fourteen and drinking pretty regularly on the weekends. We found a party spot with one of my friend's neighbors. He was twenty-eight. We were all drinking and I had a little too much and passed out. I woke up the next morning with no clothes on, and I knew something bad happened. I remember getting up and grabbing whatever clothes I could find and running out the door to my friend's house. It was early in the morning, so I had to pound on her door to wake her up, and a few other friends who were also staying over. I remember her sticking her head out the window and them all laughing at me. Whatever happened must have been witnessed because they all knew. Even though I was full of tears they were all still laughing. She would not come down to let me in, so I walked back to my house that was about six miles away. Once again, I didn't tell anyone, and I stored it deep inside.

The years passed by in the blink of an eye, and by the time I was twenty, I was a full-blown addict and alcoholic. I had also put on a lot of weight while in high school and for good reason: nobody wants the fat girl. So I was finally safe and could just be me. Fifteen years passed and I still hadn't slowed down with the drugs. It made me so numb that I didn't care about anything. I didn't have to feel any emotions. Sadly, this included the good ones.

I am now thirty-four years old and those times have haunted me through most of my life. I have been sober now for a little over three years and my healing has finally begun. It didn't begin until I let it. I have since forgiven those two men for their actions, for taking something from me I can never get back. Still I forgive them. I don't do it for them though. I do it for *me*. I am worth more than years of pain. I am worth more than years of hurt and shame. I am worth more than the torment I experienced daily. I am just worth *more*. And so are you. So are all of you. I wanted to share pieces of my story and let you know there is hope. There is happiness. There is strength. Everything that happens in this life happens for a bigger reason. You may not see it today or tomorrow, but I promise that you will see the reason. If those things had never happened to me, I would not be the person I am today. I would not be the way I am. I wouldn't care as much as I do and have so much compassion for others. I am a beautiful soul and when my life is over and I meet my maker I will stand in judgment, proud of who I am. I pray for those who have to stand in front of their maker with records like those men who raped me have.

You are a beautiful, talented young person and you have such a life in front of you. Always make the best of it. Let go of the pain. The best saying I have for that is this: holding onto resentments or pain is like drinking poison and expecting the other person to die. So let it go. Don't give them any more control over your life. No more control over your head, heart, or soul. I know we don't know each other, but I can see you. You are worth more. So please just let it go. Don't carry that pain for as long as I did. Start your life now. I am sending my love and prayers from Barberton, Ohio. Your voice is heard. Now go be the beautiful soul I know you are. And let those scumbags sit in the chaos they made. Do not sit with them. Be free.

KYLIE

It had been a month since I graduated high school when I met a guy on Facebook. We had mutual friends, so I decided to add him. We got to know each other and then met face to face with our friends, and a few weeks later he asked me to be his girlfriend. I said yes. The relationship wasn't the best. We fought a lot, broke up a lot, and he would always persuade me to come back to him. We were back together and wanted to spend the weekend together, so I went over to his house. I had spent the night with him before, so it wasn't a big deal, although I kept it from my parents, which was stupid on my part. That night I had a nightmare that he raped me. The next morning when I told him, he comforted me and took me out to breakfast. Everything seemed fine until we got back to his house and started fighting. I broke it off with him again and tried to find a way home. The only person I could find was my ex-boyfriend's mom, who would pick me up in thirty minutes. I had to wait at his house and he, like all the other times, tried to persuade me to stay. But this time he sexually assaulted me.

My ex-boyfriend's family picked me up and allowed me to stay at their house for the night. When I finally got home, I told my parents. I also told some of our mutual friends. They didn't believe me or would say that he didn't mean to do what he did. Even if he didn't mean to, I told him to stop three times and tried to push him off me but he still kept doing what he did. Some of our friends blocked me. That happened to me a year ago this month. It has been a hard year, but I feel stronger than I did the first six months after it happened. I still have nightmares about it and get panic attacks. I'm considering going back to counseling. I felt so empowered when I heard two survivors tell their stories, I try not to let my experience take over my life, but it's still hard.

LAUREN L.

If only life were all rainbows all of the time. But we can't have rainbows without a little rain (OK, a lot of rain). Before 2016, I'd really only experienced a few scattered showers, with maybe two cracks of thunder and a little lightning. Nothing too major. But then came the flood. I, once a solid brick wall, was reduced to shattered stones strewn across the bottom of a murky puddle. Every time the water began to evaporate, even more would wash in, obscuring my vision with turbid swirls of grime. I didn't know how I'd ever be clean again. I thought I would suffocate in the filth that buried me and slowly slip away into nothingness. Gone without a trace. It wasn't until the light shined down on me that I saw what I had been missing all along. It wasn't until I saw what had been right in front of me that I became unstuck from the sticky muck that held me down.

Metaphors aside, let's be real with each other. I am a high school sexual assault survivor. During my senior year of high school, at age seventeen, I was raped by a man three years older than me. To make matters worse, he sent me multiple death threats and never failed to remind me of how powerless he thought I was compared to him. Side note one: I didn't know what had actually happened to me until around three months after, so my family had no idea of what was really going on in my life. I didn't tell them until six months and three days later. So, although I wasn't alone, I felt like I was. For six months, I carried the heaviest burden I've ever had to carry on my small and weak shoulders. All on my own.

On top of that, two months after I was assaulted, I started dating a guy who I thought would "save" me from the monsters haunting me day and night. That didn't happen. Instead, he took advantage of my vulnerable state and incessantly manipulated and abused me emotionally and sexually. Side note two: It took me a long time to realize the dysfunction of the relationship, and to figure out what was wrong for the five months I was with him. I never thought I'd be a victim of sexual assault, let alone be revictimized time and time again.

After all of this, I hit rock bottom. I honestly didn't want to live anymore; I treated myself just as poorly as those two individuals did. I didn't think I deserved anything more than what had been given to me. My self-worth ceased to exist, and I just kept sinking further and further into the turbid waters. I depended on alcohol to mask my horrid thoughts and erase my memories. I swiped sharp blades across my beautiful, soft skin to release the demons swimming in my blood and to make my smooth outside match my mangled, jagged inside. I began starving myself and forcing myself to throw up after meals because I didn't think my body deserved basic care and nourishment. I stopped exercising because I didn't want to look good anymore. Maybe, just maybe, if I made myself unappealing enough no one would want to hurt me again.

It took me longer than I care to admit to realize everything I'd been telling myself was riddled with lies. Of course I deserved to have a good life—I mean, that's why I'm here, right? Alcohol just made matters worse; it doesn't erase anything, nor did it make me feel any better. Cutting my skin didn't release anything. I wish my scars could travel back in time and tell my younger self exactly that. It's OK to eat when you're hungry because food is supposed to be enjoyed. Being a victim or survivor of sexual abuse or sexual assault has nothing to do with you, including how you look. It does, however, have *everything* to do with the person who decides to take your most basic right away and violate you against your will.

I didn't just come to these realizations on my own, though. It took much coaxing and many hours of patient conversations from my family to help me know who I am in God, and I am forever thankful that they never gave up on me. By constantly pointing me back to Him, I was finally able to see His shining face and open arms. He never left my side; I just couldn't see Him fully. But now I see Him in the flowers growing along the country roads. I see Him in the grazing deer. I see Him in the sky, even when it is cloudy and gray. I delight in Him in the hurt and in the joy. And, hey, if you even *begin* to doubt how much your family loves you, remember this: my parents and sister left Florida to move to Indiana with me. No matter what you may think, your family (whether you're related by blood or by deep connection) will drop everything for you—even a well-established life in a place where everyone wishes they could be.

Please, don't give up your fight. I know you can't see the end or even the beginning of it, but trust me: God will get you to where you're meant to be. Your struggle isn't for nothing. You are not a waste of space. And you are not damaged goods. You, my friend, will change the world with your story. Just as an author chooses punctuation, use a semicolon even when you feel like a period is the better option. Stick around so you can see how the chapter only you can write will end.

MELISSA

I was sixteen at the time. I have always been chubby and quiet and kept my head in books, so any semblance of attention from a boy was like striking gold. I met him at a cosplay meet-up in the city. He was a friend of some friends, so I thought it would be fine to talk with him. He was twenty-six at the time. I was always more attracted to older men as I felt boys my age couldn't hold my attention intellectually. He was kind and funny, and although he was not that attractive, he was smart and seemed like someone I could start something with. We talked on Facebook and Skype for a few months before I decided to meet up with him in the city.

It was relatively harmless, except for a moment when we were sitting in a large grassy park area and he straddled me and started making out with me. He was so much stronger than me, so I was unable to push him off or even get him to stop kissing me. Thankfully, an older couple walked past and saw us, so he stopped and got off me. It was a little bit of a red flag, but because I was so desperate to experience something with someone for the first time (so that I could have something to talk about with my friends), I pushed it to the back of my mind and continued to hang out with him.

After a few hours, I think it was around 4:00 p.m., I was thinking of heading back to the station and going home. He asked me to go back to his place and play some video games. I asked how long and he said an hour, so I agreed.

More red flags popped up as he kept trying to distract me from seeing street names or which way we went; also, when we were in his room, I saw he had four locks on his door and he locked all of them. I relaxed my thoughts and reassured myself that it was nothing. I wish I had listened to the voice in the back of my head telling me to go.

He told me to sit back on his bed, because it was the best place to see the TV, so I did. Rather than putting a video game on, he turned on his computer and start playing one of his music playlists. I didn't say anything because I had never been in a situation like this before, so I wasn't sure what was meant to happen or how it should go. He crawled up onto the bed beside me and started kissing my neck and feeling me all over. I shakily said no a few times, but he kept reassuring me that it was fine and ignored that I felt uncomfortable and didn't want this to happen. He started to take my clothes off and told me to lay down. I tried to cover my private parts with my hands and legs, but he started kissing me again and held my hands by my sides. He started slowly kissing down my body until his head was between my thighs. I closed my thighs tightly and told him no again, shaking my head, but again he just reassured me that it was fine and pried my thighs open. He went down on me; I was so stunned with fear and confusion that I just lay there, frozen. Then he started to finger me and asked if I was a virgin because of how tight I was. I told him yes and that I felt really uncomfortable and that I didn't want this, but he just kept hushing me and reassuring me that it was fine. He came back up and started kissing and biting my neck while still fingering me. All the while my eyes were shut tightly and I was trying to transport my mind out of the current situation and distract myself from it. He stopped and sat up so that he could unzip his pants. It was the first time I had seen a penis in real life, so I was a little intrigued but also still paralyzed with fear. He grabbed my hand and put it on his penis, and he told me to start rubbing it to help it get hard. I hesitated but I knew that by now it was pointless to try to say no and get him to stop, so I just mechanically went along with what he asked so that I could get it over with quicker. Thankfully his penis was too small and too flaccid to insert into me, so he just continued to use his fingers and make out with me in an attempt to get him hard. He also sort of half grinded, half dry-humped me for twenty minutes, but he got tired and frustrated that he couldn't get it up, so he stopped and offered to put on a movie until he regained his energy to try again.

He tried two or three more times over the night. I thanked the gods that he was not successful and that I did not lose my virginity that night. In the morning he gave me back my clothes, unlocked his door, and guided me back to the main road where I could call my dad to come to pick me up and take me home.

I hadn't really told anyone about what happened until I started dating my current partner and opened up to him about it. He helped me to reach out for help and report it to the police. It was two years after it happened. I have mixed feelings about reporting, mainly because they didn't have enough evidence to take it to court. So now my family knows what happened. I'm also kind of happy that the police now know about him and have him on their radar.

The hardest part about it all is that I heard from others in my community that he has assaulted other underage girls since me. I blame myself for not reporting it sooner when I had his DNA on my body. But I'm slowly forgiving myself and trying to move on, and a big part of my recovery is thanks to my partner and his support and acceptance through the ups and downs.

I haven't run into my perpetrator again since it happened, and if I did, I'm not sure what I would do. Would I scream and verbally accuse him on the street? Would I try to hurt him as much as I could? Would I just break down and cry?

Thankfully, I never have to find out, but I also hope that someday one of his other victims will speak up and report him, and maybe even try to contact me, so that we could work together to finally get the justice that our souls need to heal.

ANONYMOUS

Unfortunately, this is not my only sexual assault experience. But it is the only one I have in high school. But I'm not 100 percent it qualifies as assault. And I know that sounds stupid. But if you read it, you will see that I said yes but I didn't mean yes. I said yes because I felt like I had no other option. My judgment was clouded by my false sense of security, my protective nature, my low self-worth, and my emotional bond to him. This piece has to deal with queer individuals (myself and him), self-worth, healing, and reframing my self-worth. High school is crazy. It is a first step toward being acknowledged in adulthood, as well as a time to find yourself. Finding yourself can be tricky because every person is different. When I was in ninth grade, I was friends with a girl who I had met through another friend. This girl identified as transgender. She was assigned female at birth (AFAB) but identified as male. So to respect transgender individuals as a group we are going to refer to them as "he." He liked me; it wasn't hard to tell. He was a grade older than me and everyone in the school knew his name because he was openly transgender and kids like to talk. One day he asked me out and I told him no, I don't date girls (AFAB). I wasn't out yet—not even to myself.

Fast forward about a year and he invites me to his Hanukkah party. I'm not Jewish, and it was just going to be just me and him. I felt bad saying no because he didn't have a lot of friends and was being so nice to me. So I went to the party, but the majority of the time was spent in his room. He sat on the bed and I sat on the floor. We sat for a while making awkward conversation and then I kissed him and immediately felt something. He was my first kiss. I had relationships in the past, but they were all with boys, and the only intimate thing to ever happen was hand-holding and hugging. I immediately felt happy. Like a real happy, something I hadn't been close to in a long time. We went and had dinner and then back to his room and continued right where we left off. This time he wanted to go further. I thought maybe he just got lost in the moment. He made a move to go further and I said no, but he didn't seem to hear, so I physically had to stop him. I said, "I don't want this." He said OK. But the next thing I know, he is making another advance for more.

And I let him do what he was trying to do.

I didn't say no that time because I was scared. It took a lot of effort to get him to stop the first time and I didn't think I would be able to stop him again. So I verbally gave him consent because I didn't feel as if I had another option. I was scared and I felt like it was safer to give my consent (even though I didn't want to) than to keep saying no, because what I wanted clearly didn't matter. He had spent the majority of his life up to that point (he was fifteen and I was fourteen) in and out of psych wards and hospitals for numerous suicide attempts. He was one of the first people I allowed myself to begin to open up to about my personal problems. I was afraid if I didn't say yes and he couldn't control himself, he would feel horrible when he realized what happened and it would cost him his life. Plus my life didn't matter to me at the time. I felt like I didn't matter so I had no right to say no.

That one night turned into two years of on-and-off dating and abuse on both sides. Even the nicest people are capable of being nasty, and we brought out the worst in each other. But that night has deeply affected me, and I am three months shy of twenty-one. I have made bad decision after bad decision with relationships and intimacy because of that night. Not only did I put someone else first, but also I made excuses for his behavior. I should have stood my ground and never said yes to something I did not want to do in order to protect him because I was hurt instead. My body is mine. Mine and mine only. I learned that day that there are times when I have to come first. *No* is a strong word and doesn't need to be explained. You are powerful even when you feel like you aren't. Never underestimate your worth and don't sacrifice your comfort, because people who truly love you would never ask you to do that.

ANGELA ROSE

The sun was shining bright on July 13, 1996, as I walked across the parking lot of a shopping mall toward my car. I was seventeen years old and had graduated high school the month before. I asked my boss if I could leave my job at the mall early that evening to attend a graduation party. My senior year of high school was a memorable one. I was a free-spirited girl with two younger sisters. I loved music, dancing, was very involved in high school theater, and much to my surprise was voted homecoming queen. I had a lot of acquaintances and one best girlfriend who was like family to me.

That fateful Saturday evening, I was walking toward my car singing out loud when something stopped me in my tracks. I felt that someone was walking behind me, so I turned around. There was a creepy-looking middle-aged man following me. I remember feeling like my cheeks turned red because I was embarrassed he had heard me singing. I felt like I should run, but I talked myself out of it. I didn't want to cause a scene or make a big deal out of nothing.

What happened in the following moments and hours completely changed the course of my life. I was kidnapped and sexually assaulted by this man. In his car, although I was physically powerless, I took control of the one thing that I could, my thoughts. I consciously catalogued details about his car and face. I spoke to him and tried to humanize myself. Several hours later, he let me go. I thought the worst was over, but I was wrong. When I went to the police station, the responding detective didn't believe me and accused me of lying. It was very retraumatizing.

Thankfully, my family and community were an incredible support network (my grandma was my rock); however, I was surprised that my very best friend stopped talking to me, and many of my friends asked me why I didn't run or get away. I began to feel like it was my fault. After the police station finally assigned new detectives to my case who were supportive and believed me, they caught my perpetrator. I learned that he was a repeat sex offender who was on parole for many crimes, including murder. I felt powerless, but I wanted to turn my pain into something positive. So I joined forces with some of his previous victims, including the mother and sister of Julie Angel, the fifteen-year-old girl he murdered.

We started a petition drive stating the need for tougher laws for repeat sex offenders. The community response was overwhelmingly positive and in a few short weeks, we gained thousands of signatures that led to a package of legislation being enacted.

During this journey, I was shocked to discover how widespread sexual assault is in our society through the countless men and women sharing their stories with me. Most people disclosed to me told me that they were hurt by someone who they knew and trusted. I felt like I had a calling.

When I went to college at the University of Wisconsin–Madison, I turned my anger into activism to help others. That's where I founded a student organization called Promoting Awareness, Victim Empowerment, or PAVE, to help prevent sexual assault and help survivors heal. I didn't want survivors to suffer in silence. We worked closely with the LGBTQ organizations on campus and the multicultural student center. I was passionate about making sure all communities felt heard.

While establishing PAVE, I still felt a sense of powerlessness and unworthiness that I funneled into creating art, film, and music. I wrote a song called "Transition to Survivor," which helped me heal. My healing journey was not a linear one. I often felt like I'd take one step forward to take two steps back. I would walk with my hand over my throat or wear scarves around my neck because he had abducted me holding a knife to my throat. When I would wash my face at night, I constantly felt like there was someone behind me. I was triggered by seeing shadows on the street or having people walk too closely behind me. At the time, I didn't realize that it was because of the abduction, though it seems so obvious to me now. I've learned that sometimes when we are in it, we can't see it.

It actually took me many years to seek professional help and counseling. I called a handful of therapists and conducted short, informational interviews because I knew what I was looking for. Faith is a huge part of my life and I needed a therapist who was holistic and inclusive of mind, body, soul. I found a trauma therapist and she introduced me to a treatment called *eye movement desensitization and reprocessing,* or EMDR. This was extremely helpful removing this invisible boulder off my chest and relieving symptoms of post-traumatic stress disorder, but it was physically exhausting. I had to practice extreme self-care after treatment and give myself permission to be extra kind to myself.

After many years, PAVE has grown into a global education and training 501(c)(3) nonprofit organization that has worked closely with the White House Task Force to Protect Students from Sexual Assault (chaired by former Vice President Joe Biden), the University of Oxford in England, and schools across the country. This was after over twenty years in the movement, though I almost gave up countless times. There were so many times when the journey felt too daunting. And then a survivor would come across my path who needed some love or guidance and it helped give me strength to help others feel like they weren't alone. I have helped guide high school survivor Chessy Prout, who wrote *I Have the Right To;* Delaney Henderson, who is in the film *Audrie & Daisy;* and Andrea Constand, who was drugged and assaulted by Bill Cosby. All of these extraordinary women and many others have become a part of my extended family.

I am passionate about self-care and have used gardening, music, and positive affirmations to feed my soul. I married my best friend, Ryan, and we have an incredible two-year-old daughter who is such a bright light in the world.

I value an attitude of gratitude—it has helped me tremendously. Louise Hay was one of my greatest mentors and she introduced me to the power of the mind–body connection. Yoga, tai chi, and other holistic modalities have been very healing for me as well. I wrote a short guide-book called *Hope, Healing and Happiness: Going Inward to Transform Your Life*. I hope you can carve out time for the things that set your soul on fire. Please give yourself permission for extreme self-care. Everyone has some aspect of trauma in their past and I want you to know that you are not alone; you are worthy, and authentic happiness can be cultivated with self-love. It's never too late to choose to heal.

Glossary of Terms

Note: The following definitions are composites of my reading and research. If I have drawn language from a particular resource, I identify it as a part of the definition.

Abusive: Characterized by physical or psychological maltreatment and violation.

Accountability: A willingness or obligation to accept responsibility for one's actions.

Acquaintance rape: Rape between two people who know each other. Also known as "date rape."

Ally: A person of one social group who stands up for members of another group, usually a member of the dominant group advocating for someone in a targeted group. Most allies work to eliminate oppressive attitudes and beliefs in themselves and others by understanding their own social privileges. If you are an ally, don't be afraid to admit when you don't know something. It's better to admit that you don't know something than to make assumptions or say something that may be mistaken or hurtful. Look for the appropriate resources that will help you learn more. Being an ally is an active practice.

Bullying: Unwanted aggressive behavior; using one's strength or influence to intimidate another into doing what they want. Bullying is repetitive and overwhelming for the victim. There are three types of bullying: verbal (saying or writing mean things); social (hurting someone's reputation or relationships); and physical (hurting a person's body or possessions).

Bystander: All of us; anyone who is not a perpetrator or victim in a given situation; this may include friends, family, teammates, teachers, peers, adults, and staff.

Clery Act: Otherwise known as the Jeanne Clery Disclosure of Campus Security Policy and Campus Crime Statistics Act. A federal law that requires higher education institutions to provide current and prospective students, employees, the public, and Department of Justice with crime statistics and information about campus crime prevention programs and policies. It requires that colleges and universities report crimes committed on campus, including sexual assault and rape. The Clery Act applies to colleges and universities, not elementary and high schools.

Consent: Permission for something to happen. An agreement.

Criminal charges: Crimes committed that could lead to potential jail or prison time, fees, and other costs. If someone is over the age of seventeen and faces criminal charges, they will be treated as an adult and the charge will be on their record permanently. Consequences for felony criminal charges can include jail time, a criminal record, probation, community service, work detail, fees, tickets, and arrest warrants.

Degrade: Treat someone with disrespect as if they are worthless or beneath consideration.

Empathy: The ability to share another person's feelings; to put yourself in someone else's shoes.

Ethical: Involving questions of right and wrong behavior. To be morally right.

Forensic interview: A trauma informed interview conducted by a qualified individual who is trained in how to be supportive of an alleged victim of sexual assault. Forensic interviews limit the amount of questioning a victim may endure to minimize the potential for retraumatization from having to recount the event(s).

Gender-based violence: A harmful act committed against a person because of their gender or sex.

Hostile: Characterized by hatred; unfriendly or antagonistic.

Incapacitated: A loss of ability to do something in the usual or desired way.

Incident: A single distinct event.

Intent: An aim or purpose in mind.

Interfere: To get involved to change or prevent something from continuing or happening.

Intimate-partner violence: Violence between individuals engaged in a sexual relationship. Also known as "dating violence" or "domestic violence."

Intimidate: To frighten or scare someone.

Investigate: To carry out an inquiry of (asking for information).

Justice: Fairness; equity.

Misdemeanor: A crime, considered less serious than a felony. Consequences for a misdemeanor usually involve a loss of privileges and/or monetary fines.

Perpetrator: Someone who has committed a crime or offense.

Post-Traumatic Stress Disorder (PTSD): A collection of long-term symptoms or long-term psychological harm from having been assaulted. PTSD can affect survivors of any trauma or horrific experience. Some symptoms may include depression, anxiety, flashbacks, substance abuse, disconnection, irrational self-blame, a preoccupation with the trauma, and difficulty concentrating and sleeping.

Predatory drugs: Drugs that are used to facilitate sexual assault. A sedative that is used by an offender with the intention of abusing the potential victim.

Predatory drugs are odorless and dissolve in liquid. They have a salty taste, so they are usually mixed into a sweetened alcoholic beverage to avoid detection. The combination of sedative and alcohol (both depressants) incapacitates whoever consumes it. Effects usually include completely impaired memory and feeling drowsy and lethargic. Many victims pass out or are incapable of resisting sexual assault. Some common predatory drugs include Rohypnol, ketamine, GHB, and Xanax. It is important to remember that alcohol is considered the most common and oldest predatory drug. Also known as "date-rape drugs."

Rape: Nonconsensual sexual behavior that usually includes some form of penetration of a bodily orifice. The legal definition of rape can vary from state to state.

Rape culture: According to Marshall University Women's Center website, it is "an environment in which rape is prevalent and in which sexual violence against women is normalized and excused in the media and popular culture." Rape culture is perpetuated through the use of misogynistic language, the objectification of women's bodies, and the glamorization of sexual violence, thereby creating a society that disregards women's rights and safety. Some examples include victim-blaming, trivializing sexual assault, tolerating sexual harassment, inflating false reporting statistics, pressuring men to "score," pressuring women to submit and be warm and welcoming, refusing to take rape accusations seriously, assuming that men do not get raped or that only "weak" men get raped, and teaching women how not to be raped instead of teaching men not to rape.

Rape kit: A kit used to collect DNA evidence from a victim's body, clothes, and other personal belongings. Is used at a medical facility, usually an emergency room, during a forensic sexual assault exam. You don't have to report a crime to have the exam. What's in the rape kit varies among states and jurisdictions.

It may contain checklists, materials, instructions, envelopes, packages, and containers for any specimens collected during the exam.

Rohypnol: Also called a "roofie." A sedative that is used to facilitate rape. It is not legally available in the United States. Known as a "date-rape drug" or "predatory drug."

Sexting: Sending sexually explicit images and messages via digital device, including text messages and social media platforms.

Sexual assault: A form of sexual violence. Any kind of nonconsensual sexual behavior during which a person is coerced or forced against their will. It includes any kind of nonconsensual sexual touching and any kind of oral, vaginal, or anal penetration.

Sexual violence: A sexual act committed against someone without that person's freely given consent.

Stalking: Unwanted or obsessive pursuit of a previous, current, or desired sex partner by an individual or group in such a way that the victim is in a state of fear. Stalking behaviors are similar to harassment and intimidation.

Statutory rape: Sexual intercourse with a person willing or unwilling who is below the age of consent according to the applicable statute. Those laws may include but aren't limited to sexual assault, sexual assault of a minor, child molestation, rape of a child, and sexual misconduct. These laws are meant to protect minors from being taken advantage of sexually by adults.

Survivors: Individuals who have been raped or sexually assaulted. Many of these individuals and their advocates prefer to use *survivor* versus *victim* because it's more empowering.

Title IX: Title IX of the Education Amendments of 1972 is a federal civil rights law that protects people from discrimination based on sex in education programs or activities that receive federal financial assistance. Title IX states: "No person in the United States shall, on the basis of sex, be excluded from participation in, be denied the benefits of, or be subjected to discrimination under any education program or activity receiving federal financial assistance." Title IX protects all people regardless of gender identity, race, religion, sexual orientation, national origin, age, disability, or undocumented status. Many people hold the misconception that Title IX only applies to student athletics; however, this is incorrect. The law prohibits gender discrimination in all educational activities, which includes everything from sexual assault to opportunities in math and science.

Trigger: A stimulus in thought, word, or action that evokes a physiological or psychological response, such as a racing heart, feeling of wanting to escalate and fight, or an urge to turn around and run away.

Victim: Someone who has been the target of a crime.

Victim-blaming: When the victim of a crime or any misconduct is held entirely or partially responsible for the wrong that happened to them.

Assaulted

What You and Your Child Need to Know if They Are Assaulted

WHAT TO DO IF YOUR TEENAGER IS ASSAULTED—HOW TO HELP YOUR CHILD
(Adapted from PAVE)

As parents, we all want the best for our kids and do what we can to keep them safe. No one expects that their child will be sexually assaulted, and research shows that it can happen to any family. When you first hear of the assault, it's normal to feel enraged that someone hurt your child, and it's important for the focus to be on the survivor's emotions. It is also common to experience self-blame, but remember that sexual assault is not your fault or your child's fault. Studies show that the first person a survivor discloses to can have a tremendous impact on their healing process. As parents, it's possible that you will be that person—the first conversation is important. Here are some guidelines to support your and your teenager's journey to healing.

Be Aware

- Different people experience and respond to trauma in different ways. During an assault, humans respond with fight, flight, or freeze. Some may fight back effectively, some may resist in habitual passive ways, and some may suddenly give in and cry. The most common, however, is the freeze instinct, or *tonic immobility*, which is a simple survival behavior and causes the body to become very still, rigid, and silent. The person may become paralyzed, faint, pass out, or dissociate.

- Depending on how a survivor responds neurologically to fear, memory can also be impacted. Memory may be fragmented or sensory-specific. This can make a victim seem like they are lying when that's not the case.

- Each person reacts differently to trauma, but here are some common reactions that may occur: nightmares or flashbacks, withdrawal or isolation, going numb or flooded with emotions, self-harm, bed-wetting, PTSD, suicidal thoughts, eating disorders, and alcohol or drug abuse.

- An assault can emotionally affect you and other family members as well. It's important to practice self-care and seek support for yourself and other family members if needed while supporting your child's recovery.

What to do

- Believe them. Use a phrase like "I believe you and am here for you" or "I'm glad you've come to me to tell me." Make sure they know that you don't think what happened was their fault.

- Ask what your child would like to share. Remember, assault is a disempowering experience; we want survivors to feel they can have autonomy as they navigate their process. Use open-ended questions and their comfort level to guide the conversation. Avoid interrogation or blame.

- Empower them to make their own choices by offering options and resources like therapeutic counseling or reporting or getting medical attention to document and collect evidence in case they want to report to law enforcement.

- Lean into the trust, love, and support you feel for your family.

What not to do

- Ask excessive questions about what they were doing, what they were wearing, if they were drinking, or why they didn't fight back or call for help. This can come across as victim-blaming.
- Decide for your child that they have to report, get counseling, or go to a medical facility without talking to them first. It is critical to the recovery process that survivors feel they have control over their own healing.
- Ask about your teenager's previous sexual activities. This can also come across as if you're blaming your teen for the assault.

FOR TEENAGERS: WHAT TO DO IF YOU ARE SEXUALLY ASSAULTED

Sexual assault can be scary and traumatic. You may feel scared, emotionally numb, depressed, angry, sad, confused, or a whole range of other emotions. It may be hard to try to figure out what you should say or do after an assault. You may feel disoriented and confused about what to do. Know that you are not alone. Here are some options for ways to take care of and to protect yourself. However, it is most important to trust your instincts and do what will make you feel safe and secure.

- Get yourself to a safe place
- If you intend on filing a police report, or if you might want to in the

future, the Rape, Abuse & Incest National Network (RAINN) recommends for the purpose of evidence collection that you:

> » Do not shower
>
> » Do not use the restroom
>
> » Do not dispose of clothes worn when the assault occurred
>
> » Do not comb your hair
>
> » Do not clean up the crime scene
>
> » Do not move anything the offender may have touched

- Whether or not there was a completed rape, consider calling the police or seeking medical attention. You can also tell a school officer, teacher, or administrator.

- Emergency rooms and sexual assault clinics provide free rape kits and resources for emotional support for sexual assault survivors. Bring a change of clothes for after the kit is done during a medical exam. The doctors and nurses who do the exam are usually well trained in sensitivity and support for sexual assault survivors. If you don't do this and then decide you want to later, depending on the time lapse, a rape kit can still be done; evidence collection is possible.

- If the perpetrator is an acquaintance, tell someone you trust what happened.

- If the perpetrator is a stranger, try to remember their appearance, clothes, details, and other people who may be able to identify them.

- Some people believe that if they froze or didn't fight back, they will be blamed. People should understand that the rape victim's main concern is to survive. Perpetrators can be successfully prosecuted without evidence that the victim fought back, even if there was no weapon involved.

- If you are on a college campus, consider reporting through Callisto, a nonprofit organization that provides technology designed to detect repeat perpetrators and empower survivors to make a reporting decision that provides different choices. In an online system that protects the survivor's anonymity, Callisto Campus offers three options: save time-stamped written records of sexual assault, report only if another victim reports the same perpetrator, and report directly to campus administrators without waiting for a match. Callisto Expansion enables survivors to identify their perpetrator with the precondition that if there is a match, a Callisto counselor will reach out to the victims separately and advise them on their reporting options in person.

- If you don't report the assault right after it happens, do so as soon as you can. The passage of time does not make the crime less serious.

- Access resources such as: PAVE, RAINN, and Culture of Respect. LGBTQ and transgender survivors, use End Rape on Campus, FORGE, and STAND in PRIDE, which is a collaboration of Community Violence Solutions, Rainbow Community Center, and STAND! For Families Free of Violence.

- Contact a sexual assault or rape crisis center or hotline: 800–656-HOPE (4673). They can provide expert advice and understanding in a confidential way. Seeking help is the best way to get in front of long-lasting trauma.

- There are a few books that may be helpful:

    » *The Sexual Healing Journey: A Guide for Survivors of Sexual Abuse* by Wendy Maltz

    » *Hope, Healing and Happiness: Going Inward to Transform Your Life* by Angela Rose

    » *Healing Sex: A Mind-Body Approach to Healing Sexual Trauma* by Staci Haines

WHAT TO DO IF SOMEONE YOU KNOW IS SEXUALLY ASSAULTED— HOW TO HELP A FRIEND

(Adapted from KnowYourIX.org and CultureOfRespect.org)

- Believe them. The most simple yet most overlooked thing one can do is to believe the survivor confiding in you. Validate their feelings about the assault and be mindful of your tone. If you sound doubtful, your friend will feel unsupported.

- Put them at ease. Let them know that you are there for them and receptive to what they are sharing with you.

- Tell your friend what happened to them was not their fault and that they didn't deserve it.

- Provide resources. You can suggest looking up your school's sexual assault policies and resource centers. You can help them find your school's advocate services as well. You can also suggest these resources to consider and figure out what they'd like to do. Each has information for how to help a friend who has been assaulted as well as information for survivors and their options:

  » PAVE

  » End Rape on Campus

  » Culture of Respect

  » RAINN

  » Know Your IX

  » National Sexual Violence Resource Center

  » Sexual Assault Hotline: 800–656-HOPE

- Empower them. Let your friend know they are in complete control over any next steps. How they proceed is entirely up to them.

- Accompany them. Offer to go with your friend or give them a ride to where they'd like to go. Ask if they need somewhere to stay or any other emotional support. It is not recommended that someone who has just been assaulted stay alone.

- Offer to help them find your school's victim advocate services. In high school, this may be a trusted teacher, school counselor, dean, or Title IX coordinator. In college, this may be the same or your school may have a resource center specifically for survivors of assault.

- Express admiration for their courage and recognize how difficult this must have been for them.

- You can also tell them about a few books that may be helpful:
  - » *The Sexual Healing Journey: A Guide for Survivors of Sexual Abuse* by Wendy Maltz
  - » *Hope, Healing and Happiness: Going Inward to Transform Your Life* by Angela Rose
  - » *Healing Sex: A Mind-Body Approach to Healing Sexual Trauma* by Staci Haines

- Continue to show support and care for your friend. This may mean listening to them talk about their experience with the assault or taking them out to spend time together and engage in activities that are enjoyable and not related to the assault. Make sure you respond to their needs. Remember that you don't have to do this alone and that you can encourage your friend to seek professional support through various resources.

- Be strong and take care of yourself as well.

Accused

What You and Your Child Need to Know if They Are Accused

WHAT TO DO IF YOUR TEENAGER IS ACCUSED OF SEXUAL ASSAULT

As parents, we all want to raise our kids to be good people, and sometimes our kids make mistakes, do bad things, and get themselves in trouble. If this happens, it is important to take responsibility legally and therapeutically. There can be severe legal consequences that aren't necessarily fair, from our perspective, relative to the crime committed. It's important to know that some sexual crimes are treated as misdemeanors and some as felonies. Sexual violence violates our humanity and should be addressed seriously.

If your teenager is accused of sexual misconduct, a good place to start is your local public defender's office. Some offices have a designated attorney who fields phone calls, provides guidance, and answers questions. If you make money beyond the limit that qualifies your family for a public defender, you may be referred to the state bar to find a private criminal attorney; however, in some states, the office thinks no minor can make an amount of money that would exempt them from services and they are the client, so it's not an issue.

If you seek private legal counsel, source your community and ask around for a highly recommended attorney who can give legal advice. Research your options and look at reviews and recommendations.

You will want a lawyer who practices juvenile law in your local jurisdiction and might specialize in criminal law as well. It can be advantageous to have an attorney who practices in the courts of the jurisdiction where the accusation and alleged crime took place. Knowing local prosecutors and judges may be helpful.

Remember:

- As far as constitutional rights and due process, your child has the right to counsel and the right to remain silent.
- Do not make a statement without an attorney present. In some counties, the police must contact the public defender's office if the alleged perpetrator is a minor. The police may not interview a minor without an attorney present. Some public defender offices have attorneys on standby 24/7 for such interviews.

Juvenile proceedings are closed to the public, except for serious offenses. If a juvenile is found guilty of a crime, the issue of which records are sealed and which are not can be complex. It does not just depend on the charge, but the age at which they were found to have committed the crime, as well as how the teen did while on probation. If they are eighteen or older, the court proceedings and records are open and public.

As discussed in this book, sexual misconduct doesn't discriminate. It can take place in all communities and demographics. However, when a case is investigated and enters the criminal justice system, a variety of political identities may influence the process of finding truth and justice.

It's important that your teenager (as well as you and other family members, if needed) seek counseling. Going through legal proceedings is challenging. It is essential to find therapeutic support, not only to manage the stress of navigating the juvenile or criminal justice system, but also to address the sexual well-being of your teenager.

Getting It Right

Practice Scenarios for You and Your Teen

Now that you've read the book, you have the information you need to discuss and assess hypothetical situations with your teenager. This practice of applying information to the complexities of social situations supports a deeper understanding. Let your teenager drive the cadence and depth of your discussions. Remember to create a context free of judgment, shame, and blame. And scaffold smaller conversations over time, so that each of them can be an opportunity to explore and infuse the values you hope to reinforce.

DECONSTRUCTION GUIDELINES

- Identify the power dynamics between and among individuals. To guide teens through this, you may ask: Is one of the characters older than the other? Who has more social power based on the information given? Is anyone incapacitated? Is anyone vulnerable because of current relationships or emotions?

- Identify and discuss the emotional and physical risks of the situation. You may ask: What is at stake for the people involved? What are the potential consequences (positive and negative) should the scenario continue?

- Identify and discuss ethical and moral considerations. You may ask: Is there a moral quandary here? Are any values at stake? Is anything ethically wrong with this situation? What do you think the right thing to do is?

- Assess if the sexual activity throughout the scenario is consensual. Why or why not? An essential question to ask: If it is not consensual, how might the outcome change if behavior changed? What could be done to establish a healthy, reciprocal, and consensual outcome? If it is consensual, when and how was consent communicated? Encourage teenagers to use concrete examples from the scenario to illustrate their thinking.

- You may then ask: Is the sexual interaction ethical? If not, what would it take to get there? Is the sexual interaction "good?" If not, what would it take to get there?

Most teenagers think the options for dealing with these scenarios are obvious. It is effective to acknowledge the worst outcome, the ideal outcome, and then the most realistic outcome. The most realistic outcome is the one to emphasize because it is the most probable. Identify and discuss what can get in the way of the most positive and realistic outcome. Encourage teenagers to "keep it real" when discussing what happens. Remind them that while people typically know what they *should* do, it doesn't always play out that way. The important questions then are why and what measures could have been taken to avoid the situation, or at least the severity of it.

SCENARIOS

1. Casey and Riley are lab partners in chemistry class. They are focused and productive, as well as flirty. Riley confides that he's going to a party on Saturday and he's hoping a certain person he's interested in will be there. Casey encourages him to go for it, but Riley doubts this person feels the same way. Casey says, "Oh, come on, anyone would go out with you." Two weeks later, Casey gets up to go to the restroom. While Casey washes her hands at the sink, someone enters. It's Riley. Surprised, Casey asks, "What are you doing in here?" Riley doesn't say anything, just walks forward, corners Casey against the wall, and starts to aggressively kiss and feel her up. Casey is shocked, starts to squirm, and pushes him away. She says, "Cut it out. Stop!" Riley backs off, smiles, and says, "Tease," and walks out. Casey returns to class and feels Riley's eyes follow her as she sits down. She doesn't want to be in class with him anymore but doesn't want to make a report and have to deal with the social scrutiny. What might she do?

2. Aidan and Steve are on the same track team at the same high school. During practice, the two run a grueling 400-meter sprint. After the finish, Aidan hunches over with his hands on his knees to catch his breath. Suddenly someone grabs his butt from behind. He exclaims, "What the fuck?" He turns around and sees Steve standing there grinning. Aidan straightens up and says, "What the hell, dude? Uncool." Steve winks, laughs it off, and walks away. Steve continues to make quiet sexual comments in passing to Aidan. Aidan feels angry and wants Steve to stop. He's afraid rumors will fly about his sexuality. What might he do?

3. Lydia is a senior teaching assistant in Drake's sophomore American

history class. She offers to help Drake with his paper after school since he is struggling with his thesis. Drake agrees. Lydia offers her house as a place to work. While working on the paper, Lydia is physically closer than usual to Drake. Her touch lingers on his arm when she wants his attention and she's flirty when they break to eat. After they edit his paper, Lydia leans into Drake's space and directly asks, "So now you wanna hook up?" Drake explains that he better not—he has a girlfriend. Lydia sits on Drake's lap and says, "No one will know—we'll keep it between us." Drake squirms a bit and stammers that he better go. Lydia's expression is mischievous, and her eyes get big. "Ooooh, are you scared?" "Nah, I just gotta go. See you at school. Thanks for the help." For the next few weeks in class, whenever Lydia circulates among the students, she brushes Drake's shoulder with her finger or manages to whisper a seductive "hey" in his ear. Drake just keeps his head down and excuses himself to the restroom whenever he sees her approaching. He really wants Lydia to stop but doesn't know what to do. He is stressed that his girlfriend will think he brought this on and that his friends will call him a "puss" for not wanting a senior girl's attention. What might he do?

4. Breena goes to a different high school than Daisy. She gets Daisy's Snap from a friend of a friend, Lorena. Breena Snaps Daisy "hey whats up." Daisy recognizes Breena from a birthday party for Lorena and responds with "hey." Breena comes back with "so i hear ridgemont girls are freaky." Daisy leaves Breena unread for about fifteen minutes. Breena Snaps again "down to hu." Daisy leaves this one unread as well. Breena responds with "what so now ur not responding," and then "bitch." Breena starts Snapping Daisy random photos and comments. Daisy wants to block Breena but knows she'll see her at

parties and worries she may make a scene or spread rumors. What might she do?

5. Elliot has returned to his high school to teach English and coach soccer. He is twenty-six, and Lena, a sophomore, is in his advisory group. The group gets together in Elliot's classroom for pizza or doughnuts during break or lunch. Someone discovers Elliot's old yearbooks and starts to share photos. The girls are talking about how hot he was, and the boys are teasing him about how ripped he is in the photo on his senior page. Lena thinks he's still incredibly good-looking and jokes with her girlfriends about how amazing it would be to date someone like him. Lena meets with Elliot often after school for tutoring. Elliot's attention feels good. Lena can't believe it when he starts to tell her how beautiful and great she is—that he's never met anyone like her before. Some days Elliot can't meet after school, so he invites Lena to his apartment to work in the evenings. Before Lena knows it, she and Elliot are engaged in a sexual relationship. Elliot makes sure Lena knows how important it is to keep their "study sessions" secret; otherwise, he won't be able to continue teaching at their school and they'll no longer be together. Lena confides in her friend, Bridget, who is concerned and knows what's happening isn't right. What might Bridget do?

6. Mia is at a residential academic summer camp on a college campus. All the students are getting to know each other through their classes. Daniel comes off as a bit different; he's seen as quirky or weird. He acts younger than a typical seventeen-year-old, so when he draws cartoon characters or acts immature, the other kids make comments and make fun of him. They'll say, "Why are you acting like a five-year-old?" or "Why do you always have to be so loud?" Mia sees the mean

behavior and tries to stop it from happening. Soon Daniel starts to follow Mia back to her dorm and the cafeterias and restaurants she goes to with friends and stares at her at dances. Mia tells the resident counselor, who informs Daniel that he needs to give Mia her space and leave her alone. Daniel's behavior doesn't change. After two weeks of this, Daniel is waiting outside of Mia's dorm room and approaches her. "You're the most beautiful girl I've ever met. I just want to be friends and talk to you." Mia is uncomfortable and scared. What might she do?

7. Monika is good friends with her ex-boyfriend Mike's best friend, Jason. They are still all in the same friend group because Monika and Mike's breakup was friendly. Monika and Jason spend a lot of time together and she finds herself getting a lot closer to Jason and being sexually attracted to him as well. There have even been a couple of times when they've been alone together and just know that they should get together but haven't because of Monika's history and Jason's friendship with Mike. What might they do?

8. Ellie and Clarke dated for a year but broke up because Clarke went to college. They continue to love each other and are still together when he returns home. They both hook up with other people, and Ellie has been hooking up with Lily while Clarke is gone. Ellie and Lily have a good time hooking up. They keep it casual because they're both seniors and just want a physical relationship; however, Lily starts to develop feelings for Ellie. Ellie and Lily talk about it. It turns out that Lily really likes Ellie, too, and thinks they should be exclusive. Ellie feels torn because she still feels love for Clarke. How should Ellie handle it?

9. Lila is a freshman. A junior boy keeps Snapchatting her. At first it's

two to three times a day, then it escalates to more and within a week, it's ten times a day. Lila's not really sure why he keeps doing it and she's a little freaked out. She doesn't want to tell anyone because the junior is actually pretty popular and she feels like it could be a joke. What might she do?

10. Linda is a high school sophomore and has recently come out as gay. She is at an outdoor concert with her older sister, Gabby, and Gabby's senior friends. They have all been drinking. They run into Alexa, also a senior, who is with some other people. Alexa identifies as bisexual and recently heard that Linda has come out. Alexa invites Linda to go smoke with her away from their friends. About fifty feet away from the group, Alexa starts to intimately touch Linda. Gabby's friend, Sophia, can see them in the distance and notices that Linda looks awkward and isn't really responding to Alexa, who is all over her. Sophia is worried and wants to intervene. What might she do?

11. Elizabeth's friend has been talking to a guy from Omegle (a website that allows you to chat with a random stranger) for a while now. She's fifteen and he's nineteen. It turns out he lives in her area so after a couple weeks of chatting with him on Omegle, she gets coffee with him. She tells Elizabeth that she's interested in him romantically and she thinks he's interested in her. Eventually, she starts going to hang out at his apartment. Every time she goes, she lies to her parents by saying she's going to another friend's house. Last night, she stayed the night at his house for the first time and she tells Elizabeth that they showered together. She doesn't say exactly how far they've gone, but Elizabeth is concerned about it because the guy sounds sketchy. What might Elizabeth do?

12. Brianna's mom is friends with Claire's mom. Brianna and Claire aren't

that close, but they hang out from time to time and are connected on Facebook. Brianna's mom asks Brianna to bring up Claire's Facebook page. She wants to see something. Brianna tells her she won't until she tells her why. Brianna's mom brings up the deal they have that at any time she wants to see Brianna's page, she can. Brianna pushes back by saying it isn't her page, it's her friend's page. Brianna's mom tells her that Claire's mom asked if she would do some "research" because Claire's mom heard from another parent that Claire posted some really compromising photos of herself. Brianna's mom threatens consequences. What might Brianna do?

13. Andrea, a sophomore, has an older sibling in the senior class, so she gets invited to upperclassmen parties. She starts hooking up with a senior guy who's really sweet and respectful. He's easygoing and never pressures her. They've also had lunch off campus a couple of times together. The two are texting about plans to meet at a party on Friday night, and he texts "how about a preview of our night together?" with a winky face emoji. Her friend Kalani is over doing homework and Andrea asks what she thinks he's asking for. Kalani's pretty sure Andrea knows, but tells her it's obvious that he's looking for a nude. Kalani warns her about the potential consequences. Andrea swears that he's a good guy and that she trusts him and that he'll just keep it for himself. Andrea asks Kalani to take the photo and reassures Kalani that the guy will delete it right after he sees it. Kalani doesn't believe it. What might she do?

14. Bethany and her friends want to score some weed for the weekend. She hears that a guy she kind of knows, TJ, can hook her up and gets his number from a friend.

Bethany: "hey whats up"

TJ: "wu"

Bethany: "i hear u hv access to weed"

TJ: "yeah i can get it for u what do u want how many grams"

Bethany: "a dime bag"

TJ: "instead of paying me how about a couple of nudes"

Bethany: "nah i don't want that going public"

TJ: "its cool dont worry ill keep em to my phone"

Bethany sends a couple of nudes.

TJ: "lets meet at mine tomorrow afternoon"

Bethany: "am good with the weed"

TJ: "were gonna meet and if you don't blow me im gonna make you a star"

Bethany leaves TJ unread to source a friend for advice.

TJ: "you'll want to be sure none of this goes public bitch"

Bethany is scared that TJ will post her pictures but doesn't want to give him a blow job. What might she do?

15. Marina and Steve have been going out and are both part of a larger group of friends who do a lot together. Nick is also part of the group, and the three of them have been having a lot of fun talking—there seems to be a connection. Steve goes up to Tahoe one weekend. Marina and Nick end up at a party together and hang out. Marina brings up the chemistry they seem to have. Nick agrees, and they have a conversation about the fact that they're attracted to each other. They also talk about Steve and not wanting to piss him off or hurt him. Marina suggests they could hook up—just a little bit—just to see if they connect "that way" too. She suggests they keep it between the two of them so that Steve doesn't get hurt. If it doesn't feel right, they could just go back to being friends. Then Steve wouldn't get

hurt. If they really have something together then they would know and could come up with the best way to tell Steve together. What might they do?

16. Marta is a mature-looking freshman. She dresses within the school dress code. Her personality isn't particularly dramatic. Every time she walks past some upperclassmen boys, she senses they are talking about her in hushed voices. Recently on Facebook, Marta's feed shows that images with her have been tagged by a bunch of different people as "Deep C" (referring to her cleavage). Marta knows lots of others see this, too, but no one says anything. It makes Marta self-conscious and she is anxious about going back to school. What might she do?

17. Tony and Caitlyn have been in a relationship for a little over a year. They love each other and have included sexual intercourse as a part of their sexual activity for the past six months. Caitlyn has never had an orgasm. She'd like to but isn't sure how to bring it up with Tony— she doesn't want to embarrass him or make him feel inadequate. How might she approach the conversation?

18. Justin and Mack are both seniors who have been secretly hooking up for months. It usually happens when they are drunk after a party. Their hookups are mostly make out sessions and grinding on each other. For the most part, clothes stay on. The last few times they've hung out, Justin has tried to go further than Mack is comfortable with, saying, "Trust me. This will feel great," while trying to undo Mack's pants. Mack can't talk to any friends and family about what's happening and is worried that if he brings it up with Justin, he'll get upset and out him at school. How should Mack approach the situation?

19. Jhalisa and Patricia have been in a casual relationship for a couple of months. Things progressed pretty quickly. They spent a lot of time together, would sleep together a couple of times a week, and have become very emotionally involved in each other's lives. Jhalisa decides that things have gotten too serious, and she tells Patricia that she wants to dial things back, hang out less, and only have a sexual relationship. While Patricia likes Jhalisa and wants to continue seeing her, she's worried that she can't have a relationship that is strictly sexual without the emotional intimacy. She knows that she told Jhalisa in the beginning that she was totally down for a casual relationship, but she isn't so sure now. She feels like she will be judged as lame or uncool if she says no to Jhalisa, and she doesn't want to lose her. What might she do?

20. Jasmine and Erik recently matched on Tinder and text for a few weeks before deciding to meet in person. While discussing what they want to do, Erik brings up that he wants to hook up with her. Jasmine is up for it and they plan to meet the next day. Meanwhile, they text about what turns them on sexually and what they want to do. The two agree that they will meet at Jasmine's, a two-hour drive for Erik. When Erik gets to Jasmine's house, they immediately start making out. As things progress, the two decide to have intercourse. During sex, Jasmine starts to feel uncomfortable and isn't getting much out of it. Jasmine wants to say something but feels guilty because Erik drove two hours to see her and they already agreed on what was going to happen. What might Jasmine do?

21. Nick is at a party at the fraternity house he is hoping to join. He and the other pledges were told to keep it quiet because they aren't members yet and underage drinking is not allowed. At the party,

there is punch available on the main floor of the house where there are a couple of poker tables and couches. The kegs and a ping-pong table are down in the basement. The music is loud and the house is packed. Nick is in the basement and sees frat members and others rallying each other as they play drinking games, throw back shots, and drink beer. As a pledge, Nick and his fellow pledges really shouldn't be there, so they are nursing their drinks on the far side of the room against the wall. People are getting sloppy drunk very quickly. Nick sees a girl on the far side of the room who is wasted. She is leaning up against a post and a fraternity brother, Mike, is in her space. His arm is around her waist; he's holding her up while talking to her. Mike leads her upstairs as she stumbles. Nick's pledge brother says, "Man, I bet he's going to tap that." Nick doesn't feel right about what's happening with the girl. What might he do?

22. Alex and Tatum walk out of the college library together at 10:30 p.m., after a study group finishes. It is quiet and dark except for the lit pathways across the quad. Alex veers off of the path to cut across the lawn toward the dorms. Tatum walks in the opposite direction. In the distance, Alex hears some noise and turns to see a group of drunk students. They are rowdy, loud, and have come across Tatum. Alex recognizes one of them. Alex sees that they enthusiastically greet Tatum and invite him to join them. Alex checks the time and wants to get back to meet friends who are going out. Someone in the group grabs Tatum's arm and says, "Aw, come on, have some fun." Tatum says, "No thanks, I really need to get back," and tries to walk away, but is cut off by someone in the group. Another starts to push at Tatum's shoulder so that Tatum is moving with them. Another pokes at Tatum's midsection and says, "'No thanks?' Come on, let's have

fun." They are all howling and laughing and pushing Tatum back and forth and grabbing at Tatum's body. Alex gets a text from a friend: "You coming? Time to go." Alex looks up one last time. Tatum makes an effort to get away again, but they keep pulling him into their small circle. Alex knows he should do something but is eager to meet his friends. What might he do?

23. Jake and Tim are both part of the Gay-Straight Alliance/Gender-Sexuality Alliance on their college campus. Jake is a freshman and Tim is a senior. They are friendly at the meetings and have partici-pated in a couple of awareness-raising events together. Tim lives in a junior–senior dorm, where his suitemates are having a small party. Tim invites Jake and tells him to be low-key about coming and to use the back entrance because freshmen aren't allowed to attend get-togethers where there's alcohol. Jake arrives and there's a bunch of people kicking back and drinking in the lounge. Tim hands Jake a drink. The two are hanging out with a few others, and it is obvious that there is some sexual tension between Tim and Jake. Later, after only two beers, while Jake is talking to a couple of girls, he is floored and can't seem to get up from his chair. An overwhelming heaviness sets in. Jake is confused because he knows he didn't drink that much. Tim comes over to join in and says, "Hey, man, you're looking pretty trashed, you want to crash in my room?" Jake manages to say, "Nah, I'm good, I'm going to head out." One of the girls, Daniella, offers to walk Jake back and helps him stand. Tim intervenes, supports Jake under his arm, and says "It's cool. I got this" to the girl and takes Jake into his room across the hall and shuts the door. Daniella doesn't think Jake can consent to anything and hopes Tim wouldn't take advantage of him sexually, but something tells her he might. What might she do?

Endnotes

1　Nagoski, Emily. *Come As You Are: The Surprising New Science That Will Transform Your Sex Life*. New York: Simon & Schuster, 2015, 154.

2　Waldinger, Robert. "What makes a good life? Lessons from the longest study on happiness." Video file. November 2015. https://www.ted.com/talks/robert _waldinger_what_makes_a_good_life_lessons_from_the_longest_study_on _happiness?language=enhttps://www.ted.com/talks/robert_waldinger_what _makes_a_good_life_lessons_from_the_longest_study_on_happiness.

3　Ward, L. M., and J. S. Aubrey, 2017. *Watching Gender: How Stereotypes in Movies and on TV Impact Kids' Development*. San Francisco, CA: Common Sense.

4　Pierce, Cindy. *Sexploitation: Helping Kids Develop Healthy Sexuality in a Porn-Driven World*. N.p.: Routledge, 2016, 166.

5　Ibid., 134.

6　Pornhub Year in Review 2017. Pornhub. https://www.pornhub.com/ insights/2017-year-in-review.

7　Cooper A, C. R. Scherer, S. C. Boies, B. L. Gordon. "Sexuality and the Internet: Surfing into the New Millennium." *Cyberpsychology and Behavior* 1, no. 2 (1998): 181–7.

8　Kerner, Ian. "When and How Should You Talk to Your Kids About Sex in the Age

of Internet Porn?" *Good in Bed* (blog). Entry posted August 2012. https://www
.goodinbed.com/blogs/sex_doctors/2012/08/when-and-how-should-you-talk-to
-your-kids-about-sex-in-the-age-of-internet-porn/

9   Jones, Maggie. "What Teenagers Are Learning from Online Porn." *New York Times
    Magazine*, February 7, 2018. https://www.nytimes.com/2018/02/07/magazine/
    teenagers-learning-online-porn-literacy-sex-education.htm.

10   Sabina, C., J. Wolak, D. Finkelhor. "The Nature and Dynamics of Internet Pornog-
    raphy Exposure for Youth." *Cyberpsychology and Behavior* 11, no. 6 (2018):
    691–693. https://scholars.unh.edu/cgi/viewcontent.cgi?referer=&httpsredir
    =1&article=1283&context=soc_facpub.

11   Leahy, Michael. *Porn University: What College Students Are Really Saying About Sex
    on Campus.* Chicago: Northfield Publishing, 2009.

12   Jones, Maggie. "What Teenagers Are Learning from Online Porn." *New York Times
    Magazine.* February 7, 2018. https://www.nytimes.com/2018/02/07/magazine/
    teenagers-learning-online-porn-literacy-sex-education.html.

13   Braun-Courville, Debra K. and Mary Rojas, "Exposure to Sexually Explicit Web
    Sites and Adolescent Sexual Attitudes and Behaviors," *Journal of Adolescent Health*
    45 (2009): 156–162.

14   Nagoski, Emily. "Is Porn Addiction for Real?" *Good in Bed* (blog). Entry
    posted December 2014. https://www.goodinbed.com/sex_nerd/2014/12/
    is-porn-addiction-for-real/.

15   Weissbourd, Richard, Trisha Ross Anderson, Alison Cachin, and Joe McIntyre.
    *The Talk: How Adults Can Promote Young People's Healthy Relationships and prevent
    Misogyny and Sexual Harassment.* Cambridge, MA: Harvard Graduate School of
    Education, 2014. https://mcc.gse.harvard.edu/files/gse-mcc/files/mcc_the_talk
    _final.pdf.

16   Pierce, Cindy. *Sexploitation: Helping Kids Develop Healthy Sexuality in a Porn-Driven
    World.* N.p.: Routledge, 2016, 94.

17   Orenstein, Peggy. *Girls and Sex: Navigating the Complicated New Landscape*. London, England: Oneworld Publications, 2016, 72.

18   Nagoski, Emily. "How Does a Fetish Develop?" *Good in Bed* (blog). Entry posted December 2014. https://www.goodinbed.com/sex_nerd/2014/12/how-does-a-fetish-develop/.

19   Pierce, Cindy. *Sexploitation: Helping Kids Develop Healthy Sexuality in a Porn-Driven World*. N.p.: Routledge, 2016, 145.

20   Weissbourd, Rick. *The Parents We Mean to Be: How Well-intentioned Adults Undermine Children's Moral and Emotional Development*. Boston: Houghton Mifflin Harcourt, 2009, 38.

21   Ibid., 2.

22   Ibid., 44.

23   Nagoski, Emily. *Come As You Are: The Surprising New Science That Will Transform Your Sex Life*. New York: Simon & Schuster, 2015.

24   "Facts and Statistics—National Sex Offender Public Website." http://www.nsopw.gov/en/Education/FactsStatistics.

25   Ibid.

26   Ibid.

27   Anderson, Nick and Scott Clement. "College Sexual Assault: 1 in 5 College Women Say They Were Violated." *Washington Post*, June 12, 2015. Krebs, C. P., C. H. Lindquist, T. D. Warner, B. S. Fisher, and S. L. Martin. *The Campus Sexual Assault (CSA) Study*. Washington, DC: National Institute of Justice, U.S. Department of Justice.; Krebs, C., C. Lindquist, T. D. Warner, B. S. Fisher, and S. L. Martin. "College Women's Experiences with Physically Forced, Alcohol- or Other Drug-enabled, and Drug-facilitated Sexual Assault Before and Since Entering College." *Journal of American College Health* 57, no. 6 (2009): 639–647. https://doi.org/10.3200/JACH.57.6.639-649.

28   Krebs et al.; *The Campus Sexual Assault (CSA) Study*.

29   Ibid.

30   Ibid.; see also Kilpatrick, D. G., H. S. Resnick, K. J. Ruggiero, L. M. Conoscenti, and
     J. McCauley. *Drug Facilitated, Incapacitated, and Forcible Rape: A National Study.*
     2007. Charleston, SC: Medical University of South Carolina, National Crime
     Victims Research & Treatment Center. https://www.ncjrs.gov/pdffiles1/nij/
     grants/219181.pdf.

31   Anderson, Nick and Scott Clement. "College Sexual Assault: 1 in 5 College
     Women Say They Were Violated." *Washington Post*, June 12, 2015. https://
     www.washingtonpost.com/sf/local/2015/06/12/1-in-5-women-say-they-were
     -violated/?utm_term=.3c6e3bf71608.

32   Exner-Cortens, D. "Longitudinal Associations Between Teen Dating Violence and
     Adverse Health Outcomes." *Pediatrics* 131, no. 1 (January 2013). https://pediatrics.
     aappublications.org/content/131/1/71.

Bibliography

Abbey, Antonia. "Alcohol-Related Sexual Assault: A Common Problem Among College Students." *Journal of Studies on Alcohol and Drugs*, no. 14 (March 2002): 118–28. Accessed August 16, 2015. http://www.jsad.com/doi/abs/10.15288/jsas.2002.s14.118.

Abbey, Antonia, Tina Zawacki, Philip O. Buck, Monique Clinton, and Pam McAuslan. "Alcohol and Sexual Assault." National Institute on Alcohol Abuse and Alcoholism, 25(1): 43–51. Accessed August 16, 2015. https://pubs.niaaa.nih.gov/publications/arh25-1/43-51.htm.

Actually, You Can Disclose That: Transparency in Sexual Assault Reporting & the Family Educational Records Privacy Act (FERPA). National Women's Law Center, 2016. https://nwlc.org/resources/actually-you-can-disclose-that-transparency-in-sexual-assault-reporting-the-family-educational-records-privacy-act-ferpa/.

Administrator Information Packet on Campus Climate Surveys. U.S. Department of Justice Office on Violence Against Women, 2017. https://www.justice.gov/ovw/page/file/929846/download.

Adolescent Sexual and Reproductive Health in the United States. Guttmacher Institute, September 2017. https://www.guttmacher.org/fact-sheet/american-teens-sexual-and-reproductive-health.

Adolescent Sexual Health and Behavior in the United States. http://advocatesforyouth
.org/storage/advfy/documents/adolescent-sexual-behavior-demographics.pdf.

"Advocates for Youth—Home." Advocates for Youth. http://www
.advocatesforyouth.org/.

"Alcohol Safety." RAINN, n.d. https://www.rainn.org/articles/alcohol-safety.

Anderson, Jenny. "National Study Finds Widespread Sexual Harassment of Students in Grades 7 to 12." Education, *New York Times*, November 7, 2011, Education. https://www.nytimes.com/2011/11/07/education/ widespread-sexual-harassment-in-grades-7-to-12-found-in-study.html.

Anderson, Nick and Scott Clement. "College Sexual Assault: 1 in 5 College Women Say They Were Violated." Washington Post, June 12, 2015.

Ashton, Jackie. "The Art of Saying No: How to Raise Kids to Be Polite, Not Pushovers." *The Washington Post*, August 31, 2016. https://www .washingtonpost.com/lifestyle/on-parenting/the-art-of-saying-no-how-to -raise-kids-to-be-polite-not-pushovers/2016/08/30/9537e5d0–696c -11e6-ba32–5a4bf5aad4fa_story.html?noredirect=on&utm_term=. 8aed52e99bd0.

Banyard, Victoria L., Elizabethe G. Plante, and Mary M. Moynihan. "Bystander Education: Bringing a Broader Community Perspective to Sexual Violence Prevention." *Journal of Community Psychology* 32.1 (2004): 61–79.

Baron, Dennis. "What's Your Pronoun?" *The Web of Language* (blog). September 4, 2015. https://blogs.illinois.edu/view/25/242099.

Bazelon, Emily. "Hooking Up at an Affirmative Consent Campus? It's Complicated." *The New York Times Magazine*, October 21, 2014. https://www .nytimes.com/2014/10/26/magazine/hooking-up-at-an-affirmative -consent-campus-its-complicated.html.

Bell, Ruth. *Changing Bodies, Changing Lives: A Book for Teens on Sex and Relationships*. 3rd ed. New York: Times Books, 1998.

Bouffard, Suzanne. "Making Your Child's School Safe and Supportive." Great! Schools, November 6, 2018. https://www.greatschools.org/gk/articles/bullying-how-to-make-school-safe-for-your-child/.

"Bringing in the Bystander." University of New Hampshire College of Liberal Arts: Preventions Innovations Research Center. Accessed August 17, 2015. http://cola.unh.edu/prevention-innovations/bystander.

Burnett, Zaron, III. "A Gentleman's Guide to Rape Culture." *Medium*, May 29, 2014. https://medium.com/human-parts/a-gentlemens-guide-to-rape-culture-7fc86c50dc4c.

———. "A Gentleman's Guide to Sexual Misconduct…and Enthusiastic Consent." *Medium*, November 26, 2017. https://medium.com/@zaron3/a-gentlemans-guide-to-sexual-misconduct-and-enthusiastic-consent-9a0b750bc93e.

———. "A Gentleman's Guide to Street Harassment." *Medium*, November 12, 2014. https://medium.com/human-parts/a-gentlemans-guide-to-street-harassment-fbab3410b340.

———. "Stand Up to Sexual Harassment and Abuse: How Men Can Help Women." *Teen Vogue*, October 24, 2017. https://www.teenvogue.com/story/how-men-can-help-avoid-sexual-harassment.

———. "You Wanna Compare Rape Culture to Racism? Okay, Let's Do That!" *Medium*, July 16, 2014. https://medium.com/human-parts/you-wanna-compare-rape-culture-to-racism-okay-lets-do-that-88024d8a7b54.

Bystander Intervention Tips and Strategies. National Sexual Violence Resource Center, February 19, 2018. http://nsvrc.org/sites/default/files/2018–02/publications_nsvrc_tip-sheet_bystander-intervention-tips-and-strategies_1.pdf.

Cacioppo, John T., and Stephanie Cacioppo. "Social Relationships and Health: The Toxic Effects of Perceived Social Isolation." *HHS Author Manuscripts*, February 4, 2014. https://www.ncbi.nlm.nih.gov/pmc/articles/PMC4021390/.

Caldwell, Patrick. "The Absolute Best Podcasts about Sex." *The Daily Dot*,

November 5, 2012. https://www.dailydot.com/upstream/best-sex-podcasts/.

Cantalupo, Nancy Chi. "Accurate Reporting of Sexual Assault on Campus Without Shame." *New York Times,* January 3, 2017. https://www.nytimes.com/roomfordebate/2014/08/12/doing-enough-to-prevent-rape-on-campus/accurate-reporting-of-sexual-assault-on-campus-without-shame.

———. "For the Title IX Civil Rights Movement: Congratulations and Cautions." *Yale Law Journal* 125 (2015). https://www.yalelawjournal.org/forum/for-the-title-ix-civil-rights-movement-congratulations-and-cautions.

———. "Rape Victims Need Title IX: Opposing View." *USA Today,* May 6, 2014. https://www.usatoday.com/story/opinion/2014/05/06/sexual-assault-colleges-universities-title-ix-editorials-debates/8786319/.

Carmichael, Cheryl L., Harry T. Reis, and Paul R. Duberstein. "In Your 20s It's Quantity, in Your 30s It's Quality: The Prognostic Value of Social Activity Across 30 Years of Adulthood." *HHS Author Manuscripts,* March 1, 2016. https://www.ncbi.nlm.nih.gov/pmc/articles/PMC4363071/.

Chambers, R. Andrew, Jane R. Taylor, and Marc N. Potenza. "Developmental Neurocircuitry of Motivation in Adolescence: A Critical Period of Addiction Vulnerability." *American Journal of Psychiatry* 160, no. 6 (June 2003): 1041–52.

Clup-Ressler, Tara. "What 'Affirmative Consent' Actually Means." Think Progress. Last modified June 25, 2014. Accessed August 25, 2015. http://thinkprogress.org/health/2014/06/25/3453041/affirmative-consent-really-means/.

"Coaching Boys into Men." Futures Without Violence. http://www.futureswithoutviolence.org/engaging-men/coaching-boys-into-men/.

Columbia University. "Go Ask Alice." Go Ask Alice! http://www.goaskalice.columbia.edu/.

Columbia University in the City of New York. "Healthy versus Unhealthy Relationships." Go Ask Alice! Accessed July 28, 2015. http://goaskalice.columbia.edu/answered-questions/healthy-versus-unhealthy-relationships.

Committee on Public Education. "Media Education." American Academy of Pediatrics, August 1999, 104(2). http://pediatrics.aappublications.org/content/pediatrics/104/2/341.full.pdf.

"Community Violence Solutions: Ending Sexual Assault and Family Violence." Community Violence Solutions. http://www.cvsolutions.org/.

Corinna, Heather. "Driver's Ed for the Sexual Superhighway: Navigating Consent." Scarleteen: Sex Ed for the Real World. Accessed August 25, 2015. http://www.scarleteen.com/article/abuse_assault/drivers_ed_for_the_sexual_superhighway_navigating_consent.

Corinna, Heather. *S.E.X.: The All-You-Need-to-Know Progressive Sexuality Guide to Get You through High School and College.* New York: Da Capo, 2007.

———. *Sexual Response & Orgasm: A Users Guide.* Scarleteen.com, 2000. http://www.scarleteen.com/article/sexuality/sexual_response_orgasm_a_users_guide.

Corty, E. W., and J. M. Guardiani. "Canadian and American Sex Therapists' Perceptions of Normal and Abnormal Ejaculatory Latencies: How Long Should Intercourse Last?" *Journal of Sexual Medicine* 5, no. 5 (May 2008): 1251–56. https://www.ncbi.nlm.nih.gov/pubmed/18331255.

Covenant Eyes, comp. *Porn Stats 2018.* 2018. https://www.covenanteyes.com/pornstats/

Cullen, F., B. Fisher, and M. Turner, *The Sexual Victimization of College Women* (NCJ 182369). December 2000. Retrieved from the U.S. Department of Justice Office of Justice Programs, National Institute of Justice: https://www.ncjrs.gov/pdffiles1/nij/182369.pdf

DeGue, Sarah, comp. *Preventing Sexual Violence on College Campuses: Lessons from Research and Practice.* n.p., 2014. Accessed August 17, 2015. https://www.notalone.gov/assets/evidence-based-strategies-for-the-prevention-of-sv-perpetration.pdf.

DeMaria, A. L., M. Flores, J. M Hirth., and A. B. Berenson. "Complications Related to Pubic Hair Removal." *American Journal of Obstetrics & Gynecology* 210, no. 6 (June 2014). https://www.ncbi.nlm.nih.gov/pubmed/24486227.

Dickson, Caitlin. "Can Affirmative Consent Apps Combat Campus Sexual Assault?" *Yahoo Finance.* Last modified May 26, 2016. https://finance.yahoo.com/news/can-affirmative-consent-apps-combat-campus-sexual-assault-222724569.html.

Dione, Evette. "5 of Michelle Obama's Most Powerful Speeches Ever." *Teen Vogue,* November 27, 2016. https://www.teenvogue.com/story/michelle-obama-first-lady-best-speeches.

Dockterman, Eliana. "Can Bad Men Change? What It's Like Inside Sex Offender Therapy." *Time,* May 10, 2018, 38–46. http://time.com/5272337/sex-offenders-therapy-treatment/.

"Dove Evolution." Video file. YouTube. Posted by Tim Piper, October 6, 2006. https://www.youtube.com/watch?v=iYhCn0jf46U.

"Dove—Onslaught." Video file. YouTube. Posted by Bornsquishy, April 3, 2008. https://www.youtube.com/watch?v=9zKfF40jeCA.

Elgersma, Christine. *The Facts About Online Predators Every Parent Should Know.* Common Sense Media, 2017. https://www.commonsensemedia.org/blog/the-facts-about-online-predators-every-parent-should-know.

End Rape on Campus. Accessed August 13, 2015. http://endrapeoncampus.org.

"The Evaluation of Campus-Based Gender Violence Prevention Programming: What We Know about Program Effectiveness and Implications for Practitioners," 2015. July 31, 2015. http://www.vawnet.org/assoc_files_vawnet/ar_evaluationcampusprogramming.pdf.

Exner-Cortens, D. "Longitudinal Associations Between Teen Dating Violence and Adverse Health Outcomes." *Pediatrics.* January 2013, 131(1). https://pediatrics.aappublications.org/content/131/1/71.

"Facts for Families: Teens: Alcohol and Other Drugs." The American Academy of Child and Adolescent Psychiatry. Last modified July 2013. Accessed August 17, 2015. https://www.aacap.org/App_Themes/AACAP/docs/facts_for_families/03_teens_alcohol_and_other_drugs.pdf.

Fessler, Leah. "A Lot of Women Don't Enjoy Hookup Culture—So Why Do We Force Ourselves to Participate?" *Quartz*, May 17, 2016. https://qz.com/685852/hookup-culture/.

Fessler, Leah Marie. "Can She Really 'Play That Game, Too'?" Unpublished manuscript, Middlebury College, Middlebury, VT, May 2016.

"Fifty Shades of Gay." Video file. TED.com. Posted by IO Tillet Wright, 2012. https://www.ted.com/talks/io_tillett_wright_fifty_shades_of_gay?language=en.

Finkelhor, David, Heather Turner, Richard Ormrod, Sherry Hamby, and Kristen Kracke. *Children's Exposure to Violence: A Comprehensive National Survey.* October 2009. https://www.ncjrs.gov/pdffiles1/ojjdp/227744.pdf.

For Educators: Digital Citizenship Resource List. Cambridge, MA: Harvard Graduate School of Education, 2014. https://mcc.gse.harvard.edu/files/gse-mcc/files/social_media_resource_list_0_0.pdf.

For Educators: Supporting LGBTQIA Youth Resource List. Cambridge, MA: Harvard Graduate School of Education, 2014. https://mcc.gse.harvard.edu/files/gse-mcc/files/lgbtq_resource_list_0.pdf.

For Families: 5 Tips for Parents: Guiding Teens and Young Adults in Developing Healthy Romantic Relationships. Cambridge, MA: Harvard Graduate School of Education, 2014. https://mcc.gse.harvard.edu/files/gse-mcc/files/mcc_the_talk_loveparenttips.pdf.

Forge. "Safe Dating Tips." Accessed August 13, 2015. http://forge-forward.org.

"Frances Jensen: Why Teens Are Impulsive, Addiction-Prone and Should Protect Their Brains." NPR KQED Public Radio, Fresh Air, Shots: Health News from NPR. Podcast audio. January 28, 2015. Accessed August 25, 2015. http://www.npr.org/sections/health-shots/2015/01/28/381622350/ why-teens-are-impulsive-addiction-prone-and-should-protect-their-brains.

Freitas, Donna. *The End of Sex: How Hookup Culture Is Leaving a Generation Unhappy, Sexually Unfulfilled, and Confused about Intimacy*. New York: Basic Books, 2013.

Friedland, Roger. "Looking Through the Bushes: The Disappearance of Pubic Hair." *Huffington Post*, June 13, 2011. https://www.huffingtonpost.com/ roger-friedland/women-pubic-hair_b_875465.html.

Futures Without Violence. "Beyond Title IX: Guidelines for Preventing and Responding to Gender-based Violence in Higher Education." Accessed August 16, 2015. https://www.futureswithoutviolence.org/beyond-title -ix-guidelines-for-preventing-and-responding-to-gender-based-violence -in-higher-education/.

Gasch, Renee. "The Hunting Ground Action Toolkit." Futures Without Violence. Accessed August 16, 2015. https://www.futureswithoutviolence .org/the-hunting-ground-action-toolkit-2/.

Gavrieli, Ran. "Why I Stopped Watching Porn." Video file. TEDxJaffa, October 26, 2013. https://www.youtube.com/watch?v=gRJ_QfP2mhU.

"Gender Based Violence and Harassment: Your School, Your Rights." American Civil Liberties Union. Last modified May 2011. Accessed August 16, 2015. https://www.aclu.org/files/assets/genderbasedviolence_factsheet_0.pdf.

"Get Statistics." National Sexual Violence Resource Center, 2018. https://www .nsvrc.org/statistics.

Gibbons, Roberta E., and Julie Evans. "The Evaluation of Campus-Based Gender Violence Prevention Programming: What We Know about Program Effectiveness and Implications for Practitioners." VAWnet.org; National Online Resource Center on Violence. January 2013. Accessed August 17, 2015.

https://vawnet.org/material/evaluation-campus-based-gender-violence
-prevention-programming-what-we-know-about-program.

Ginsburg, Eric. "Ten Best Ways to Practice Consent." I Don't Do Boxes.
Accessed August 25, 2015. http://www.idontdoboxes.org/ten-best-ways
-to-practice-consent/.

"'Girls & Sex' and the Importance of Talking to Young Women about Pleasure."
Audio file. Fresh Air, Shots: Health News from NPR. March 29, 2016.
https://www.npr.org/sections/health-shots/2016/03/29/472211301/
girls-sex-and-the-importance-of-talking-to-young-women-about-pleasure.

GLSEN, Inc. Gay, Lesbian, & Straight Education Network. https://www.glsen
.org/.

Golanty, Eric, and Gordon Edlin. *Human Sexuality: The Basics.* Sudbury, MA:
Jones & Bartlett Learning, 2012.

Gray, Emma. "From Sex to Love: Emotional Attachment and Sexual Desire
Originate in Overlapping Parts of the Brain." *Huffington Post.* July 9,
2012. https://www.huffingtonpost.com/2012/07/09/from-sex-to-love
-emotional-attachment-sexual-desire-brain-dating_n_1659334.html.

Green, Matthew. "Before #MeToo: The Long Struggle Against Sexual Harassment
at Work (with Interactive Timeline and Lesson Plan)." *The Lowdown* (blog).
KQED News, December 14, 2017. https://www.kqed.org/lowdown/29228/
timeline-a-short-history-of-the-long-fight-against-sexual-harassment.

Grinberg, Emanuella, and Victoria Larned. "This Is What Happens When Gender
Roles Are Forced on Kids." CNN Health. September 20, 2017. https://www
.cnn.com/2017/09/20/health/geas-gender-stereotypes-study/index.html.

H. S. Resnick, K. J. Ruggiero, L. M. Conoscenti, and J. McCauley. *Drug Facilitated,
Incapacitated, and Forcible Rape: A National Study.* Charleston, SC: Medical
University of South Carolina, National Crime Victims Research & Treatment
Center, 2007.

Haffner, Debra W. *Beyond the Big Talk: Every Parent's Guide to Raising Sexually Healthy Teens—from Middle School to High School and Beyond.* New York: Newmarket Press, 2002.

———. *What Every 21st-Century Parent Needs to Know: Facing Today's Challenges with Wisdom and Heart.* New York: William Morrow Paperbacks, 2009.

Harris Interactive. *Hostile Hallways.* Edited by Jodi Lipson. May 2001. https://www .aauw.org/files/2013/02/hostile-hallways-bullying-teasing-and-sexual -harassment-in-school.pdf

Hay, Mark. "How and Why Pubic Hair Is Back in Porn." Vice Channels. Last modified June 6, 2017. https://www.vice.com/en_us/article/xw8dzn/ bush-is-back-in-porn-baby.

Hess, Amanda. "The Sex-Ed Queens of YouTube Don't Need a Ph.D." *New York Times,* September 30, 2016. https://www.nytimes.com/2016/10/01/arts/ the-sex-ed-queens-of-youtube-dont-need-a-phd.html.

Hill, Catherine and Elena Silva. "Drawing the Line: Sexual Harassment on Campus." 2005. American Association of University Women. http://www .aauw.org/files/2013/02/drawing-the-line-sexual-harassment-on-campus.pdf

Hill, Catherine, and Holly Kearl. "Crossing the Line: Sexual Harassment at School." American Association of University Women. Last modified November 2011. Accessed August 16, 2015. https://www.aauw.org/research/ crossing-the-line/.

Hoffman, Jan. "Many Women Prefer to Groom, Citing Hygiene (and Baffling Doctors)." *Well* (blog). *New York Times,* June 29, 2016. https://well .blogs.nytimes.com/2016/06/29/most-women-prefer-to-go-bare- citing-hygiene-and-baffling-doctors/.

"How Do You Know if Someone Wants to Have Sex with You? Planned Parenthood Video." Video file. YouTube. Posted by Planned Parenthood, September 21, 2015. https://www.youtube.com/watch?v=qNN3nAevQKY.

"How 7 Things that Have Nothing to Do with Rape Perfectly Illustrate the Concept of Consent." Updated October 16, 2018. http://www.upworthy .com/how-7-things-that-have-nothing-to-do-with-rape-perfectly-illustrate -the-concept-of-consent.

"How to File a Title IX Sexual Harassment or Assault Complaint with the U.S. Department of Education." National Women's Law Center, June 2016. https://nwlc.org/resources/how-to-file-a-title-ix-sexual-harassment-or -assault-complaint-with-the-u-s-department-of-education/.

The Hunting Ground Official Website. Accessed August 17, 2015. http://www .thehuntinggroundfilm.com/.

Hyatt, Katarina. "Supporting a Survivor: The Basics." Know Your IX. Accessed August 16, 2015. https://www.knowyourix.org/for-friends-and-fami/ supporting-survivor-basics/

Inaba, Darryl, and William E. Cohen. *Uppers, Downers, All Arounders: Physical and Mental Effects of Psychoactive Drugs.* 8th ed. Medford, OR: CNS Productions, 2014.

Internet Crimes. University of New Hampshire Crimes Against Children Research Center, n.d. http://unh.edu/ccrc/internet-crimes/.

"It's Time to Incorporate the Bystander Approach into Sexual Violence Prevention." 2011. http://www.nsvrc.org/sites/default/files/Publications _NSVRC_Factsheet_Bystander-SAAM-2011.pdf.

Jackson Katz, PhD, website, accessed August 16, 2015. http://www.jacksonkatz .com/

Jamie. "Losing It." *Rookie Magazine*, April 12, 2012. http://www.rookiemag .com/2012/04/losing-i/.

Jhally, Sut. "Dreamworlds—Desire, Sex, and Power in Music Videos." Thought Maybe. Last modified 2007. https://thoughtmaybe.com/ dreamworlds-desire-sex-and-power-in-music-videos/.

Johnson, Joshua. "The Controversy Over Comprehensive Sex Ed." *1A*. Podcast audio. July 24, 2017. https://the1a.org/shows/2017-07-24/the-controversy-over-comprehensive-sex-ed.

Jones, Maggie. "What Teenagers Are Learning from Online Porn." *New York Times Magazine*, February 7, 2018. https://www.nytimes.com/2018/02/07/magazine/teenagers-learning-online-porn-literacy-sex-education.html.

Keierleber, Mark. "The Younger Victims of Sexual Violence in School." *Atlantic*, August 10, 2017. https://www.theatlantic.com/education/archive/2017/08/the-younger-victims-of-sexual-violence-in-school/536418/.

Kim, Mina. "STD Rates in California, U.S. Soar." Audio file. KQED.org. October 27, 2016. https://www.kqed.org/forum/2010101857279/std-rates-in-california-u-s-soar.

Kimmel, Michael. *Guyland: The Perilous World Where Boys Become Men*. New York: Harper Perennial, 2008.

Kirkham, Alli. "What If We Treated All Consent like Society Treats Sexual Consent?" *Everyday Feminism*, June 23, 2015. https://everydayfeminism.com/2015/06/how-society-treats-consent/.

Krakauer, Jon. *Missoula: Rape and the Justice System in a College Town*. New York: Doubleday, 2015.

Krebs, C. P., C. H. Lindquist, T. D. Warner, B. S. Fisher, and S. L. Martin. *The Campus Sexual Assault (CSA) Study*. Washington, DC: National Institute of Justice, U.S. Department of Justice, 2007.

Krebs, C., C. Lindquist, T. D. Warner, B. S. Fisher, and S. L. Martin. "College Women's Experiences with Physically Forced, Alcohol- or Other Drug-enabled, and Drug-facilitated Sexual Assault Before and Since Entering College." *Journal of American College Health* 57, no. 6 (2009): 639–647. https://doi.org/10.3200/JACH.57.6.639-649

Krebs, Christopher, Christine Lindquist, Marcus Berzofsky, Bonnie Shook-Sa,

Kimberly Peterson, Michael Planty, Lynn Langton, and Jessica Stroop. *Campus Climate Survey Validation Study Final Technical Report.* January 2016. https://www.bjs.gov/content/pub/pdf/ccsvsftr.pdf.

Laville, Sandra. "Most Boys Think Online Pornography Is Realistic, Finds Study." *Guardian,* June 14, 2016. https://www.theguardian.com/culture/2016/jun/15/majority-boys-online-pornography-realistic-middlesex-university-study.

Levay, Simon, and Janice Baldwin. *Human Sexuality.* 4th ed. Sunderland, MA: Sinauer Associates, 2012.

"LGBTQ Youth Sexual Health Information." GSA Network, n.d. https://gsanetwork.org/sexualhealth.

Liew, Jonathan. "All Men Watch Porn, Scientists Find." *Telegraph,* December 2, 2009. https://www.telegraph.co.uk/women/sex/6709646/All-men-watch-porn-scientists-find.html.

Martin, Courtney E. "This Isn't About Bad Apples; It's About Our Broken Sexual Culture." On Being, December 7, 2017. https://onbeing.org/blog/courtney-martin-this-isnt-about-bad-apples-its-about-our-broken-sexual-culture/.

The Mask You Live In. Directed by Jennifer Siebel Newsom. Screenplay by Jessica Anthony and Jessica Congden. Performed by Joe Herman, Michael Kimmel, and Caroline Heldman. The Representation Project, 2015.

Maxwell, Sharon. *The Talk: A Breakthrough Guide to Raising Healthy Kids in an Oversexualized, Online, In-You-Face World.* New York, NY: Penguin Group, 2008.

McLaughlin, Julia Halloran. "Crime and Punishment: Teen Sexting in Context." *Penn State Law Review* 115, no. 1 (Summer 2010): 135–81. http://www.pennstatelawreview.org/print-issues/articles/crime-and-punishment-teen-sexting-in-context/.

McNamara, Brittney. "Google Launches Trans Voices Campaign with GLAAD."

Teen Vogue, November 15, 2016. https://www.teenvogue.com/story/ glaad-google-stories-voices-campaign.

McNeely, Clea, and Jayne Blanchard. "The Teen Years Explained: A Guide for Healthy Adolescent Development." Johns Hopkins Bloomberg School of Public Health; Center for Adolescent Health. Last modified 2009. Accessed August 17, 2015. https://www.jhsph.edu/research/centers-and-institutes/ center-for-adolescent-health/_docs/TTYE-Guide.pdf.

Men Can Stop Rape. Accessed August 17, 2015. http://www.mencanstoprape .org/.

Mineo, Liz. "Good Genes Are Nice, but Joy Is Better." *Harvard Gazette*, April 11, 2017. https://news.harvard.edu/gazette/story/2017/04/over-nearly-80 -years-harvard-study-has-been-showing-how-to-live-a-healthy-and-happy -life/.

Miss Representation. Directed by Jennifer Siebel Newson and Kimberlee Acquaro. Performed by Pat Mitchell, Jackson Katz, and Jim Steyer. Screenplay by Jacoba Atlas and Jessica Congden. Girl's Club Entertainment, 2011.

MK, Alex. "To Shave or Not to Shave Down There? I Won't Let Porn Trends Decide." *Guardian*, July 7, 2018. https://www.theguardian.com/ commentisfree/2018/jul/07/porn-pubic-hair-fashionable-pornography -feminism.

Mogel, Wendy. *The Blessing of a B Minus: Using Jewish Teachings to Raise Resilient Teenagers*. New York: Scribner, 2011.

Moreton, Cole. "Children and the Culture of Pornography: 'Boys Will Ask You Every Day Until You Say Yes.'" *Telegraph*, January 27, 2013. https:// www.telegraph.co.uk/women/sex/9828589/Children-and-the-culture-of -pornography-Boys-will-ask-you-every-day-until-you-say-yes.html?fb.

Moynihan, Mary M., Victoria L. Banyard, Alison C. Cares, et. al., "Encouraging Responses in Sexual and Relationship Violence Prevention." *Journal of*

Interpersonal Violence 30, no. 1 (January 1, 2015): 110-132. http://jiv .sagepub.com/content/30/1/110.refs.

Mustankski, Brian. "Queer Sex Ed." Impact Program. http://www .impactprogram.org/research/past-research-projects/queer-sex-ed/.

Nagoski, Emily. *Come As You Are: The Surprising New Science That Will Transform Your Sex Life*. New York: Simon & Schuster, 2015.

———. "Good in Bed: How Does a Fetish Develop?" *Good in Bed* (blog). Entry posted December 2014. https://www.goodinbed.com/sex_nerd/2014/12/ how-does-a-fetish-develop/.

———. "Is Porn Addiction for Real?" *Good in Bed* (blog). Entry posted December 2014. https://www.goodinbed.com/sex_nerd/2014/12/ is-porn-addiction-for-real/

———. "Pleasure is the Measure: The Science of Sex and Desire." Relationships Alive podcast number 123. Interview by Neil Sattin. NeilSattin. January 1, 2018. https://www.neilsattin.com/ blog/2018/01/123-pleasure-measure-science-sex-desire-emily-nagoski/.

National Sexual Violence Research Center. 2012. "False Reporting." http://nsvrc .org/sites/default/files/Publications_NSVRC_Overview_False-Reporting .pdf.

New, Jake. "Bystander Intervention Helps Prevent Sexual Assault in High Schools, Study Shows." *Teen Vogue*, March 10, 2017. https://www.teenvogue .com/story/bystander-intervention-sexual-assault-prevention-high-schools.

"The Next Generation of Title IX: Harassment and Bullying Based on Sex." National Women's Law Center, June 2012. https://nwlc.org/resources/ next-generation-title-ix-harassment-and-bullying-based-sex/.

Noelle, Nica. "Do I Make 'Feminist Porn'?" *Huffington Post*, April 3, 2013. https://www.huffingtonpost.com/nica-noelle/do-i-make-feminist -porn_b_3002905.html.

Not Alone: The First Report of the White House Task Force to Protect Students from Sexual Assault. Accessed August 16, 2015. https://www.notalone.gov/.

O'Leary, Amy. "How to Talk to Your Kids about Pornography: Parents' Stories and Expert Advice." *New York Times.* https://archive.nytimes.com/www .nytimes.com/interactive/2012/05/10/garden/porn-intro.html?_r=2.

———. "How to Talk with Your Kids about Pornography, Example 4: The Filtered Family." *New York Times.* https://archive.nytimes.com/www .nytimes.com/interactive/2012/05/10/garden/porn-filter.html.

Olejniczak, Nick. "Brain Activity in Sex Addiction Mirrors That of Drug Addiction." University of Cambridge Research. July 11, 2014. https://www.cam.ac.uk/research/news/brain-activity-in-sex -addiction-mirrors-that-of-drug-addiction.

Olshen, Elyse, Katharine H. McVeigh, Robin A. Wunsch-Hitzig, and Vaughn I. Rickert. "Dating Violence, Sexual Assault, and Suicide Attempts Among Urban Teenagers." *JAMA Pediatrics* 161, no. 6 (June 1, 2007). Accessed August 16, 2015. http://archpedi.jamanetwork.com/article.aspx?articleid=570505.

"1 In 5 College Women Say They Were Violated." 2015. 12 Aug. 2015 http:// www.washingtonpost.com/sf/local/2015/06/12/1-in-5-women-say-they -were-violated/.

Orenstein, Peggy. *Girls and Sex: Navigating the Complicated New Landscape.* London, England: Oneworld Publications, 2016.

"The Other Freshman 15: Action Plan for Students." Futures Without Violence. Last modified November 1, 2014. Accessed August 17, 2015. http://www .futureswithoutviolence.org/action-plan-alumni-preventing-college-sexual- assault-2/.

"Parents Held Responsible for Underage Drinking." *Wall Street Journal.* December 30, 2011.

Parker, Imogen. Progressive Policy Think Tank, comp. *Young People, Sex and*

Relationships: The New Norms. August 27, 2014. https://www.ippr.org/files/ publications/pdf/young-people-sex-relationships_Aug2014.pdf.

Partnership News Service Staff. "Liability Laws Make Parents Responsible for Underage Drinking in Their Home." *Partnership for Drug-Free Kids* (blog). Posted January 3, 2012. https://drugfree.org/learn/drug-and-alcohol-news/ liability-laws-make-parents-responsible-for-underage-drinking-in-their-home/.

Pierce, Cindy. *Sexploitation: Helping Kids Develop Healthy Sexuality in a Porn-Driven World.* N.p.: Routledge, 2016.

Planned Parenthood. "For Teens." https://www.plannedparenthood.org/learn/ teens.

The Porn Conversation. *A Guide for Parents with Teens over 15 Years.* The Porn Conversation, n.d. http://thepornconversation.org/wp-content/ uploads/2017/05/TPC-Guidekids15.pdf.

Prevention and Protection Podcast. Podcast audio. https://www.ue.org/ risk-management/prevention-and-protection-podcast/.

"Protecting Survivors of Sexual Assault on Campus: Myths and Facts." National Women's Law Center, April 2014. https://nwlc.org/resources/ protecting-survivors-sexual-assault-campus-myths-and-facts/.

"Providing Additional Information Online: Resources and Materials." Centers for Disease Control and Prevention. Accessed August 16, 2015. http://www .nsopw.gov/en/education/resourcesmaterials.

"Questions and Answers on Title IX and Sexual Violence." United States Department of Education Office for Civil Rights, 2012. https://www2 .ed.gov/about/offices/list/ocr/docs/qa-201404-title-ix.pdf.

Rainbow Community Center. Accessed August 17, 2015. http://rainbowcc.org/.

"Raising Awareness about Sexual Abuse: Facts and Statistics." National Sex Offender Public Website. http://www.nsopw.gov/en/Education/ FactsStatistics.

Rape, Abuse & Incest National Network. https://www.rainn.org/.

Remez, Lisa. "Oral Sex Among Adolescents: Is It Sex or Is It Abstinence?" Guttmacher Institute, 2000. https://www.guttmacher.org/sites/default/files/pdfs/pubs/journals/3229800.pdf.

Rideout, Victoria, and Michael B. Robb. *Social Media, Social Life: Teens Reveal Their Experiences.* 2018. https://www.commonsensemedia.org/research/social-media-social-life-2018.

Riera, Michael. *Uncommon Sense for Parents with Teenagers.* 3rd ed. Berkeley: Ten Speed Press, 2012.

Riera, Michael, and Joseph Diprisco. *Field Guide To The American Teenager: A Parent's Companion.* N.p.: Da Capo Press, 2009.

"Risk Management." United Educators. https://www.ue.org/risk-management/.

Roffman, Deborah. *Talk to Me First: Everything You Need to Know to Become Your Kids' "Go-To" Person about Sex.* New York: Da Capo Press, 2012.

Rookie Magazine. http://www.rookiemag.com/.

Rutgers University. Sex, Etc. https://sexetc.org/.

S, Sylvia. *Vocabulary Lists: Harassment in the Workplace.* Vocabulary.com, June 6, 2013. https://www.vocabulary.com/lists/270037.

Sabina, C., J. Wolak, D. Finkelhor. "The Nature and Dynamics of Internet Pornography Exposure for Youth." *Cyberpsychology and Behavior* 11, no. 6 (2018): 691–693. https://scholars.unh.edu/cgi/viewcontent.cgi?referer=&httpsredir=1&article=1283&context=soc_facpub.

Sales, Nancy Jo. *American Girls: Social Media and the Secret Lives of Teenagers.* New York: Alfred A. Knopf, 2016.

———. "Tinder and the Dawn of the 'Dating Apocalypse.'" *Vanity Fair*, September 2015. https://www.vanityfair.com/culture/2015/08/tinder-hook-up-culture-end-of-dating.

Scaccia, Annamarya. "What Trump's Abstinence-Only Education Budget Means for Young People." *Teen Vogue*, February 21, 2018. https://www.teenvogue.com/story/trumps-abstinence-only-education-budget-means-for-young-people.

Scarleteen. Scarleteen: Sex Ed for the Real World. http://www.scarleteen.com/.

"Sex Needs a New Metaphor. Here's One…" Video file, 08:17. TED: Ideas Worth Sharing. Posted by Al Vernacchio, March 2012. Accessed August 16, 2015. https://www.ted.com/talks/al_vernacchio_sex_needs_a_new_metaphor_here_s_one?language=en.

"Sexual Harassment." *United States Equal Employment Opportunity Commission Laws, Regulations & Guidance*. United States Equal Opportunity Commission. https://www.eeoc.gov/laws/types/sexual_harassment.cfm.

Sexual Violence: Facts at a Glance. National Center for Injury Prevention and Control Division of Violence Prevention, 2012. https://www.cdc.gov/violenceprevention/sexualviolence/fastfact.html.

Sexual Violence in Youth: Findings from the 2012 National Intimate Partner and Sexual Violence Survey. https://www.cdc.gov/violenceprevention/pdf/2012FindingsonSVinYouth.pdf.

"Sexual Violence: Prevention Strategies." Centers for Disease Control and Prevention. Accessed August 16, 2015. http://www.cdc.gov/violenceprevention/sexualviolence/prevention.html.

"The Sexy Lie: Caroline Heldman at TedxYouth @ San Diego." TED video. Posted by TEDxYouth, January 20, 2013. https://www.youtube.com/watch?v=kMS4VJKekW8.

Sharp, Catherine. "Consent and Sexual Entitlement: A Case for Truly Comprehensive Sexuality Education." Planned Parenthood Advocates of Arizona. Last modified November 6, 2017. http://advocatesaz.org/2017/11/06/consent-and-sexual-entitlement-a-case-for-truly-comprehensive-sexuality-education/.

6 Tips for Parents: Reducing and Preventing Misogyny and Sexual Harassment Among Teens and Young Adults. Cambridge, MA: Harvard Graduate School of

Education, 2014. https://mcc.gse.harvard.edu/files/gse-mcc/files/mcc_the _talk_misogynyparenttips.pdf.

Social-Emotional Learning (SEL). Cambridge, MA: Harvard Graduate School of Education, 2014. https://mcc.gse.harvard.edu/files/gse-mcc/files/sel_and _common_core_1.pdf.

Speciale M. (Producer). (2018, September 12). Sexual Healing After #MeToo: Conversations on what Counselors Need to Know [Audio Podcast]. The Thoughtful Counselor. Retrieved from https://wp.me/p7R6fn-rQ.

Spiegel, Amy Rose. "Age of Consent." *Rookie Magazine*, June 17, 2014. http:// www.rookiemag.com/2014/06/age-of-consent/.

Stein, Nan. *Sexual Harassment in Schools*. 2000. https://mainweb-v.musc.edu/ vawprevention/research/sexharass.shtml.

Steps You Can Take to Prevent Sexual Assault. RAINN, n.d. https://www.rainn .org/articles/steps-you-can-take-prevent-sexual-assault.

"Step Up Your Game." The Consensual Project. http://www.theconsensualproject .com/action/your-game.

Steyer, James P., and Amy Guggenheim Shenkan. *Watching Gender: How Stereotypes in Movies and on TV Impact Kids' Development*. 2017. https:// www.commonsensemedia.org/research/watching-gender.

"Stop Sexual Violence: A Sexual Violence Bystander Intervention Toolkit." New York State Department of Health. Accessed August 16, 2015. https://www .health.ny.gov/publications/2040.pdf.

"Straight for Equality: Trans Allies." Straight for Equality. https://www .straightforequality.org/trans.

"Take Back the Night." Take Back the Night. Accessed August 17, 2015. http:// takebackthenight.org/.

Talpert, Susan F., Lisa Caldwell, and Christina Burke. "Alcohol and the Adolescent Brain—Human Studies." National Institute on Alcohol Abuse and Alcoholism. Accessed August 17, 2015. http://pubs.niaaa.nih.gov/ publications/arh284/205–212.htm.

Taylor, Kate. "Sex on Campus: She Can Play That Game, Too." *New York Times*, July 12, 2013. https://www.nytimes.com/2013/07/14/fashion/sex-on -campus-she-can-play-that-game-too.html.

Teenage Choices and Legal Consequences. 35th District Court, State of Michigan, September 7, 2018. http://35thdistrictcourt.org/Forms/Juvenile/ Teenage%20Choices%20and%20Legal%20Consequences.pdf.

"The Teen Brain: Still Under Construction." NIH: National Institute of Mental Health. Last modified 2011. Accessed August 16, 2015. http://www.nimh .nih.gov/health/publications/the-teen-brain-still-under-construction/index. shtml.

Theoharis, Mark. "Teen Sexting." Criminal Defense Lawyer. https://www .criminaldefenselawyer.com/crime-penalties/juvenile/sexting.htm.

Thrash, Maggie. "A Guide to Internet Privacy Policies." *Rookie Magazine*, March 13, 2015. http://www.rookiemag.com/2015/03/94259/.

"Tips for Allies of Transgender People." GLAAD, 2018. https://www.glaad.org/ transgender/allies.

Title IX Protections from Bullying and Harassment in School: FAQs for Students. N.p.: National Women's Law Center, n.d.

"Title IX Requires Schools to Address Sexual Violence." National Women's Law Center. June 2016. https://nwlc.org/resources/ title-ix-requires-schools-to-address-sexual-violence/.

Title IX Resource Guide. U.S. Department of Education Office for Civil Rights. April 2015. https://www2.ed.gov/about/offices/list/ocr/docs/dcl-title-ix -coordinators-guide-201504.pdf.

Tolentino, Jia. "Is There a Smarter Way to Think About Sexual Assault on Campus?" *The New Yorker*, February 12, 2018. https://www.newyorker

.com/magazine/2018/02/12/is-there-a-smarter-way-to-think-about -sexual-assault-on-campus.

Ullman, Sarah E., George Karabatsos, and Mary P. Koss. "Alcohol and Sexual Assault in a National Sample of College Women." *Journal of Interpersonal Violence,* June 1, 1999. Accessed August 16, 2015. http://jiv.sagepub.com/ content/14/6/603.short.

United States. Committee on Home Land Security & Governmental Affairs Subcommittee on Financial and Contracting Oversight. Written testimony for *Roundtable on "Campus Sexual Assault: The Administrative Process & the Criminal Justice System".* June 19, 2014. Statement of Nancy Chi Cantalupo, esq. https://www.hsgac.senate.gov/subcommittees/fco/hearings/roundtable -discussion-on-campus-sexual-assault-the-role-of-title-ix.

United States Department of Education; Office for Civil Rights, Dear Colleague Letter, Doc. (2011). https://www2.ed.gov/about/offices/list/ocr/letters/ colleague-201104.pdf.

United States Government. "Sextortion Help Us Locate Additional Victims of an Online Predator." FBI. Last modified July 7, 2015. https://www.fbi.gov/ news/stories/sextortion.

———. "Sexual Predator Sentenced to 29 Years, Targeted Young Victims Through Social Media." FBI. Last modified July 30, 2015. https://www.fbi .gov/news/stories/sexual-predator-sentenced-to-29-years.

United Way. "Check in First: How to Talk about Sexual Consent." Teen Health Source. Accessed August 25, 2015. http://teenhealthsource.com/sex/ sconsent/.

US Department of Justice. "Raising Awareness about Sexual Abuse: Facts and Statistics." National Sex Offender Public Website. Last modified 2014. Accessed July 13, 2015. https://www.nsopw.gov/en/Education/ FactsStatistics?AspxAutoDetectCookieSupport=1.

Utt, Jaimie. "Want the Best Sex of Your Life? Just Ask!" Everyday Feminism. Last modified December 13, 2012. http://everydayfeminism.com/2012/12/want-the-best-sex-of-your-life-just-ask/.

Vernacchio, Al. *For Goodness Sex: Changing the Way We talk to Teens About Sexuality, Values, and Health.* New York, NY: Harper Collins, 2014.

"Violence Against Women: It's a Men's Issue." Video file, 17:40. TED. Posted by Jackson Katz, November 2012. Accessed August 16, 2015. http://www.ted.com/talks/jackson_katz_violence_against_women_it_s_a_men_s_issue?language=en.

Waldinger, M. D., P. Quinn, M. Dilleen, R. Mundayat, D. H. Schweitzer, and M. Boolell. "A Multinational Population Survey of Intravaginal Ejaculation Latency Time." *Journal of Sexual Medicine* 2, no. 4 (July 2005): 492–97. https://www.ncbi.nlm.nih.gov/pubmed/16422843.

Waldinger, Robert. "What Makes a Good Life? Lessons from the Longest Study on Happiness." Video file. November 2015. https://www.ted.com/talks/robert_waldinger_what_makes_a_good_life_lessons_from_the_longest_study_on_happiness?language=en.

"Want 'Consent Is Sexy' for Your College or University?" ConsentIsSexy.com. Accessed August 25, 2015. http://www.consentissexy.net/consent.

Ward, L. M., and J. S. Aubrey. *Watching Gender: How Stereotypes in Movies and on TV Impact Kids' Development.* 2017. San Francisco, CA: Common Sense.

Weissbourd, Richard, Trisha Ross Anderson, Alison Cachin, and Joe McIntyre. *The Talk: How Adults Can Promote Young People's Healthy Relationships and prevent Misogyny and Sexual Harassment.* Cambridge, MA: Harvard Graduate School of Education, 2014. https://mcc.gse.harvard.edu/files/gse-mcc/files/mcc_the_talk_final.pdf.

Weissbourd, Richard, Suzanne M. Bouffard, and Stephanie M. Jones. *School Climate and Moral and Social Development.* February 2013. https://www.schoolclimate .org/themes/schoolclimate/assets/pdf/practice/sc-brief-moral-social.pdf.

Weissbourd, Richard. *The Parents We Mean to Be: How Well-intentioned Adults Undermine Children's Moral and Emotional Development.* Boston: Houghton Mifflin Harcourt, 2009.

Weschler, Toni. *Cycle Savvy: The Smart Teen's Guide to the Mysteries of Her Body.* New York: Collins, 2006.

West Virginia Foundation for Rape Information & Services, comp. *Campus Sexual Violence.* 2012. http://www.fris.org/CampusSexualViolence/ CampusSexViolence.html.

"When Someone Definitely Wants to Have Sex | Planned Parenthood Video." Video file. YouTube. Posted by Planned Parenthood, September 21, 2015. https://www.youtube.com/watch?v=VmcGigHzpK0.

"When Someone Doesn't Want to Have Sex: What is Consent? | Planned Parenthood Video." Video file. YouTube. Posted by Planned Parenthood, September 21, 2015. https://www.youtube.com/watch?v=QSDjSetlGiw.

"When Someone Isn't Quite Sure If They Want to Have Sex | Planned Parenthood Video." Video file. YouTube. Posted by Planned Parenthood, September 21, 2015. https://www.youtube.com/watch?v=D-8isMT2u9A.

White House Task Force to Protect Students From Sexual Assault, Bystander-Focused Prevention of Sexual Violence, Exec. Doc. Accessed August 17, 2015. https://www.notalone.gov/assets/bystander-summary.pdf.

"Who Are You?" Video file, 8:07. Who Are You.co.nz. Accessed August 17, 2015. http://www.whoareyou.co.nz/.

Williams, Macy Cate. "Yes, 'Stealthing' Is Sexual Assault, and We Should Be Prosecuting the Men Who Practice It." Pop Sugar, May 24, 2017. https:// www.popsugar.com/love/What-Stealthing-43462655.

Wilson, Gary. "Gary's TEDx talk—'The Great Porn Experiment' (2012)."

Video file. Your Brain on Porn. https://www.yourbrainonporn.com/about /your-brain-on-porn-in-the-news/garys-tedx-talk-the-great-porn -experiment-2012/.

Winerip, Michael. "Stepping Up to Stop Sexual Assault." *New York Times*, February 7, 2014, Education/Life. https://www.nytimes.com/2014/02/09/ education/edlife/stepping-up-to-stop-sexual-assault.html.

Wiseman, Rosalind. *Masterminds and Wingmen: Helping Our Boys Cope with Schoolyard Power, Locker-room Tests, Girlfriends, and the New Rules of Boy World.* New York: Harmony Books, 2014.

Ybarra, Michele L., and Kimberly J. Mitchell. "Prevalence Rates of Male and Female Sexual Violence Perpetrators in a National Sample of Adolescents." *JAMA Pediatrics* 167, no. 12 (December 2013). Accessed August 16, 2015. http://archpedi.jamanetwork.com/article.aspx?articleid=1748355.

"Youth Risk Behavior Surveillance: United States, 2013." *Morbidity and Mortality Weekly Report* 63, no. 4 (June 13, 2014). Accessed August 16, 2015. http:// www.cdc.gov/mmwr/pdf/ss/ss6304.pdf.

Index

Acknowledgments

We all stand on the shoulders of others. It is with humility, gratitude, and love that I write this piece, appropriately placed at the end of the book, symbolizing the end of this part of my journey. There have been so many who mentored, taught, and supported me along the way. People who provided me with stepping stones and pointed me in the direction of substance and truth, and allowed for my questions and mistakes. Each one of you has walked alongside me as a student, colleague, friend, family member, or coach, and I am profoundly grateful.

To my students, thank you for sharing what's real with such open honesty and heart. Your thoughtful generosity and spirit are in every word of this book. And to all of their parents, thank you for all of the questions, conversation, enthusiasm, recognition, confidence, and most importantly, for showing up!

To Cate School and the Walden House, two communities that empowered me with the foundation to teach. I am thankful whenever I call on that education.

To Bodie Brizendine, thank you for embracing my promise and setting me up for success.

To Michael Riera, as a mentor and friend, your enthusiasm and support has been bedrock on which I still stand. Thank you for your unconditional belief in me.

To my Aim High Family, thank you for eighteen years of professional opportunity, the capacity to give, and the most meaningful ways to make a difference. To grow up with you has been an immense privilege.

To my Urban family, past and present, I am humbled and proud that you are my colleagues and friends. Your scholarship, passion, dedication, creativity, and love for young people inspires me every day. I am so fortunate to work in such a phenomenal community where education is so much more than just school.

To Jenn Epstein, especially, health educator extraordinaire, I couldn't ask for a better work partner, confidant, and playmate. Thank you for always having my back.

To Annie Roney and Kirby Dick, thank you for putting me on this path.

To Susan Wels, thank you for the beginnings of this book. Your skill and talent organized and developed years of work and captured my voice. I owe you a debt of gratitude.

To Connie Matthiessen, I am forever grateful for your incredible writing partnership. Your insight, expertise, and guidance have made all the difference with this project.

To my Review Crew for the book, you are da bomb! Words cannot express what a privilege it's been to work with each one of you on this book. Your unbelievable generosity, commitment, and thoughtful feedback has enriched and shaped this process in every way.

To Becky Marcus-Woods, Julie Deardorff, Danny Chiu, Amy Killy, Rick Weissbourd, Debbie Roffman, Kelsey Vrooman, Debra Wilson,

Dave Mochel, André Salvage, and Angela Rose, thank you for your professional and personal support. Your belief in me and this work means more than you know.

To Liz Trupin-Pulli, my literary agent, I am so deeply appreciative for you walking me through this publishing process and for persistently nurturing this project forward.

To Anna Michels, my publishing editor, and Sourcebooks, thank you for making this dream a reality.

To Peggy Orenstein, your generosity, writing prowess, and tremendous heart has inspired me beyond measure. I am so deeply grateful for all that you have shared and how it always comes back to LOVE.

To Katherine Kennedy, star storyteller, I value our friendship and your wisdom. I am seven times grateful for all of the truth, love, and generous guidance you give.

To my Cate girls, to be in sisterhood with you sustains me. I wouldn't have made it through our own adolescence without you. Thank you for over thirty years of cheerleading. It is through our bond that I first learned how to treat people right and love unconditionally. You're the best.

To all of my cherished friends, you are tremendous. I am eternally grateful for the joy and grace you so generously share. This life would not be the same without you. Aylin, you are deeply missed and written into these pages with love.

To my family, Zalooms, Wongs, Lims, Neeces, Bucks, and Piacentinis, extended and close, I thank you for all of your support and care. I am so blessed and grateful to each one of you.

To my parents, Vivian and Tony, I appreciate you for being my biggest fans. You are the reason I live my life with integrity and a sense of justice.

And to my brother, Ken, you are my touchstone. I can always count on you. I am so grateful for your loyalty and that you always look out for me, even though you will always be my baby brother.

To my children, Mei Lan, Kyle, and Maddie, you are truly my life's finest blessing. You inspire me to bring my best loving self to every day. May you always live true to your hearts as you journey through life one spirited adventure at a time.

And finally, to my husband, Brian, the love of my life. I couldn't ask for a better partner, lover, and friend. I am grateful beyond expression for the life we are building together.

About the Author

Shafia Zaloom is a health educator and consultant whose work centers on human development, community building, ethics, and social justice. Her approach involves creating opportunities for students and teachers to discuss the complexities of teen culture and decision-making with straightforward, open, and honest dialogue. In her twenty-five-year career, Zaloom has worked with thousands of children and their families in her role as teacher, coach, administrator, board member, and certified outdoor educator. Zaloom is currently the health teacher at the Urban School in San Francisco, and she develops curricula and trainings for schools across the country. Her work has been featured in the *New York Times*, *USA Today*, and on NPR and PBS. She lives in California with her husband and three children.

Photo credit: Hillary Hood